SECOND EDITION

# The Bill of Rights
## *A User's Guide*

*Linda R. Monk*

**Close Up Publishing**

## Close Up Foundation
## Stephen A. Janger, President

The Close Up Foundation is a nonprofit, nonpartisan organization that encourages responsible participation in the democratic process through educational programs and publications in government and citizenship. Since its founding in 1970, Close Up has been committed to developing new and better ways for young people, teachers, and a widening circle of citizens of all ages to gain a practical understanding of how public policy affects their lives and how individual and collective efforts affect public policy. For information about other Close Up Publishing educational materials, call 800-765-3131.

**Library of Congress Cataloging-in-Publication Data**

Monk, Linda R.
   The Bill of Rights : a user's guide / written by Linda R. Monk—2nd ed.
     p.  cm.
   Includes bibliographical references and index.
   Summary: Describes the history and development of the first ten
Constitutional amendments, also known as the Bill of Rights, and
presents stories of the many people who have helped to keep it a
living document.
   ISBN 0-932765-67-X (pbk.)
   1. United States—Constitutional law—Amendments—1st-10th.—
Juvenile literature. 2. Civil rights—United States—Juvenile
literature. 3. Civil rights movement—United States—History—
Juvenile literature. [1. United States.—Constitutional law—
Amendments—1st-10th. 2. Civil rights.] I. Title.
KF4750.M66 1995
342.73'085—dc20
[347.30285]                             95-31455
                                          CIP
                                          AC

*Cover Photos by*
   Virginia Department of Corrections
   Peralandra Services/Patsy Lynch
   UPI/Bettmann

*"America has always been about rights. . . . While many nations are based on a shared language or ethnic heritage, Americans have made rights the foundation of their national identity."*

—Commission on the Bicentennial of the United States Constitution

## ACKNOWLEDGMENTS

Many people at the Close Up Foundation have been instrumental in the development of this second edition. Stephen A. Janger, Close Up's president, created a vision of civic education that has inspired the Foundation's mission for twenty-five years. Charles M. Tampio, vice president of the Programs Division, and Cindy Graff Hobson, director of the Publications Department, supported the project from beginning to end. Charles R. Sass edited the manuscript, and Marcia Thompson kept the project running smoothly. Kimberly Couranz copyedited and proofread the book, and Amy Rowland and Pherabe Kolb coordinated photo research and reprint permissions. Judy Myers served as the second edition's designer, and Steven Waxman shepherded the project from the written word to the printed page.

A scholarly review panel helped ensure the book's accuracy and provided important ideas for the final manuscript. James A. Henretta, Ph.D., Burke Professor of History at the University of Maryland, lent his expertise in American colonial and legal history. Eric N. Lindquist, Ph.D., of Alexandria, Virginia, offered many helpful comments on the English background. Mary Jane Turner, Ph.D., director of Close Up's Curriculum Department, offered keen insights based on her experience as author of several civics textbooks. John W. Winkle III, Ph.D., associate professor of political science at the University of Mississippi, extensively reviewed the book's analysis of American constitutional law—and it was he who first instilled in the author an enduring love for our nation's charter.

## ABOUT THE AUTHOR

Linda R. Monk is a graduate of Harvard Law School with an emphasis in constitutional law. She has written numerous articles on legal issues for newspapers nationwide—including the *Washington Post,* the *Baltimore Sun,* the *Chicago Tribune,* the *Denver Post,* the *Des Moines Register,* the *Miami Herald,* the *St. Louis Post-Dispatch,* and the *San Francisco Chronicle.* Her other books—*The First Amendment: America's Blueprint for Tolerance* and *Ordinary Americans: U.S. History Through the Eyes of Everyday People*—are also available from Close Up Publishing.

# CONTENTS

# Congress OF THE United States

### begun and held at the City of New-York, on
### Wednesday the Fourth of March, one thousand seven hundred and eighty nine

THE Conventions of a number of the States, having at the time of their adopting the Constitution, expressed a desire, in order to prevent misconstruction or abuse of its powers, that further declaratory and restrictive clauses should be added: And as extending the ground of public confidence in the Government, will best ensure the beneficent ends of its institution.

RESOLVED by the Senate and House of Representatives of the United States of America, in Congress assembled, two thirds of both Houses concurring, that the following Articles be proposed to the Legislatures of the several States, as amendments to the Constitution of the United States, all, or any of which Articles, when ratified by three fourths of the said Legislatures, to be valid to all intents and purposes, as part of the said Constitution; viz.

ARTICLES in addition to, and Amendment of the Constitution of the United States of America, proposed by Congress, and ratified by the Legislatures of the several States, pursuant to the fifth Article of the original Constitution.

**Article the first.** .... After the first enumeration required by the first Article of the Constitution, there shall be one Representative for every thirty thousand, until the number shall amount to one hundred, after which, the proportion shall be so regulated by Congress, that there shall be not less than one hundred Representatives, nor less than one Representative for every forty thousand persons, until the number of Representatives shall amount to two hundred, after which the proportion shall be so regulated by Congress, that there shall not be less than two hundred Representatives, nor more than one Representative for every fifty thousand persons.

**Article the second.** .... No law, varying the compensation for the services of the Senators and Representatives, shall take effect, until an election of Representatives shall have intervened.

**Article the third.** .... Congress shall make no law respecting an establishment of religion, or prohibiting the free exercise thereof; or abridging the freedom of speech, or of the press; or the right of the people peaceably to assemble, and to petition the Government for a redress of grievances.

**Article the fourth.** .... A well regulated Militia, being necessary to the security of a free State, the right of the people to keep and bear Arms, shall not be infringed.

**Article the fifth.** .... No Soldier shall, in time of peace be quartered in any house, without the consent of the owner, nor in time of war, but in a manner to be prescribed by law.

**Article the sixth.** .... The right of the people to be secure in their persons, houses, papers, and effects, against unreasonable searches and seizures, shall not be violated, and no Warrants shall issue, but upon probable cause, supported by oath or affirmation, and particularly describing the place to be searched, and the persons or things to be seized.

**Article the seventh.** .... No person shall be held to answer for a capital, or otherwise infamous crime, unless on a presentment or indictment of a Grand jury, except in cases arising in the land or naval forces, or in the Militia, when in actual service in time of War or public danger; nor shall any person be subject for the same offence to be twice put in jeopardy of life or limb; nor shall be compelled in any criminal case to be a witness against himself, nor be deprived of life, liberty, or property, without due process of law; nor shall private property be taken for public use, without just compensation.

**Article the eighth.** .... In all criminal prosecutions, the accused shall enjoy the right to a speedy and public trial, by an impartial jury of the State and district wherein the crime shall have been committed, which district shall have been previously ascertained by law, and to be informed of the nature and cause of the accusation; to be confronted with the witnesses against him; to have compulsory process for obtaining witnesses in his favor, and to have the assistance of counsel for his defense.

**Article the ninth.** .... In suits at common law, where the value in controversy shall exceed twenty dollars, the right of trial by jury shall be preserved, and no fact tried by a jury, shall be otherwise re-examined in any court of the United States, than according to the rules of the common law.

**Article the tenth.** .... Excessive bail shall not be required, nor excessive fines imposed, nor cruel and unusual punishments inflicted.

**Article the eleventh.** .... The enumeration in the Constitution, of certain rights, shall not be construed to deny or disparage others retained by the people.

**Article the twelfth.** .... The powers not delegated to the United States by the Constitution, nor prohibited by it to the States, are reserved to the States respectively, or to the people.

ATTEST,

Frederick Augustus Muhlenberg, Speaker of the House of Representatives.

John Adams, Vice-President of the United States, and President of the Senate.

John Beckley, Clerk of the House of Representatives.

Sam. A. Otis Secretary of the Senate.

# FOREWORD

Drafted in 1787, the U.S. Constitution is the oldest written constitution still in use. Many of the Constitution's supporters (James Madison, the Constitution's principal author, among them) had initially argued that a Bill of Rights was unnecessary. In *Federalist* 84, Alexander Hamilton wrote that bills of rights "are, in their origin, stipulations between kings and their subjects, . . . reservations of rights not surrendered to the prince." No need, Hamilton asserted, for such a document in a constitution "founded upon the power of the people, and executed by their immediate representatives and servants"; here, "the people surrender nothing; and as they retain everything, they have no need of particular reservations."

But Madison, Hamilton, and the other Federalists could not win over the opposition on this point. As one of the great compromises that helped assure passage of our founding document, the first Congress passed a terse Bill of Rights, adopting provisions submitted by Madison himself. Ratified by the states in 1791, the Bill of Rights contains ten amendments. Since then, the Constitution has been amended only seventeen times.

Neither the original Constitution, nor the Bill of Rights, bestows any rights on individuals. To the Framers, no document could perform that task. In their view, individual rights antedated the state and thus were not the state's to confer. As Jefferson wrote in our principal rights-declaring document, the Declaration of Independence: "We hold these truths to be self-evident, that all men are created equal, that they are endowed by their Creator with certain unalienable Rights, that among these are Life, Liberty, and the pursuit of Happiness." Thus, the Bill of Rights assumes the existence of fundamental human rights—for example, freedom of speech, press, and assembly—and simply instructs the state not to interfere with those rights.

Madison recognized that if the Bill of Rights was not to be a mere "parchment barrier" to the will of the majority, the judiciary would have to play a central role. "If [a Bill of Rights is] incorporated into the Constitution, independent tribunals of justice will consider themselves in a peculiar manner the guardians of those rights; they will be an impenetrable bulwark . . . naturally led to resist every encroachment upon rights."

While that sentiment has brightened the spirit of the men and women privileged to serve on the federal bench, the judiciary does not stand alone in guarding against governmental interference with fundamental rights. Responsibility for securing those rights is a charge we share with the Congress, the president, the states, and with the people themselves. As one of our greatest jurists, Judge Learned Hand, put it, the spirit of liberty that infuses our Constitution—a spirit that is not too sure it is right, one that seeks to understand the minds of other men and women and to weigh the interests of others alongside its own without bias—must lie, first and foremost, in the hearts and minds of the men and women who compose this great nation.

It manifests no disrepect for the Constitution to note that the Framers were gentlemen of their time, and therefore had a distinctly limited vision of those who counted among "We the People." Not until adoption of the post-Civil War Fourteenth Amendment did the word "equal," in relation to the stature of individuals, even make an appearance in the Constitution. But the equal dignity of all persons is nonetheless a vital part of our constitutional legacy, even if the culture of the Framers held them back from fully perceiving that universal ideal. We can best celebrate that legacy by continuing to strive to form "a more perfect Union" for ourselves and the generations to come.

Ruth Bader Ginsburg
Associate Justice
Supreme Court of the United States

# A **LIVING** *Bill of Rights*

America is a nation based on an idea. That idea, as expressed in the Declaration of Independence, is that all people are endowed "with certain unalienable Rights" and that the purpose of government is "to secure these rights." Rights are at the center of Americans' national identity. Rights are why many people make America their home.

In 1791, Americans added a list of their rights to the Constitution. These first ten amendments became known as the Bill of Rights. But putting rights on paper is not enough. As the late Learned Hand, one of America's greatest judges, said: "Liberty lies in the hearts of men and women; when it dies there, no constitution, no law, no court can save it." In Hand's opinion, the real protectors of liberty were not constitutions or courts, but citizens.

Justice William O. Douglas of the U.S. Supreme Court, in his book *A Living Bill of Rights,* agreed with Judge Hand:

> What our Constitution says, what our legislatures do, and what our courts write are vitally important. But the reality of freedom in our daily lives is shown by the attitudes and policies of people toward each other in the very block or township where we live. There we will find the real measure of *A Living Bill of Rights*.

The purpose of this "user's guide" to the Bill of Rights is to help citizens make the Bill of Rights a living document. Unfortunately, the Bill of Rights did not come with an instruction manual. The language of 1791 can often be difficult to understand and apply more than 200 years later. Therefore, this guide describes the history of each right in the Bill of Rights and explains how the Supreme Court has interpreted those rights. It also tells the stories of many "ordinary" people who have helped keep the Bill of Rights a living document—not just an artifact stored under glass at the National Archives in Washington, D.C. Making the Bill of Rights come alive in our communities is the best way to secure those rights for the next 200 years.

BILL OF RIGHTS

FREEDOM of SPEECH

FREEDOM of ASSEMBLY

FREEDOM of RELIGION

FREEDOM of The PRESS

Howard Chandler Christy

# The **BIRTH** of the Bill of Rights

The first ten amendments to the United States Constitution became known as the Bill of Rights because they contained many of the fundamental freedoms vital to Americans. These rights were so important that the American people insisted they be added to the new Constitution written in 1787. But the Bill of Rights did not suddenly appear when it was ratified by the states in 1791. It was the result of more than a century of experience with rights in America, and many centuries before that in England.

To understand the Bill of Rights and its history, one must first understand the principles underlying the idea of rights. What is a right? Where do rights come from? Who protects rights? This section helps answer those questions. By understanding both the underlying principles and the historical background of the Bill of Rights, Americans can exercise more fully the rights it guarantees them.

# The **IDEA** of Rights

Calvin, the boy in the cartoon below, thinks he has a "right" to give the wrong answer on his homework. "It's a free country," he says; "I've got my rights!" But what is a right, and where do rights come from? Does Calvin really have a *right* to ignore the rules of mathematics?

Even in America, a country based on the protection of rights, Calvin has to do his homework. His rights as an American do not include freedom from math. But there are many other rights that he *does* have because he lives in the United States. What are rights? Where do they come from? How are rights protected in the United States? The answers to these questions help define the rights of all Americans.

## WHAT IS A RIGHT?

A right is a power or privilege that a person has a just claim to, that belongs to a person by law, nature, or tradition. The first part of this definition—a power or privilege that a person has a just claim to—means to some people that their own individual ideas of fairness determine their rights. That is why Calvin claims he has a right to ignore the rules of math. But one person's belief that a right exists does not necessarily mean another person must respect it. Calvin's teacher probably will not respect Calvin's "right" to be wrong.

Calvin and Hobbes Copyright 1990 Universal Press Syndicate. Reprinted with permission. All rights reserved.

Therefore, the second part of the definition—a power or privilege that belongs to a person by law, nature, or tradition—is equally important. A right is supported by law, nature, or tradition and can therefore be enforced against others. Individuals can claim rights based on their own sense of fairness, but without the support of law, nature, or tradition, other people and the government may not recognize or enforce those rights.

## WHERE DO RIGHTS COME FROM?

Are you born with rights, or does the government give them to you? The answer to this question determines how a society views rights. The first view, that people are born with rights, is the theory of natural rights. The second view, that rights come from the government, is the theory of legal rights.

### NATURAL RIGHTS

Natural rights are based on the principle that all people by nature have certain rights simply by being human. These rights are higher than any human political system. Natural rights do not come from government. Because they do not come from government, government cannot legitimately take them away. But because they do not come from government, government does not always protect them either.

John Locke, an English political philosopher of the late 1600s, developed a very influential theory of natural rights. He believed that people do not give up their "rights of nature" when they create a government. Moreover, he said that government exists to protect the natural rights of its citizens. Locke's idea of natural rights had a great impact on the development of rights in America. Thomas Jefferson relied on Locke's theories when he wrote the Declaration of Independence. It stated that people have "certain unalienable Rights"—including "Life, Liberty, and the pursuit of Happiness"—and that the purpose of government is "to secure these rights."

### LEGAL RIGHTS

Legal rights come from the laws, statutes, and court decisions of a society's government. A right is a legal right when it is protected by law. A popular saying in the law is "there is no right without a remedy." This means that a right does not legally exist unless other people are required

*John Locke (1637-1704) was an English political philosopher whose work,* Two Treatises on Civil Government *(1690), greatly influenced the Declaration of Independence and the U.S. Constitution.*

to respect that right or are held responsible if they violate it. Legal rights are rights created by the government. However, if a government gives a right, it can also take that right away.

## FROM NATURAL RIGHTS TO LEGAL RIGHTS

In America, many natural rights have become legal rights as well. Since colonial times, Americans have wanted to make sure that their rights were protected by law. They began listing their rights in the written laws of the colonies and of the states created after independence from England. Americans relied on statutory law, the written codes or statutes created by their legislatures. England used the common law, which was based on custom and the decisions of the courts but was not written down in a legal code. Americans were afraid that if their rights were not written in the law, government officials could violate those rights. Therefore, the American people would not accept the new Constitution of 1787 unless a bill of rights was added. Rights thus were recognized under constitutional law, the highest and most fundamental law in a legal system.

*The words "Equal Justice Under Law" appear at the top of the U.S. Supreme Court building in Washington, D.C.*

The rights in the Bill of Rights are both natural rights and legal rights. The Bill of Rights differs from the Declaration of Independence in this respect. Because the Declaration of Independence is not a law, the natural rights listed in it are not protected by the government. For instance, a person cannot sue in the courts for violations of the right to the "pursuit of Happiness." But the Bill of Rights is part of the U.S. Constitution, and the rights it contains are enforced by the courts. The Constitution and the Bill of Rights are the "supreme law of the land" that all other laws, including state constitutions and statutes, must follow.

However, state constitutions can grant more expansive rights than the U.S. Constitution. Recently, the Supreme Court has tended to protect fewer individual rights under the U.S. Constitution, so more Americans are pursuing their rights under state constitutions. Thus, Americans have two sets of constitutional rights: those under the U.S. Constitution and those under the constitution of the state in which they live.

## HOW ARE RIGHTS PROTECTED IN AMERICA?

The courts have a unique role in protecting rights in America. All government officials, including the president and members of Congress, take an oath to support the Constitution and the Bill of Rights. But what happens if they break that oath, or if they disagree about the meaning of a right? In such cases, the courts have the authority to decide what the Constitution requires.

## JUDICIAL REVIEW

*At the end of his presidency (1797-1801), John Adams made the infamous "midnight appointments" that led to Marbury v. Madison (1803).*

Only the courts have the power of judicial review, which means that they can declare a law unconstitutional and make it void. The Supreme Court upheld the power of judicial review in *Marbury v. Madison* (1803).

In that case, William Marbury asked the Court to issue a writ of mandamus—a legal order forcing government officials to carry out their duties—as it had been authorized to do by the Judiciary Act of 1789. The writ would force Secretary of State James Madison to give Marbury his commission as a justice of the peace. Marbury was one of former President John Adams's "midnight appointments"—judicial appointments Adams made as he was leaving office in an attempt to increase the influence of his political party, the Federalists. But in the press of business, John Marshall, Adams's secretary of state, had failed to deliver seventeen of the commissions—among them Marbury's. President Thomas Jefferson, a Democratic-Republican, ordered his secretary of state, James Madison, not to deliver the commissions that were still left when Jefferson assumed office.

Now on the Supreme Court as chief justice, John Marshall heard the case that resulted from his errors as secretary of state. Writing for a unanimous Court, Marshall held that the Judiciary Act of 1789 was unconstitutional. The Act authorized the Supreme Court to issue writs of mandamus as part of its original jurisdiction—that is, people could go directly to the Supreme Court for the writ, without having to go to a lower court first and then appeal to the Supreme Court. But the Constitution clearly did not include writs of mandamus in the Supreme Court's original jurisdiction; changing the Court's jurisdiction required a constitutional amendment, not an act of Congress. By declaring the Judiciary Act of 1789 unconstitutional, Marshall and the Supreme Court established that "it is emphatically the province and duty of the judicial department to say what the law is" and that "a law repugnant to the Constitution is void." Marbury did not get his commission, but the Supreme Court got its most important power.

# Case Study: Marbury v. Madison (1803)

*In this case, the Supreme Court established the power of judicial review by declaring the Judiciary Act of 1789 unconstitutional, because the act changed the original jurisdiction of the Court.*

*I*t is, emphatically, the province and duty of the judicial department, to say what the law is.

## Chief Justice Marshall
delivered the opinion of the Court. . . .

. . . The Constitution vests the whole judicial power of the United States in one Supreme Court, and such inferior courts as Congress shall, from time to time, ordain and establish. . . .

In the distribution of this power, it is declared, that "the Supreme Court shall have original jurisdiction, in all cases affecting ambassadors, other public ministers and consuls, and those in which a state shall be a party. In all other cases, the Supreme Court shall have appellate jurisdiction." . . .

. . . If Congress remains at liberty to give this Court appellate jurisdiction, where the Constitution has declared their jurisdiction shall be original; and original jurisdiction where the Constitution has declared it shall be appellate; the distribution of jurisdiction, made in the Constitution, is form without substance. . . .

. . . The Constitution is either a superior paramount law, unchangeable by ordinary means, or it is on a level with ordinary legislative acts, and, like other acts, is alterable when the legislature shall please to alter it. If the former . . . be true, then a legislative act, contrary to the Constitution, is not law; if the latter part be true, then written constitutions are absurd attempts, on the part of the people, to limit a power, in its own nature, illimitable. . . .

It is, emphatically, the province and duty of the judicial department, to say what the law is. Those who apply the rule to particular cases, must of necessity expound and interpret that rule. If two laws conflict with each other, the courts must decide on the operation of each. So, if a law be in opposition to the Constitution; if both the law and the Constitution apply to a particular case, so that the court must decide that case, conformably to the law, disregarding the Constitution; or conformably to the Constitution, disregarding the law; the court must determine which of these conflicting rules governs the case: this is of the very essence of judicial duty. If then, the courts are to regard the Constitution, and the Constitution is superior to any ordinary act of the legislature, the Constitution, and not such ordinary act, must govern the case to which they both apply. . . .

Thus, the . . . Constitution of the United States confirms and strengthens the principle, supposed to be essential to all written constitutions, that a law repugnant to the Constitution is void; and that courts, as well as other departments, are bound by that instrument.

*The justices of the U.S. Supreme Court for the 1994/95 term were, left to right: Antonin Scalia, Ruth Bader Ginsburg, John Paul Stevens, David H. Souter, William H. Rehnquist, Clarence Thomas, Sandra Day O'Connor, Steven G. Breyer, and Anthony M. Kennedy.*

Collection, The Supreme Court Historical Society

## JUDICIAL RESTRAINT VS. JUDICIAL ACTIVISM

Experts disagree about how the courts should exercise the power of judicial review. Some argue that judges should use judicial restraint—rarely overturning previous court decisions, or precedents, and statutes enacted by popularly elected legislatures. Advocates of judicial restraint say that courts should not take such drastic action and thus initiate broad changes in public policy. Otherwise, they maintain, unelected judges are just imposing their own political values on the rest of the nation.

Supporters of judicial activism are less hesitant to overturn laws and precedents. They argue that the judiciary, no less than the executive and the legislative branches, has an important role in shaping public policy. An unelected judiciary is designed to protect unpopular rights, they say, and if changes in public policy are necessary to protect those rights, then those changes are within the judicial power.

Judicial activism is not restricted to liberals, nor is judicial restraint limited to conservatives. Judges can be very conservative in their political philosophy, but very activist in their approach to judicial review. Similarly, judges can be very liberal politically, but still exercise judicial restraint.

Experts disagree about the role of politics in the judiciary. Some say that the law is, or should be, based on neutral principles. A good judge, they say, is immune to politics. Others argue that no human beings, including judges, are ever immune to politics. According to these scholars, judges always interpret the law based on their own personal values.

The Supreme Court has shown certain trends based on the political leanings of its members. When the Court was led by Chief Justice Earl Warren (1953-1969), for instance, it tended to be more activist and liberal. The Warren Court upheld many rights for criminal defendants and gave broad protections to civil liberties. The Burger Court, led by Chief Justice Warren Burger (1969-1986), was divided, issuing both liberal and conservative rulings. Since William Rehnquist became chief justice in 1986, the Court has taken a decidedly conservative, and some critics say activist, turn.

### THE SUPREME COURT IN ACTION

When the Supreme Court reaches a decision in a case, it issues an opinion—a written explanation of the reasons for the decision. The majority opinion gives the decision of the Court and the reasons why the majority of the Court supported it. A concurring opinion is written by justices who agree with the majority's decision but for different reasons. A dissenting opinion is written by justices who disagree with the Court's decision.

The Supreme Court, as the highest court in the land, has the final say on what the Constitution and the Bill of Rights mean. Congress cannot pass a law to change a decision of the Supreme Court on constitutional issues, nor can the president alter it. Only the people, by amending the Constitution itself, can change how the Supreme Court interprets a right in the Bill of Rights.

### RIGHTS IN A DEMOCRACY

Rights take on added importance in a democracy, a form of government in which the majority rules. As James Madison, the principal author of the Bill of Rights, pointed out:

> Wherever the real power in a government lies, there is the danger of oppression. In our government, the real power lies in the majority of the community, and the invasion of private rights is *chiefly* to be feared, not from acts of government contrary to the sense of its constituents, but from acts in which the government is the mere instrument of the major number of constituents.

The Bill of Rights is designed to protect minority rights in a system of majority rule. It is a document in which "We, the People" have agreed to limit ourselves, to say that some rights are so important that they cannot be voted on. Thus, the United States has a constitutional democracy—a government in which the people rule, but with certain limits. The Bill of Rights sets forth those limits.

# The HISTORY *of the Bill of Rights*

Rights in America did not begin in 1791 with the Bill of Rights. Colonial Americans began protecting rights almost as soon as they arrived in the new world. This chapter traces the Bill of Rights from its roots in England, through its beginnings in colonial America, to its final form in the new nation.

James Madison, who played a key role in drafting both the Constitution and the Bill of Rights, wrote to a friend in 1834: "You give me a credit to which I have no claim in calling me 'the writer of the Constitution of the U.S.' This was not like the fabled goddess of wisdom the offspring of a single brain. It ought to be regarded as the work of many heads and many hands."

This quote is no less true of the Bill of Rights. While Madison was the principal author of the Bill of Rights, he relied almost totally upon the existing provisions in state bills of rights—which were themselves the result of hundreds of years of human experience about rights.

## ENGLISH ROOTS

The history of rights in America begins with the history of rights in England. Since the United States began as English colonies, many of the rights the colonists demanded were rights they believed they had as Englishmen. These rights came from three major English documents: the Magna Carta, the Petition of Right, and the English Bill of Rights.

### MAGNA CARTA (1215)

A group of English barons, tired of heavy taxes and arbitrary actions by the king, forced King John to sign the Magna Carta (Latin for "great charter") at Runnymede in 1215. It guaranteed such fundamental rights as trial by jury and due process of law, a requirement that government be fair in its actions. Originally, these rights applied only to noblemen, but over time they were extended to all English people. By today's standards, the Magna Carta did not contain many fundamental rights, but it established the principle that the monarch's power is not absolute. As the modern British leader Winston Churchill stated, "here is a law which is above the King and which even he must not break."

*William and Mary of Orange, a region in the Netherlands, were invited to assume the British throne only if they agreed to the English Bill of Rights of 1689.*

## PETITION OF RIGHT (1628)

The monarchs of England did not always respect the Magna Carta in the 400 years that followed its signing. Parliament, the English legislature, gradually grew in influence during that time. In 1628, Parliament enacted a statute limiting the power of the king, Charles I, and refused to approve more taxes until the king signed the law. This statute, known as the Petition of Right, prohibited the king from arresting people unlawfully and quartering troops in private homes without the owners' consent. The Petition of Right challenged the divine right of kings by reasserting that even the monarch must obey the law of the land.

## BILL OF RIGHTS (1689)

Charles's arbitrary behavior led to a civil war and his execution in 1649. His son, Charles II, was restored to the throne in 1660, but disputes continued between the monarch and his subjects. James II, Charles's brother, became king in 1685, but he also alienated his subjects with his promotion of Catholicism and violations of the law. In 1688, James was forced to abdicate as part of the Glorious Revolution, and Parliament offered the crown to William of Orange and his wife, Mary.

As a condition of their rule, William and Mary had to agree to an act of Parliament in 1689 known as the Bill of Rights. It guaranteed the right of British subjects to petition the king and to bear arms, as well as prohibited excessive bails and fines and cruel and unusual punishment. The English Bill of Rights was the first document to be called a bill of rights, but it protected far fewer individual rights than the American Bill of Rights of 1791.

The term "bill of rights" refers to the English document's origin in Parliament as a bill, the first step in making a law. While the American Bill of Rights uses the same name, it is part of the U.S. Constitution, not a statute like the English Bill of Rights. A constitution is the most important, most fundamental law of the land, whereas a statute is part of everyday lawmaking. A statute can be changed by a simple majority of the legislature, whereas the U.S. Constitution can only be amended by a two-thirds majority in both houses of Congress (or a national convention called by two-thirds of the states) and a three-fourths majority of the states. Therefore, rights protected by the Constitution are more secure than rights protected by a statute because they are more fundamental and cannot be taken away as easily.

## AMERICAN BEGINNINGS

Early Americans built on their English heritage when developing rights in the new land. But they also went beyond it. In fact, many colonies had laws protecting rights long before the English Bill of Rights that far exceeded its scope. Americans protected rights in the founding charters of the colonies and in the constitutions of the state governments formed after independence from England.

Rights were crucial to America's founding. Because their rights in England were threatened, many future Americans left their homeland to form new colonies in a strange land. And because their rights were threatened, the colonists declared independence from England and created a new nation to secure those rights.

## COLONIAL CHARTERS AND LAWS

Many of the first English colonists in America sought to escape violations of their rights in their native land. Not surprisingly, then, these colonists worked to guarantee individual rights in their new home. Colonial governments protected rights both in their colonial charters, or constitutions, and in the statutes enacted by the colonial assemblies, or legislatures.

Several colonial charters guaranteed the rights of Englishmen for the colonists. The rights of Americans were not to be inferior to those of their English siblings. Other colonies attracted settlers by going beyond the rights of Englishmen. Maryland, for example, was founded as a haven for Catholics, but, needing more settlers, extended the right of religious toleration to other Christians as well. It was the first American colony to recognize some degree of freedom of conscience. "Without religious toleration," wrote the third Lord Baltimore, a descendant of Maryland's founder, "in all probability this province had never been planted."

Most colonies were not as generous as Maryland. Indeed, colonies founded to escape religious persecution in England, such as the Puritan colony of Massachusetts Bay, were often quick to deny religious freedom to others in America. But overall, the colonial charters and laws protected a broad sweep of rights. In 1641, Massachusetts Bay enacted the first detailed protection of rights in America, the Massachusetts Body of Liberties. Other colonies also protected rights, either in their charters or in their laws.

The colonial charters and laws provided far more detailed protection for individual rights than did the English documents guaranteeing rights.

These colonial laws covered many of the rights later protected by the American Bill of Rights. However, rights under colonial law were less secure than those in the U.S. Bill of Rights because, like the English laws, the colonial charters and laws could be changed more easily than the U.S. Constitution. Even the colonial charters could be altered by the king or Parliament at will.

## REVOLUTIONARY DECLARATIONS

With the American Revolution came more documents declaring the rights of the colonists. The Stamp Act Congress, composed of delegates from nine colonies, met in 1765 to protest England's imposition of the first direct tax on its American colonies. The tax covered various printed documents, including newspapers—all of which had to carry a special stamp. The Congress issued a "Declaration of Rights and Grievances," which stated that the colonists were entitled to all the rights of Englishmen. It also asserted the rights of petition and jury trial for the colonists.

In 1772, the Boston Town Meeting issued "The Rights of the Colonists and a List of Infringements and Violations of Rights." This document restated the principle that the colonists were entitled to the rights of Englishmen. It also asserted some new rights not listed in the colonial charters. One of these was the protection from general warrants, which later appeared in the Fourth Amendment of the Bill of Rights. A general warrant allowed the British officials to search colonial homes and businesses at will, without any restrictions, to look for smuggled goods on which import duties had not been paid.

Delegates from every colony except Georgia met at the First Continental Congress in September 1774. Samuel Adams urged the Congress to "agree in one general bill of rights" to address the grievances of the colonists. The congress issued its "Declaration and Resolves," which yet again claimed the rights of Englishmen for the colonists. It also listed other specific rights, among them the right to trial by jury in the local area—protesting the British power to send Americans back to England to be tried for some offenses. One printing of the "Declaration and Resolves" entitled it "The Bill of Rights," reflecting a popular conception that it was the American equivalent of the English Bill of Rights of 1689. This was the first use of the term "bill of rights" to refer to an American document.

By 1776, the momentum had shifted toward independence, and the colonists were more concerned about their rights as *Americans* than as

Colonial Williamsburg Foundation

*Colonial opposition to the Stamp Act took various forms, including this teapot.*

*Colonial protesters in 1776 pull down a statue of King George III, which was melted down for ammunition.*

Englishmen. The Second Continental Congress voted to declare independence from Britain on July 2, 1776, and approved Thomas Jefferson's draft of the Declaration of Independence on July 4, 1776. Jefferson relied on John Locke's theory of natural rights to justify the American case for independence. The Declaration stated that all people are entitled to "certain unalienable Rights" (rights that cannot be taken or given away) and that the purpose of government is "to secure these rights." While the Declaration of Independence was not a bill of rights as such, it did list some basic rights violated by King George, including the right to trial by jury in the local community and the prohibition on quartering troops in private homes without the owners' consent.

None of the revolutionary documents stating the rights of the colonists had the status of law. They were declarations of principles, not actual bills of rights. The colonists had no authority to provide legal protections for rights until they established new governments for the states and the nation after independence from Britain.

### STATE CONSTITUTIONS

The first colony to form a new government as a state was Virginia. In June 1776, even before the Declaration of Independence, Virginia adopted a new constitution, prefaced by a declaration of rights. The Virginia Declaration of Rights contained a comprehensive list of rights, including many that would later appear in the U.S. Bill of Rights. George Mason, a Virginia planter self-taught in the law, drafted the Virginia Declaration. Mason was able to write the document quickly and with little opposition because he drew on the consensus that had developed among the colonists about the rights that should be protected by a constitution.

The Virginia Declaration of Rights of 1776 is sometimes called the first real bill of rights in America because, like the U.S. Bill of Rights, it was not a statute, but part of a constitution adopted by a popularly elected convention. It served as a model for eight of the twelve other states that formed new constitutions during the revolutionary period. Like Virginia, their constitutions included specific bills of rights at the very beginning. The other four state constitutions also contained provisions protecting rights, but they were spread throughout the documents, not listed separately at the outset—the same method followed by the original U.S. Constitution of 1787. All of the basic individual rights that later became part of the U.S. Bill of Rights were included in these state constitutions of the revolutionary period.

## ARTICLES OF CONFEDERATION

While the new state governments protected individual rights, the new national government did not. The Articles of Confederation, the first constitution of the United States, contained no separate bill of rights, nor any provisions equivalent to those in the state constitutions. One reason for this lack of protection was that the Articles of Confederation created a very weak national government. States retained virtually all powers, so a national bill of rights did not seem necessary.

While the national government had no power over rights in the states, it did control the new territories created from lands formerly claimed by some states. Some of this land—the future states of Ohio, Indiana, Illinois, Michigan, and Wisconsin—was called the Northwest Territory. To govern this territory, the Confederation Congress enacted the Northwest Ordinance, which contained the first bill of rights enacted by the federal government. The Northwest Ordinance protected many of the traditional rights covered by the state declarations of rights. But a bill of rights that applied to all regions and all powers of the national government came only when the national government itself was changed.

*George Washington presided over the 55 delegates from 12 states that composed the Constitutional Convention, which met from May 25 to September 17, 1787, at Independence Hall in Philadelphia, Pennsylvania.*

## RIGHTS AND THE NEW CONSTITUTION

The weak national government under the Articles of Confederation created many problems. In 1787, these problems finally led to a convention to draft a new charter for the national government, the Constitution of the United States. But the Constitution's lack of a bill of rights became the main reason many people opposed it. Many states refused to ratify the Constitution until they were assured a bill of rights would be added. Even after three-fourths of the states ratified the Constitution in 1788, some states threatened to call a second convention to weaken its powers. The struggle did not end until a bill of rights was finally added to the Constitution.

## THE CONSTITUTIONAL CONVENTION

The Confederation Congress called a convention in 1787 to amend the Articles of Confederation. The convention, which met in Philadelphia from May to September, soon abandoned the Articles and began to draft a new Constitution for the United States. This document greatly increased the powers of the national government, but it did not contain a separate bill of rights.

The Constitution did protect several individual rights in its text, however. Among them were:

- the right of habeas corpus, which prevents arbitrary imprisonment by government officials
- the right of trial by jury in criminal cases
- a ban on bills of attainder, which are legislative acts that convict a person of a crime without a trial
- a ban on ex post facto laws, which make actions criminal after they have been committed
- a guarantee that the citizens of each state are entitled to the privileges and immunities of citizens of other states
- a ban on religious tests for officials of the national government

### THE MASON-GERRY MOTION

Despite the protections of individual rights in the text of the Constitution, some delegates to the convention believed strongly that a separate bill of rights should be added. George Mason of Virginia, the author of the Virginia Declaration of Rights, brought up the subject on September 12, in one of the final sessions of the convention. He wished that "the plan had been prefaced with a Bill of Rights and would second a motion made for the purpose." Elbridge Gerry of Massachusetts made a motion "to appoint a committee to prepare a Bill of Rights," which Mason seconded. But the motion was defeated unanimously, with the delegates voting as state units.

Why did the convention totally reject Mason's proposal for a bill of rights? Some scholars argue that the plan was presented too late in the convention, when delegates were exhausted by one of the hottest summers in Philadelphia history (in an age before air conditioners and deodorants). But Mason argued at the convention that a bill of rights would not take long to draft, that "with the aid of the state declarations, a bill might be prepared in a few hours." This, indeed, had been Mason's experience when drafting the Virginia Declaration of Rights, again reflecting the consensus that had developed as to what individual rights should be protected by a constitution.

Roger Sherman, a delegate from Connecticut, stated that a bill of rights was unnecessary. The state declarations of rights offered sufficient protection, he said, and the national government had no power to violate the rights protected by the states. But as George Mason noted, the Supremacy Clause of the Constitution made it and laws of the United

# The Courage of Their Convictions: George Mason

*George Mason*

George Mason (1725-1792) lived on his plantation at Gunston Hall in Fairfax County, Virginia, a few miles down the Potomac River from George Washington's home at Mount Vernon. Washington and Mason were close friends as well as neighbors.

Mason is best known as the author of the Virginia Declaration of Rights. Although he was not formally trained in the law, Mason had read widely about political and legal issues. James Madison said that Mason had "the greatest talents for debate of any man I have ever seen or heard speak."

George Mason represented Virginia at the Constitutional Convention in 1787. He advocated abolishing the slave trade, calling it "diabolical in itself and disgraceful to mankind"—although he himself held slaves. Mason also made a motion to add a bill of rights to the new Constitution. Defeated on both the slave trade and the bill of rights issues, Mason refused to sign the Constitution.

Leading the opposition to the new Constitution, Mason gave his principal objection: "There is no declaration of rights." Mason drafted Virginia's proposed amendments to the Constitution, which Madison relied upon heavily, along with the Virginia Declaration of Rights, in drafting the Bill of Rights.

Mason lived to see the Bill of Rights be added to the Constitution, but he paid a price for his stand: George Washington never forgave him for opposing the Constitution. Mason sacrificed his longtime friendship with Washington to secure a bill of rights for his country.

States the "supreme law of the land," superior to the state declarations of rights. Thus, Mason later wrote, "the declarations of rights in the separate states are no security."

After the convention, another attempt was made to add a bill of rights to the new Constitution. Richard Henry Lee of Virginia made a motion in the Confederation Congress to amend the Constitution with a bill of rights before it was submitted to the states for ratification, or formal approval. Congress, however, rejected Lee's motion.

To take effect, the Constitution had to be ratified by nine states. Special state conventions were elected to decide if the Constitution should be ratified. These conventions became arenas for the struggle between the Federalists, who supported the Constitution, and the Anti-Federalists, who opposed it.

## THE FEDERALISTS

Federalists supported the Constitution because of the increased powers of the new federal government. James Madison was one of the most important Federalist leaders because of the critical role he played in drafting the Constitution. Other Federalists included John Jay and Alexander Hamilton of New York. Together with Madison, they wrote the *Federalist* papers, a lengthy series of newspaper articles defending the new Constitution.

In *Federalist* 84, Alexander Hamilton outlined the reasons why Federalists opposed adding a bill of rights to the Constitution. He pointed out that several states had no bill of rights in their constitutions, including New York—one of the largest and most influential states. He also emphasized that the proposed federal Constitution protected a number of individual rights in its text. Beyond being unnecessary, Hamilton argued, a bill of rights could well prove dangerous because it might imply powers that the government did not have. "Why declare things that shall not be done," Hamilton asked, "which there is no power to do?" Finally, Hamilton argued, "the constitution is itself in every rational sense, and to every useful purpose, a Bill of Rights" because it specified "the political privileges of the citizens in the structure and administration of the government."

## THE ANTI-FEDERALISTS

Anti-Federalists opposed the Constitution because they feared the expanded powers of the federal government. They worried that the federal government under the Constitution would be just as tyrannical as the British king they had recently opposed. Key Anti-Federalist leaders included George Mason and Patrick Henry of Virginia.

The Anti-Federalists were the chief advocates for a bill of rights, and the absence of one in the new constitution became the greatest stumbling block to its ratification. Anti-Federalists pointed out that the new government would have all powers "necessary and proper" to carry out its expressed powers. They feared that this implied power was unlimited and could easily be used to repress individual rights.

## STATE RATIFYING CONVENTIONS

The state conventions held to ratify the Constitution became a battleground between Federalists and Anti-Federalists. Support for a bill of rights was so strong in some states that many Federalists, among them James Madison, conceded the issue. The question then became whether

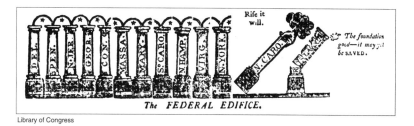

The FEDERAL EDIFICE.

Library of Congress

states should ratify the Constitution before a bill of rights was added, assuming one would later be proposed by the first federal Congress, or refuse to ratify it until a bill of rights was added by a second constitutional convention. Federalists feared that another convention would give some Anti-Federalists the opportunity to strip the new government of its important powers. They urged states to ratify the Constitution with no conditions, but to recommend possible amendments to the first Congress that would convene after the Constitution was ratified by nine states.

The Federalist position finally prevailed. Only one state, North Carolina, refused to ratify the Constitution until a bill of rights was added. Five other states ratified with a recommendation for later amendments, including both Virginia and New York, two large and influential states. Of these, Virginia proposed the most comprehensive list of amendments. The amendments proposed by the states included almost all of the individual rights that would later be protected in the federal Bill of Rights.

When New Hampshire became the ninth state to ratify on June 21, 1788, the Constitution went into effect. The Confederation Congress passed a law establishing New York as the capital of the new government. It also set dates early in 1789 for the presidential election and for the meeting of the first federal Congress. The new government was about to begin.

## CREATING THE BILL OF RIGHTS

Despite the clear mandate from many states for a federal bill of rights, the new Congress delayed acting on the measure. Only with the prodding of James Madison, then a U.S. representative from Virginia, did Congress finally submit a bill of rights to the states for ratification. Madison's action stopped the momentum for a second constitutional convention, and the new government under the Constitution was finally secure.

# Letters of Liberty

*Thomas Jefferson and James Madison enjoyed a lifelong friendship. In letters written from 1787 to 1789, while in Paris as U.S. minister to France, Jefferson convinced Madison that a bill of rights was necessary.*

*A bill of rights is what the people are entitled to against every government on earth.*

### Thomas Jefferson to James Madison, December 20, 1787

. . . I will now add what I do not like [about the U.S. Constitution]. First the omission of a bill of rights providing clearly . . . for freedom of religion, freedom of the press, protection against standing armies, restriction against monopolies, the eternal and unremitting force of the habeas corpus laws, and trials by jury in all matters of fact triable by the laws of the land. . . . Let me add that a bill of rights is what the people are entitled to against every government on Earth, general or particular, and what no just government should refuse, or rest on inference. . . .

### James Madison to Thomas Jefferson, October 17, 1788

. . . My own opinion has always been in favor of a bill of rights, provided it be so framed as not to imply powers not meant to be included. . . . At the same time I have never thought the omission a material defect, nor been anxious to supply it even by *subsequent* amendment, for any other reason than that it is anxiously desired by others. I have favored it because I supposed it might be of use, and if properly executed could not be of disservice. I have not viewed it in an important light. . . .

Experience proves the [ineffectiveness] of a bill of rights on those occasions when its control is most needed. Repeated violations of these parchment barriers have been committed by overbearing majorities in every state. In Virginia I have seen the bill of rights violated in every instance where it has been opposed to a popular current. . . . Wherever the real power in a government lies, there is the danger of oppression. In our government, the real power lies in the majority of the community, and the invasion of private rights is *chiefly* to be [feared], not from acts of government contrary to the sense of its constituents, but from acts in which the government is the mere instrument of the major number of the constituents. . . . Wherever there is an interest and power to do wrong, wrong will generally be done, and not less readily by a powerful and interested party than by a powerful and interested prince. . . .

### Thomas Jefferson to James Madison, March 15, 1789

. . . In the arguments in favor of a declaration of rights, you omit one which has great weight with me, the legal check which it puts into the hands of the judiciary. This is a body, which if rendered independent, and kept strictly to their own department merits great confidence for their learning and integrity. . . .

. . . Experience proves the [ineffectiveness] of a bill of rights. True. But [though] it is not absolutely [effective] under all circumstances, it is of great potency always. . . . A brace the more will often keep up the building which would have fallen with the brace the less.

Although James Madison was the principal sponsor of the Bill of Rights in Congress, he had at first opposed adding a bill of rights to the Constitution. As a Federalist, and one of the chief authors of the Constitution, Madison saw a bill of rights as unnecessary. But Madison's friendship with Thomas Jefferson helped change his mind. Even though Jefferson wrote the Declaration of Independence, he had not participated in the Constitutional Convention because he was then U.S. Minister to France. Madison and Jefferson wrote letters to each other discussing the merits of a bill of rights.

Jefferson argued that "a bill of rights is what the people are entitled to against every government on earth, general or particular, and what no just government should refuse, or rest on inference." Madison believed that a bill of rights would be little more than a "parchment barrier" against the will of the majority. But Jefferson reminded Madison that one great strength of a bill of rights was "the legal check which it puts into the hands of the judiciary." Madison repeated Jefferson's point when he introduced his draft of the Bill of Rights in Congress, saying: "independent tribunals of justice will consider themselves in a peculiar manner the guardians of those rights."

Madison had reversed his original opposition to a bill of rights by the time he ran for Congress from Virginia against James Monroe. A key to Madison's victory over Monroe was his promise to work for passage of a bill of rights in Congress.

When the new Congress convened, Madison quickly acted to fulfill his campaign pledge. On May 4, 1789, Madison announced to the House of Representatives his intention to propose amendments to the Constitution protecting individual rights. The next day both Virginia and New York applied to Congress to call a second constitutional convention. Madison was able to delay immediate action on the applications. He worried that some Anti-Federalists were using the lack of a bill of rights as an excuse to call a constitutional convention that would take away the government's powers. The momentum for a second convention finally ended when Madison introduced his suggested amendments in June.

Despite the states' demands for a bill of rights, Madison had difficulty convincing Congress to act. At the time, Congress was preoccupied with import duties, which were necessary to finance the government. Some legislators believed that proposed amendments should wait until more experience was gained about the specific flaws in the new government. But Madison warned that if Congress continued to postpone action, the public "may think we are not sincere in our desire to incorporate such

*Doodling by Thomas Lloyd, a stenographer, on his notes of debates in the First Congress indicates that he might have been an unreliable record-keeper. Unfortunately, Lloyd's notes, printed as the* Congressional Register, *are the chief source of information regarding the intentions of the framers of the Bill of Rights.*

Library of Congress

amendments in the constitution as will secure those rights, which they consider as not sufficiently guarded." Finally, on June 8, Madison introduced his proposed amendments.

## THE FIRST DRAFT

Madison's first draft for the Bill of Rights was not a separate bill of rights as such. Rather, he intended for his amendments to be inserted into the actual text of the Constitution at the appropriate places. Madison based his proposals on the amendments recommended by the state ratifying conventions, in particular those from Virginia. One might say that Madison was the editor of the Bill of Rights, not its author. He did not rely on his own original ideas, but rather selected among the nearly 100 different provisions offered by the states. Madison chose amendments on which there was a consensus among the states. He specifically avoided any that might prove controversial, which would delay their ratification in the states and make a second constitutional convention more likely.

One big difference between Madison's proposed protections of rights and similar provisions in the states was the tone of the language. State declarations of rights said that rights such as free speech "ought" not be denied. Madison's version said that rights "shall" not be denied. Saying

# A "Nauseous Project"

*James Madison*

James Madison (1751-1836) was a reluctant supporter of the Bill of Rights, although he is credited as its author. As a Federalist, Madison initially opposed adding a bill of rights to the Constitution. But his friend Thomas Jefferson and the voters of Virginia convinced Madison that a bill of rights was both philosophically sound and politically necessary.

Madison faced an uphill battle getting the Bill of Rights through the first Congress. When the legislators finally agreed to hear Madison's suggested amendments, they criticized his proposals unmercifully. Opponents referred to Madison's amendments as "milk and water" and "water gruel" designed to cure the imaginary illnesses of the public.

Some Anti-Federalists in Congress accused Madison of more ominous motives. By offering the people meaningless amendments, they argued, Madison was distracting attention from the serious dangers to liberty posed by a strong central government. Madison's critics charged that his amendments were "a tub thrown out to a whale"—referring to sailors' practice of throwing out a wooden tub to distract the whale and prevent it from attacking the ship itself.

Even George Mason, the chief advocate of a bill of rights, offered Madison little support. Mason commented that Madison had become, after his election to Congress, the "patron of amendments." Mason added, "perhaps some milk and water propositions may be made . . . by way of throwing out a tub to the whale; but of important and substantial amendments, I have not the least hope."

Congressional debates over the Bill of Rights were, in Madison's words, "extremely difficult and fatiguing" and "exceedingly wearisome." Indeed, members of Congress challenged each other to duels at one passionate point in the debates. After months of congressional deliberations, Madison wrote to a friend that the Bill of Rights had become a "nauseous project." But Madison's skill as a lobbyist finally paid off, and Congress approved the final version of the Bill of Rights on September 25, 1789.

a right "ought" not be denied implied that it could be violated if necessary; saying a right "shall" not be denied meant that it could never be legally violated. "Ought" said that a right was just a good idea; "shall" said that it was a command.

### THE HOUSE AND SENATE VERSIONS

Madison's original draft contained every provision that became part of the U.S. Bill of Rights. But during congressional debate, the format of

Madison's proposal was changed, and several of Madison's suggested amendments were eliminated. Those eliminated were a general declaration of the theory of popular government, a prohibition of state violations of certain individual liberties, a limit on appeals to the Supreme Court, and a statement of the separation of powers doctrine.

The House of Representatives adopted Roger Sherman's motion that Madison's amendments be added to the end of the Constitution, not incorporated within the text. On August 24, 1789, the House passed seventeen proposed amendments, making few changes to the substance of Madison's original proposals. The Senate reduced those amendments to twelve by combining some and eliminating others. The Senate also weakened the language on religious freedom, but the conference committee that reconciled the House and Senate versions restored the religious liberty protections. On September 25, 1789, Congress asked the president to send the twelve proposed amendments to the states for ratification.

## RATIFICATION

Most states moved quickly to ratify the Bill of Rights. Nine states had ratified the Bill of Rights by the end of June 1790—most importantly North Carolina and Rhode Island, which had previously refused to join the Union. When Vermont became a state in 1791, however, the number of states needed to ratify the Bill of Rights increased to eleven.

Anti-Federalists in the states charged that the proposed Bill of Rights only distracted people from the real problem of increased governmental powers. Nonetheless, the amendments met with popular approval, and only two failed to be ratified: one changing the apportionment of Congress and the other forbidding congressional pay raises to take effect until after the next election. The Bill of Rights thus became ten amendments, not twelve. On December 15, 1791, Virginia became the eleventh state to ratify the Bill of Rights, and it became part of the law of the land. Three of the original states—Massachusetts, Georgia, and Connecticut—did not ratify the Bill of Rights until 1939, celebrating the 150th anniversary of the submission of the Bill of Rights to the states for ratification.

And in 1992, enough states had finally ratified—over a period of 200 years—the proposed amendment about congressional pay raises. It became the Twenty-seventh Amendment to the Constitution.

## THE SCOPE OF THE BILL OF RIGHTS

As the Supreme Court held in *Barron v. Baltimore* (1833), the Bill of Rights applied only to the national government, not the states. Thus, only the national government was forbidden to pass laws abridging those freedoms listed in the Bill of Rights. Madison had initially proposed an amendment prohibiting the states from violating "the rights of conscience, or the freedom of the press, or the trial by jury in criminal cases." Congress defeated the amendment, although Madison viewed it as "the most valuable amendment in the whole list."

When the Fourteenth Amendment was added to the Constitution in 1868, however, the status of the Bill of Rights regarding the states began to change. The primary author of the Fourteenth Amendment had argued that it made the Bill of Rights applicable to the states. Yet the Supreme Court waited almost thirty years before slowly extending, one by one, most of the guarantees of the Bill of Rights to the states. Only then was the birth of the Bill of Rights finally complete.

"Let me give you a lesson in American history: James Madison never intended the Bill of Rights to protect riffraff like you."

# The **FIRST** Ten Amendments

The Bill of Rights, in the words of President Franklin D. Roosevelt, is "the great American charter of personal liberty and human dignity." The Bill of Rights is less than 500 words long, but these first ten amendments to the Constitution contain many rights.

The Bill of Rights has two major groups of rights. The first group is commonly known as "First Amendment Freedoms." These rights are fundamental to each citizen's full participation in American government; they include freedom of religion, speech, press, assembly, and petition. The second group of rights, by far the largest, consists of those that protect persons accused of crimes. These rights are stated in the Fourth, Fifth, Sixth, and Eighth amendments. Early Americans took great care to ensure the rights of criminal defendants, because they had been defendants themselves under British rule. While most of the Bill of Rights deals with criminal law, in which the government accuses a person of a crime, other rights have to do with civil law, which involves disputes between private parties over such issues as contracts and injuries to persons and property.

Originally, the Bill of Rights only limited the national government and did not apply to the states. But after the Fourteenth Amendment was ratified in 1868, the Supreme Court began incorporating the Bill of Rights, the process of applying its provisions—one by one—to the states. Most of the rights in the Bill of Rights now restrict the states as well as the federal government. This section explores the history of each right in the Bill of Rights and describes how the Supreme Court has interpreted those rights.

# The **FIRST** Amendment

**CONGRESS** *shall make* **NO LAW** *respecting an* **ESTABLISHMENT OF RELIGION**, *or prohibiting the* **FREE EXERCISE** *thereof; or abridging the* **FREEDOM OF SPEECH**, *or of the* **PRESS**, *or the right of the people* **PEACEABLY TO ASSEMBLE**, *and to* **PETITION THE GOVERNMENT** *for a redress of grievances.*

The First Amendment is often considered the most important amendment in the Bill of Rights. It protects many rights Americans hold most dear: freedom of religion, of speech, of the press, of assembly, and of petition. The Supreme Court has held that the First Amendment also protects freedom of association, which is not mentioned but is linked to other First Amendment freedoms.

Some people argue that these rights are more important than others in the Bill of Rights because they come first. When Congress sent the Bill of Rights to the states for ratification, however, two other amendments came before what is now the First Amendment. But those amendments were not ratified by the states and did not deal with individual liberties. Thus, the freedoms listed in the First Amendment always came before other rights in the Bill of Rights, even in its original version.

The rights in the First Amendment are essential to democratic government. Without freedom of religion, members of unpopular faiths can be denied civil freedoms, as was done in colonial America. And without the freedoms of speech, press, assembly, petition, and association, citizens cannot be fully informed about important issues or take action on them.

# STATE ACTION

**CONGRESS** *shall make* **NO LAW** . . .

Although this opening phrase does not guarantee a specific right, it is very important. It says that *Congress* is forbidden to make certain laws—not the states or local communities. James Madison included a provision in his original draft of the Bill of Rights to make certain rights apply to the states, but that amendment was defeated in Congress. Consequently, the Supreme Court ruled in *Barron v. Baltimore* (1833) that the Bill of Rights applied only to the national government, not the states. Only after the Fourteenth Amendment was ratified did the Supreme Court begin to apply the Bill of Rights to the states.

Now, the Bill of Rights restricts federal, state, and local governments—or those who act under their authority. This principle is known as the state action requirement. The Bill of Rights applies to all actions of government (the state), but it does not apply to *private* actions. For instance, a private employer who forbids employees to talk on the job does not violate freedom of speech. The First Amendment says that *"Congress* shall make no law" violating those rights; it does not mention the actions of private citizens.

While the opening phrase in the First Amendment says that Congress shall make *no* law regarding those rights, in practice very few rights are that absolute. Justice Hugo Black, however, often argued that "no law means *no law.*" Nonetheless, Congress frequently passes laws that affect the rights in the Bill of Rights. The Supreme Court determines whether those laws restrict individual freedom so much that they must be declared unconstitutional.

# FREEDOM OF RELIGION

. . . *respecting an* **ESTABLISHMENT OF RELIGION**, *or prohibiting the* **FREE**

**EXERCISE** *thereof;* . . .

The very first right mentioned in the First Amendment is freedom of religion, indicating its importance to the American people. As protected by the First Amendment, freedom of religion consists of two parts: the Establishment Clause and the Free Exercise Clause. The Establishment Clause forbids the government from creating—or establishing—an official church, formally supporting religious activities, or giving preference to religion. But under the Free Exercise Clause, the government also cannot interfere with the expression of religious beliefs. Sometimes these two rights conflict.

## RELIGIOUS LIBERTY BEFORE 1791

During colonial times and still today, England has an established church, the Church of England, that is officially supported by the government. Many of the American colonists fled England to escape persecution by its established church, yet they quickly established churches of their own in the New World.

Library of Congress

*In her Boston home, Anne Hutchinson preached that people could commune directly with God, rather than through Puritan ministers. She was banished from the Massachusetts Colony in 1638 for heresy and joined Roger Williams in Rhode Island.*

**COLONIAL PRACTICES.** In most of colonial America, church and state were not separate. Colonies with established churches required citizens to support those churches through their taxes, regardless of their beliefs. Furthermore, colonists sometimes could not vote unless they belonged to a church. Colonists were also required to go to church on Sunday, and, in early Virginia, could be whipped if they failed an examination in the faith. Thus, under established religion a sin became a crime.

In New England, the Congregational religion was the established church. In southern colonies, the Church of England (which became the Episcopal Church after the Revolution) was the established religion. Only four colonies—Delaware, New Jersey, Pennsylvania, and Rhode Island—did not have established churches. Some colonies, such as Maryland, tolerated other religions even though they had established churches. A haven for Catholics, Maryland protected the rights of all persons "professing to believe in Jesus Christ" in its Toleration Act of 1649. But toleration was not the same as freedom of religion. The very word "toleration" meant that religious beliefs were not a right but a privilege, subject to the "tolerance" of others.

One of the greatest colonial advocates of religious freedom was Roger Williams. A Puritan minister, Williams was expelled from Massachusetts in 1635 for his controversial ideas—among them that government had no right to enforce religious laws. Instead, Williams advocated that "a permission of the most Paganish, Jewish, Turkish, or Antichristian consciences and worships be granted to all men in all nations and countries." Williams founded the colony of Rhode Island in 1636 to guarantee religious liberty for all creeds.

**THE VIRGINIA STATUTE OF RELIGIOUS LIBERTY.** By the time of the American Revolution, the idea of religious freedom was gaining momentum. Virginia, for example, moderated some of its earlier punishments against religious dissenters, although it still jailed those who denied the doctrine of the trinity or the divinity of the Bible. Thomas Jefferson decried such practices. Government should only penalize actions that harmed other people, he thought, not punish beliefs. "It does me no injury for my neighbor to say that there are twenty gods, or no god," Jefferson declared. "It neither picks my pocket nor breaks my leg."

Jefferson helped lead the struggle in Virginia for freedom of religion. Although the Virginia Declaration of Rights of 1776 included a provision for religious freedom, many prominent Virginians such as George Washington and Patrick Henry advocated a tax to support all Christian churches in the state. Thomas Jefferson and James Madison opposed the tax. Jefferson drafted a law, the Statute of Religious Liberty, to guarantee freedom of religion in Virginia. Madison wrote his "Memorial and Remonstrance Against Religious Assessments," an essay that helped convince the Virginia legislature to pass Jefferson's statute in 1786.

The Virginia Statute of Religious Liberty provided the most extensive protections of religious freedom of its time. The law stated that "whereas Almighty God hath created the mind free . . . no man shall be compelled to frequent or support any religious worship." Furthermore, the law held that "all men shall be free to profess . . . their opinion in matters of religion, and that the same shall in no wise . . . affect their civil capacities." No longer could Virginians be denied the right to vote and participate in government because of their religious beliefs. Thomas Jefferson was so proud of this law that he had his authorship of it, along with the Declaration of Independence, listed on his tombstone.

**RELIGION AND THE CONSTITUTION.** By the time the U.S. Constitution was written in 1787, religious freedom had gained importance at the national level. Indeed, it was one of the few individual liberties protected in the text of the original Constitution. Article VI states that "no religious test shall ever be required as a qualification to any office or public trust under the United States." Consequently, government jobs could not be limited to certain religious groups.

However, many people believed that the original Constitution did not provide enough protection. Six of the eight states that proposed amendments to the Constitution recommended that religious freedom be included. Therefore, Madison included the Establishment Clause and the Free Exercise Clause when he proposed the Bill of Rights in Congress. The Senate tried to weaken the language of the Establishment Clause, allowing government to aid religion in general if it did not prefer one religion over another, but Madison's original version prevailed.

# From Toleration to Freedom

*President George Washington visited Newport, Rhode Island, in 1790. There he was presented with an address by the Hebrew Congregation of Newport, who had built the Touro Synagogue. Washington's reply emphasized that freedom of religious belief, not mere toleration, was the standard of the new nation.*

Touro Synagogue, Newport, Rhode Island

*The Touro Synagogue is America's oldest surviving Jewish house of worship.*

## To the President of the United States of America

*Sir.*

Permit the children of the Stock of Abraham to approach you with the most cordial affection and esteem for your person and merits, and to join with our fellow citizens in welcoming you to Newport. . . .

Deprived as we heretofore have been of the invaluable rights of free citizens, we now . . . behold a Government, erected by the Majesty of the People.—a Government, which to bigotry gives no sanction, to persecution no assistance—but generously affording to All liberty of conscience, and immunities of Citizenship:—deeming every one, of whatever Nation, tongue, or language equal parts of the great governmental machine. . . .

— *Moses Seixas, Warden*

## To the Hebrew Congregation in Newport, Rhode Island

*Gentlemen.* . . .

The Citizens of the United States of America have a right to applaud themselves for having given to mankind examples of an enlarged and liberal policy: a policy worthy of imitation. All possess alike liberty of conscience and immunities of citizenship. It is now no more that toleration is spoken of, as if it was by the indulgence of one class of people, that another enjoyed the exercise of their natural rights. For happily the Government of the United States, which gives to bigotry no sanction, to persecution no assistance, requires only that they who live under its protection should demean themselves as good citizens, in giving it on all occasions their effectual support.

. . . May the Children of the Stock of Abraham, who dwell in this land, continue to merit and enjoy the good will of the other Inhabitants; while every one shall sit in safety under his own vine and figtree, and there shall be none to make him afraid. . . .

— *G. Washington*

# THE ESTABLISHMENT CLAUSE

*. . . respecting an* **ESTABLISHMENT OF RELIGION,** *. . .*

This clause, or phrase, of the First Amendment is known as the Establishment Clause. It restricts the relationship between the government and the church. The Establishment Clause forbids the government from creating, or establishing, an official church; nor can it support one religion over another, or religion over nonreligion.

**A WALL OF SEPARATION.** In a letter to the Baptists of Danbury, Connecticut, Thomas Jefferson wrote that the Establishment Clause erects "a wall of separation between church and state." Therefore, the Establishment Clause is often said to require "separation of church and state." Those words, however, do not actually appear in the First Amendment.

The Supreme Court did not rule on the meaning of the Establishment Clause until *Everson v. Board of Education* (1947), which incorporated the clause to apply to the states. In *Everson,* the Court set forth a definition of the Establishment Clause:

> Neither a state nor the federal government can set up a church. Neither can pass laws which aid one religion, aid all religions, or prefer one religion over another. Neither can force . . . a person to go to or to remain away from church against his will, or force him to profess a belief or disbelief in any religion.

The Court also held that government may not participate in religious affairs nor impose taxes for their support. "In the words of Jefferson," said the Court, the Establishment Clause "was intended to erect 'a wall of separation between church and state.'"

**HOW HIGH A WALL?** But how high should the "wall of separation" be? Most public officials take their oaths of office in the name of God. Military chaplains serve every branch of the armed forces. "In God We Trust" appears on American money. Church property and contributions to religious organizations are exempt from taxes. Sessions of Congress and of many state legislatures and city councils open with a prayer. Should these practices be prohibited by the Establishment Clause?

Some people say yes, arguing that the Constitution requires a strict separation between church and state. These separationists oppose any mingling of church and state functions. Other people known as accommodationists believe that government must at times accommodate,

*This 1871 cartoon by Thomas Nast, entitled* Church and State—No Union Upon Any Terms, *shows Columbia rejecting the pleas of various religious denominations.*

or make allowances for, the role of religion in society. Otherwise, they say, government would be hostile to religion and risk violating the Free Exercise Clause. At times the Supreme Court has been more separationist about Establishment Clause issues, and at other times more accommodationist.

In *Lemon v. Kurtzman* (1971), the Supreme Court set forth a three-part test, based on its holdings in previous cases, for determining whether a government policy violates the Establishment Clause:

1. The policy's purpose must be secular, not religious.
2. The policy's primary effect must neither advance nor inhibit religion.
3. The policy must avoid an "excessive entanglement" of government and religion.

Using this test, the Supreme Court struck down many government policies as violations of the Establishment Clause. But in the 1990s, Chief Justice William Rehnquist and other members of the Supreme Court openly opposed the *Lemon* test. However, the Court refused to overturn *Lemon.* Thus, while the *Lemon* test is not always popular with the Supreme Court, it has not yet been entirely abandoned.

**RELIGION AND THE SCHOOLS.** Most cases under the Establishment Clause involve religion and education. Since public schools are agencies of the government, any religious programs in them raise Establishment Clause issues, as does government aid to private religious schools.

*Released Time.* Many states have allowed students to be "released" during school time to attend religious classes. These "released-time" programs were examined by the Supreme Court in two major cases. In *McCollum v. Board of Education* (1948), the Court struck down an Illinois released-time program. In that program, religious teachers came into the public school classrooms, and students who did not wish to participate were required to leave their classrooms and go to study hall instead.

But in *Zorach v. Clauson* (1952), the Supreme Court upheld a released-time program in New York that allowed students to leave school property and attend religious classes in private facilities. Writing for the Court's majority, Justice William O. Douglas declared:

> We are a religious people whose institutions presuppose a Supreme Being. . . . [Government] respects the religious nature of our people and accommodates the public service to their spiritual needs. To hold that it may not would be to find in the Constitution a requirement that the government show a callous indifference to religious groups. That would be preferring those who believe in no religion over those who do believe.

*Parochaid.* Government aid to parochial, or religious, schools is often known as "parochaid." This financial support can take many forms: tax deductions for parents with children in private religious schools, bus transportation and textbooks for parochial students, and providing public school teachers for parochial school classes. Supreme Court rulings about parochaid have been confusing and contradictory.

In *Everson v. Board of Education* (1947), the Supreme Court ruled that New Jersey could reimburse parents for bus transportation to church-supported schools. Such practices, the Court said, did not primarily aid religion, but ensured child safety—similar to providing police protection at school crossings. The Court's reasoning in this case became known as the "child benefit theory."

However, in the *Lemon* case, the Supreme Court struck down a Pennsylvania law that reimbursed private schools for teachers' salaries, textbooks, and other teaching materials. The Court held that the program directly benefited religious schools and required such close state supervision that it created an "excessive entanglement" with religion.

The Court tends to be more lenient about aid to religious colleges and universities, as opposed to elementary and secondary schools, on the theory that college students are less likely to be influenced by religious doctrines. In *Tilton v. Richardson* (1971), the Court allowed federal grants to sectarian, or religious, colleges for erecting academic buildings as long as the buildings were never used for religious purposes.

The Supreme Court has ruled on parochaid issues in a variety of other cases. The Court has held that tax deductions for both public and private educational expenses are acceptable, but that tuition tax credits only for parochial schools are not. And the Court has ruled that states may lend textbooks to parochial school students, but may not lend such items as movie projectors, films, tape recorders, maps, and globes. The Court has forbidden government funding for bus transportation for field trips by religious schools, but upheld bus rides to and from school. As one constitutional expert commented, these parochaid cases leave "lawyer and layman alike . . . wondrously perplexed."

In more recent cases, the Rehnquist Court has generally taken an accommodationist stance toward parochaid. The Court upheld the provision of a state-sponsored interpreter for a deaf student attending Catholic school in *Zobrest v. Catalina Foothills School District* (1993). For the first time, the Court allowed a public employee to participate in religious instruction. But in *Kiryas Joel School District v. Grumet* (1994), the Supreme Court struck down a New York law that created a special school district to benefit the disabled children in the village of Kiryas Joel—a community of very conservative Jews, the Satmar Hasidim, who segregate themselves from modern society. The Court held that the New York law was not neutral to religion and instead benefited a single sect.

*School Prayer.* Perhaps the most controversial Establishment Clause issue involves prayer in public schools. In *Engel v. Vitale* (1962), the Supreme Court prohibited the use of a nondenominational prayer composed by the New York State Board of Regents to open the school day. The Court held that "in this country it is no part of the business of government to compose official prayers for any group of the American people to recite as part of a religious program carried on by government."

In *Abington School District v. Schempp* (1963), the Supreme Court also struck down a Pennsylvania law requiring the school day to begin with Bible readings and the Lord's Prayer. And in *Wallace v. Jaffree* (1985), the Court declared unconstitutional Alabama's "moment of silence" law, which set aside a period of silence in public schools for "meditation or voluntary prayer." The Court held that the law had no legitimate secular purpose because its legislative history indicated that "the state intends to

# The Courage of Their Convictions: Ishmael Jaffree

*Ishmael Jaffree wanted his children to be "free from programmed thinking." Below Jaffree describes what happened after he filed a lawsuit challenging Alabama's "moment of silence" law. The Supreme Court overturned the law in* **Wallace v. Jaffree** *(1985).*

UPI/Bettmann

*Ishmael Jaffree*

That's when the publicity really started. The school-board president thought he could make political points and he started attacking me, and the local media just had a field day. I got a lot of hostile reaction. The black community was up in arms that some black person had done this. I got portrayed as a person who was trying to take God out of the public schools. The talk shows in Mobile were filled with people who said, Why doesn't he go back to Africa where he came from. I got all kinds of nasty letters, and I got nasty phone calls at all times of night. I used to talk with people and try to let them understand why I did this—that it was a matter of principle and the schools shouldn't be promoting anybody's religion. People in the neighborhood stopped their children from associating with my children. My children got jumped on, laughed at, talked about in school. My children started turning against me; they said it was a stupid lawsuit. They especially turned against me when Judge Hand [the lower court judge] ruled against me. They told me the judge had said what I was doing was stupid. . . .

As soon as Judge Hand ruled, everybody started having prayer sessions in school. The school-board president even called in the media and led children in prayer at lunch. This was all focused on my children. One of them used to bury his head when the media came around. We got more threats on my life. Some of the black people would see me at the mall and criticize me. I was considered a misfit. It wasn't until the court of appeals ruled in my favor that the attitude among blacks started to change slightly. . . .

I had never been in the Supreme Court before, and I was aware of a sense of awe, the sense of serenity of the place, the power that these justices have. Everything was so solemn and quiet. It was like a church.

While I was there at the argument, sitting at the counsel table, I really wanted to answer some of the questions. They asked whether the "moment of silence" statute had ever been implemented, and whether the Jaffree children had suffered any injuries, and whether there was a case or controversy. I knew the answers to all of those questions, and it was frustrating that I couldn't answer them. I wanted to say something so they could see I was a real human being with flesh and blood, I wanted to tell them about my children. . . .

The Supreme Court decision created a great deal of joy in my children. They suddenly realized that I had won, and that the whole case was over. That was it! The teachers in my children's schools stopped saying the prayers, although I found out they were still praying in other schools. But they are very careful not to pray in my children's schools, because they know that I, more than any other person in Mobile, would raise the issue all over again.

Reprinted with permission of The Free Press, a division of Macmillan, Inc., from *The Courage of Their Convictions: Sixteen Americans Who Fought Their Way to the Supreme Court* by Peter Irons. Copyright 1988 by Peter Irons.

characterize prayer as a favored practice." Furthermore, in *Lee v. Weisman* (1992), the Supreme Court ruled that official prayers at public school graduation ceremonies violated the Establishment Clause.

In sum, the Supreme Court's decisions have prohibited school sponsorship of religious exercises. The Court has never banned prayer in public schools if it is done voluntarily by individual students. Nor has the Court forbidden the study of religion or the Bible, as long as such study is done in a secular, or nonreligious, manner. However, opponents of the Supreme Court's decisions advocate an amendment to the Constitution to allow government-sponsored prayer in public schools. And despite the Court's rulings, school-sponsored prayer and Bible readings still continue in many public school classrooms.

*Evolution.* State laws that prohibit the teaching of evolution, which conflicts with the biblical version of creation, also raise Establishment Clause issues. In the famous "monkey trial" of 1925, John Scopes was convicted of teaching evolution in violation of Tennessee law. Scopes's conviction was overturned by the state supreme court on a technicality, so the U.S. Supreme Court did not rule on the issue of antievolution laws until 1968.

In *Epperson v. Arkansas* (1968), the Supreme Court struck down an Arkansas law that prohibited the teaching of evolution. The Establishment Clause, said the Court, "forbids alike the preference of a religious doctrine or the prohibition of theory which is deemed antagonistic to a particular dogma." Furthermore, the Court held, "the state has no legitimate interest in protecting any or all religions from views distasteful to them." In *Edwards v. Aguillard* (1987), the Supreme Court also struck down a Louisiana law that required the teaching of biblical "creation science" in conjunction with the scientific theory of evolution.

*Equal Access.* One particularly thorny issue is whether a public school or university violates the Establishment Clause when it gives religious groups "equal access" to school facilities on the same basis as other student groups. In *Widmar v. Vincent* (1981), the Supreme Court held that a university regulation denying student use of university facilities for religious purposes violated the students' freedom of speech, by discriminating against religious speech. (The Free Speech Clause, discussed later, forbids government to prohibit speech based on its content.) In *Widmar,* the Court held that an equal access policy did not violate the Establishment Clause because "[u]niversity students are, of course, young adults. They are less impressionable than younger students and should be able to appreciate that the university's policy is one of neutrality toward religion."

Fred Veleba

*Bridget Mergens wanted "equal access" for her Bible club at Westside High School in Nebraska.*

In 1984, Congress extended the *Widmar* principle to high school students by passing the Equal Access Act. The law forbade public high schools that received federal funds and allowed student groups not related to the curriculum, such as chess clubs and social groups, to meet from discriminating against such groups "on the basis of the religious, political, philosophical, or other content of the speech at such meetings." Thus, if a school allowed a chess club to meet, it had to allow a Bible club to meet as well. The law specifically provided that teachers or other school officials could not participate in student religious groups.

In *Westside Community Schools v. Mergens* (1990), the Supreme Court held that the Equal Access Act did not violate the Establishment Clause. Said the Court:

> [T]here is a crucial difference between *government* speech endorsing religion, which the Establishment Clause forbids, and *private* speech endorsing religion, which the Free Speech and Free Exercise Clauses protect. We think that secondary school students are mature enough and are likely to understand that a school does not endorse or support student speech that it merely permits on a nondiscriminatory basis.

The Supreme Court extended the equal access doctrine in *Lamb's Chapel v. Center Moriches Union Free School District* (1993), when it held that if a school allows nonschool adult groups to use its facilities after school hours, religious groups must be allowed to use the property as well. And in *Rosenberger v. University of Virginia* (1995), the Court held that if a university subsidizes other student publications, it cannot exclude a Christian magazine.

# The Courage of Their Convictions: Bridget Mergens

*Bridget Mergens wanted to start a Bible club at her high school. In the process, she tested the boundaries between the Establishment Clause and the Free Speech Clause. Her case became a landmark decision of the Supreme Court,* Westside Community Schools v. Mergens *(1990). This article was printed a few months before the Supreme Court's decision.*

Bridget Mergens never thought of herself as an activist. Active, yes. By the time she was a senior at Westside High School, in Omaha, Nebraska, Bridget was an officer of the school drama club and a member of the choir, and she was carrying a full load of advanced placement classes. But she wasn't the political type. She had never been to a rally or demonstration. And all she knew about America's legal system was what she picked up watching *L.A. Law.* She certainly never imagined that she could ignite a legal battle that would land in the chambers of the Supreme Court of the United States.

But that's just what happened . . . at the beginning of her senior year in high school. Bridget's legal odyssey began one morning when she approached her homeroom teacher—"a close pal"—who was also Westside's principal. "I asked him if I could start an afterschool Bible club," Bridget recalls.

Bridget figured the principal, James Findlay, would be delighted to hear that she and a group of her Christian friends wanted to stay after school for a Bible-discussion group. "There are a lot of problems with teenagers in Omaha," Bridget explains. "There are drug gangs here, the Crips and the Bloods from Los Angeles. Kids are getting killed in malls and on the street. Drugs are all over the place. It's a really hard time for young people. I thought the school would be happy that a bunch of students wanted to sit around after school and talk about the Bible."

Bridget was wrong. "Dr. Findlay said that we absolutely could not meet," she remembers. "I was shocked."

Findlay didn't object to Bridget's basic idea of a Bible-discussion group. He actually encouraged it. But he said he couldn't allow her to hold the meetings at school, even after hours. Findlay believed that letting Bridget's Bible group meet at school would be in direct violation of U.S. laws forbidding the mixing of church and state—or in this case, bringing religion into public schools.

Bridget accepted Findlay's decision at first. As a firm believer in religious freedom, she's strongly opposed to the idea of school prayer or any other move that would require students to practice a religion they don't believe in. "If anyone ever told me I had to pray," she says, "I'd tell them to take a jump. I also think it's wrong for parents to force their kids to go to church. Religion is something that each person has to decide on their own."

But as Bridget mulled over her disappointment, she began to wonder whether it was logical to compare her idea of a voluntary Bible club with school prayer, in-class Bible reading, or any other mandatory religious study. "Our Bible club wasn't going to be adults telling students they had to pray or read the Bible," says Bridget. "It was just students joining because they wanted to exchange ideas with each other." . . .

. . . "I really believed we were being treated unfairly," says Bridget. "We weren't asking for special treatment. And if we wanted to do something destructive, like sacrifice dogs or cats or mess up the school, I could understand it. But all we wanted to do was meet like any other club."

Although not everyone in school agreed with Bridget, she found that both her teachers and fellow students respected her decision to stand up for what she believed. "Some of the younger punk-rocker types would walk by me in the hall and say, 'Hey, let's go sacrifice a cow after school,' or, 'Let's go worship Satan,'" Bridget recalls with a laugh. "And some of my more liberal teachers called me 'Fundy,' for fundamentalist. But they were joking. And most people were really supportive. My social-studies teachers thought it was the greatest thing to talk about in class." . . .

The Court's decision will no longer have any direct bearing on Bridget's life. She's married now, attending college, . . . and even has a new last name—Mayhew.

But the outcome of her case will affect virtually every public school in America. . . . Bridget says she's proud to have started it all. "I have a different name now," she says. "So when people are talking about the *Mergens* case, they won't even know it's me. But I'll always know."

---

Excerpt from "From High School to the High Court" by Lauren Tarshis, *UPDATE,* January 26, 1990. Copyright 1990 by Scholastic, Inc. Reprinted by permission of Scholastic, Inc.

As the equal access cases illustrate, Establishment Clause issues can be very difficult. In trying to ensure separation of church and state, the government can risk violating the free exercise of religion and freedom of speech.

**RELIGION IN THE PUBLIC SQUARE.** The Establishment Clause is also involved when religion enters the public square, such as the town hall and the state legislature. The Court has been more inclined to permit religious expression in these official settings, since the impressionable nature of schoolchildren is not an issue. But government endorsement, or official support, of religion is prohibited in the public square as well as the public classroom.

*Holiday Displays.* Many local governments put up displays and decorations celebrating Christmas, a religious holiday for Christians. Some also commemorate Hanukkah, a Jewish holiday. In *Lynch v. Donnelly* (1984), the Supreme Court upheld the use of a Christmas nativity scene by the city of Pawtucket, Rhode Island, because the display included secular symbols of the season as well, such as a Santa and his reindeer. Critics of the decision called it the "two reindeer rule."

Similarly, the Court in *Allegheny County v. Greater Pittsburgh ACLU* (1989) upheld a holiday display by a local government that contained a Hanukkah menorah, a Christmas tree, and a sign calling the display a "salute to liberty." The Court said that such a display recognized cultural diversity, rather than endorsed religion. However, in that same case, the Court disallowed a nativity scene inside the county courthouse that had no other secular symbols. Such a display in a public building, held the Court, implied government endorsement of religion. But in *Capitol Square Review v. Pinette* (1995), the Supreme Court upheld the right of private organizations to place religious displays on public property. The Court affirmed the right of the Ku Klux Klan (KKK) to erect a cross on a public square next to the Ohio state capitol.

*Prayer in Legislatures.* While official prayer is forbidden in the public schools, it is allowed in Congress and the state legislatures. Both houses of Congress and most state legislatures begin their daily sessions with prayer, often led by chaplains paid with public funds. The Supreme Court upheld this practice in *Marsh v. Chambers* (1983), a case involving the Nebraska legislature. The Court noted the historical roots of prayers in legislative bodies and distinguished between schoolchildren and legislators, who are not "susceptible to religious indoctrination or peer pressure."

Close Up Foundation/Renée Bouchard

*Does this Easter display, erected by a private group on the steps of the U.S. Capitol, violate the Establishment Clause?*

**GOVERNMENT REGULATIONS THAT BENEFIT RELIGION.** General government ment regulations can often benefit religion. Such government action violates the Establishment Clause only if its purpose and effect are to sponsor or advance religion.

*Sunday Closing Laws.* Originally, laws that require businesses to close on Sunday, known as "blue laws," were designed to aid religions that honored Sunday as their sabbath. Jewish merchants, for instance, preferred to close on Saturday, the Jewish sabbath, and use Sunday as a normal business day. Nonetheless, the Supreme Court held in *McGowan v. Maryland* (1961) that Sunday closing laws served the secular purpose of creating a uniform day of rest and relaxation.

*Tax Exemptions.* All states and the federal government exempt religious property from taxation. The Supreme Court upheld this practice in *Walz v. Tax Commission* (1970), noting that tax exemptions were also provided for other educational and charitable organizations. Such exemptions indicated government's "benevolent neutrality" toward religion, not its official support.

## THE FREE EXERCISE CLAUSE

*. . . or prohibiting the* **FREE EXERCISE** *thereof; . . .*

This part of the First Amendment is known as the Free Exercise Clause. While cases under the Establishment Clause involve government policies that *aid* religion, cases under the Free Exercise Clause challenge government policies that *burden* religion. Most laws that are contested under the Free Exercise Clause today do not discriminate against a particular religion directly, but rather impose a hardship when applied to certain religious groups.

**BELIEF VS. ACTION.** Freedom of religious *belief* is one of the very few absolute rights in the Bill of Rights. But religious belief often involves *action,* which government can regulate.

The very first Supreme Court case involving the Free Exercise Clause, *Reynolds v. United States* (1879), distinguished between belief and action. Reynolds was a Mormon living in Utah who had more than one wife, a practice known as polygamy. The Mormon church advocated polygamy for its members, but federal law prohibited it. The Supreme Court upheld Reynolds's conviction under federal law despite his religious beliefs. The Free Exercise Clause, said the Court, did not protect actions

*These four wives in a polygamous Mormon family were arrested by police during the 1950s in Short Creek, Arizona. Some fundamentalist Mormon sects continue to practice polygamy.*

Utah State Historical Society

that were "violations of social duties or subversive of good order." The Court noted, for example, that religious beliefs in human sacrifice would not exempt an individual from being prosecuted for murder. Similarly, the Supreme Court in later cases upheld laws that required schoolchildren to be vaccinated despite their parents' religious beliefs and that prohibited the use of poisonous snakes in religious ceremonies. Also, parents who deny their children medical treatment for religious reasons may be prosecuted as criminals.

In *Cantwell v. Connecticut* (1940), which incorporated the Free Exercise Clause to apply to the states, the Supreme Court again distinguished between belief and action. The Court held that free exercise of religion "embraces two concepts—freedom to believe and freedom to act. The first is absolute but, in the nature of things, the second cannot be." Nonetheless, the Court struck down a state law that required solicitors for religious groups to be licensed. Cantwell was a Jehovah's Witness, a fundamentalist group known for actively promoting its beliefs. Jehovah's Witnesses have been involved in many of the Supreme Court's religion cases.

**THE FLAG-SALUTE CASES.** One of the most controversial cases involving Jehovah's Witnesses was *Minersville School District v. Gobitis* (1940). Lillian Gobitis, 12, and her brother William, 10, refused to salute the U.S. flag, as required in many states, and were suspended from school. The Gobitis family believed that saluting the flag was idolatry, forbidden by the Ten Commandments. But the Supreme Court, in a decision issued while World War II was being fought in Europe, upheld the flag-salute law and said that "religious liberty must give way to political authority."

Public outcry against the *Gobitis* decision was great, and in only three years the Supreme Court overturned it. In *West Virginia State Board of Education v. Barnette* (1943), which also involved Jehovah's Witness children, the Court struck down the flag-salute laws on both free exercise and free speech grounds. In an oft-quoted opinion, Justice Robert H. Jackson wrote for the Court:

> Freedom is not limited to things that do not matter much. That would be a mere shadow of freedom. The test of its substance is the right to differ as to things that touch the heart of the existing order.

> If there is any fixed star in our constitutional constellation, it is that no official, high or petty, can prescribe what shall be orthodox in politics, nationalism, religion, or other matters of opinion or force citizens to confess by word or act their faith therein.

Forcing students to salute the flag and recite the Pledge of Allegiance was contrary to the Bill of Rights, the Court held. Furthermore, added Justice Jackson: "To believe that patriotism will not flourish if patriotic ceremonies are voluntary and spontaneous instead of a compulsory routine is to make an unflattering estimate of the appeal of our institutions to free minds."

**THE TEST.** The Supreme Court has set forth the following test to decide whether a religious practice is protected by the Free Exercise Clause. First, the Court determines whether the beliefs are "sincerely held." To do so, however, the Court cannot consider whether or not the beliefs are factually true. As held in *United States v. Ballard* (1944): "Men may believe what they cannot prove." If the religious beliefs are sincere, the Court then balances the burden on the individual's religious practice against the government's interest in the challenged action. Traditionally, the government could win only if its interest was "compelling"—a very strict test.

However, for the Free Exercise Clause to apply at all, individuals must first prove that the government *forces* them to violate their religious beliefs. In *Lyng v. Northwest Indian Cemetery Protective Association* (1988), the Supreme Court upheld a logging road through national forestlands, even though the government admitted that the road would cause irreparable damage to the sacred areas of American Indians. The Supreme Court held that the government did not have to prove a compelling interest in the road, because the American Indians did not own the land and because the government was not actively forcing them to violate their beliefs.

**VIOLATIONS OF FREE EXERCISE.** In the examples below, government actions were struck down as violations of the Free Exercise Clause under the "compelling interest" test.

*Unemployment Benefits.* The government may not deny unemployment benefits to people who quit their jobs because of conflicts with their religious beliefs. In *Sherbert v. Verner* (1963) and *Hobbie v. Florida* (1987), Seventh-Day Adventists had been fired because they refused to work on Saturdays, their sabbath.

Pennsylvania Dutch Visitors Bureau

*Amish children do not have to attend school past the eighth grade, held the Supreme Court in* Wisconsin v. Yoder *(1972).*

*Compulsory Education.* The government may not require compulsory education beyond the eighth grade for the Amish, who believe in separating themselves from the modern world. Many Amish do not send their children to school beyond the eighth grade, despite state laws requiring further compulsory school attendance. In *Wisconsin v. Yoder* (1972), the Supreme Court held that the Amish did not have to comply with a Wisconsin compulsory attendance law because the "self-sufficient agrarian lifestyle essential to their religious faith is threatened . . . by modern education." The Court held that the "state's interest in universal education" did not outweigh the free exercise rights of the Amish.

**NOT VIOLATIONS OF FREE EXERCISE.** Government actions in the following examples were upheld under the "compelling interest" test against charges that they violated the Free Exercise Clause.

*Conscientious Objectors.* The Supreme Court has never ruled that the Free Exercise Clause requires that persons who oppose war on religious grounds must be exempt from the draft. And, in *Gillette v. United States* (1971), the Court held that a law restricting religious exemptions to those opposed to war in any form, rather than a particular war, is justified by the government's interest in a uniform draft system with few exceptions.

*Social Security.* The government can require the Amish to pay Social Security taxes, as do all other employers, even though the Amish have a religious practice of self-sufficiency and taking care of their own, as held the Supreme Court in *United States v. Lee* (1982).

*Racial Discrimination.* The government may deny tax-exempt status to private schools that practice racial discrimination based on religious beliefs, as held in *Bob Jones University v. United States* (1983).

*Military Dress.* The military's interest in uniformity and discipline outweighs an individual's free exercise rights. A Jewish Air Force captain who wore a yarmulke (skullcap) on duty was disciplined for violating regulations prohibiting nonmilitary apparel. The Supreme Court upheld the regulations in *Goldman v. Weinberger* (1986).

**A NEW TEST.** The Supreme Court recently changed the traditional "compelling interest" test in free exercise cases. In *Employment Division v. Smith* (1990), the Court ruled that the state does not need a compelling interest to justify a general criminal law (as opposed to one that targets specific religious practices). In *Smith,* the Court upheld an Oregon law prohibiting the use of peyote, a hallucinogenic drug some American Indians use in religious ceremonies.

The Supreme Court applied the *Smith* test in *Church of the Lukumi Babalu Aye v. City of Hialeah* (1993) to overturn laws prohibiting animal sacrifice. The Court held that four Florida cities had passed laws that specifically targeted the Santeria religion, which practices animal sacrifice as a form of prayer.

Many religious groups opposed the *Smith* decision because they believed it limited religious liberty, particularly for minority religions. They supported the Religious Freedom Restoration Act (RFRA), a federal law enacted in 1993 that restores the pre-*Smith* test for free exercise cases involving the national government. The RFRA requires the federal government to demonstrate a compelling interest if any of its laws place a burden on a religious group.

## FREEDOM OF SPEECH

*. . . or abridging the* **FREEDOM OF SPEECH***, . . .*

Freedom of speech is closely linked to the rights that follow it in the First Amendment, including freedom of the press, of assembly, and of petition. These rights are referred to collectively as freedom of expression. Supreme Court decisions dealing with freedom of speech often apply to other rights of free expression as well.

Freedom of expression is essential to democratic government. Without free speech, citizens cannot debate the actions and policies of their elected officials, nor can they be well informed about current issues. Thus, some people argue that the First Amendment protects only political speech. But others maintain that freedom of speech is not limited to politics, but includes art, music, literature, science, and business.

Freedom of speech seems simple at first. Government may not prohibit the right of free speech. But what is "speech"? Does freedom of speech

Don Wright, *The Palm Beach Post*

mean spoken words alone, or does it also include actions, such as rock concerts and flag burnings? Also, the right to free speech has been limited by the courts. What, if any, limits on free speech should be allowed in a democracy?

## HISTORICAL BACKGROUND

As long as there have been governments, there has been censorship, the official denial of free expression. Censorship has taken different forms— among them banned books, laws against certain types of speech, and imprisonment or death for dissenters.

In sixteenth-century England, for example, a subject of Henry VIII would be sent to prison for saying, "I like not the proceedings of this realm." In earlier times, the sentence would have been even harsher— death for treason. England also had a very restrictive system of licensing for publications. None of the great English documents of liberty, including the Magna Carta and the 1689 Bill of Rights, protected freedom of speech or of the press.

In America, freedom of speech was first mentioned in the Massachusetts Body of Liberties in 1641. After the Revolutionary War, several states included freedom of speech in their constitutions. But only three states recommended that this freedom be included in amendments to the U.S. Constitution. Nonetheless, freedom of speech was included when the Bill of Rights was ratified in 1791.

**THE SEDITION ACT OF 1798.** Americans upheld the right of free speech only imperfectly, however. Just a few years after the First Amendment was ratified, the national government passed the Sedition Act, part of the infamous Alien and Sedition Acts of 1798. Sedition is the urging of resistance to lawful authority or rebellion against the government. The Sedition Act made it a crime to write, print, or say "any false, scandalous, and malicious" statements against the government and its officials or "to incite against them the hatred of the good people of the United States." The act was designed by President John Adams and his Federalist allies in Congress primarily to suppress dissent by their political opponents, the Democratic-Republicans led by Thomas Jefferson. One of the first persons convicted under the act was a member of Congress, who accused President Adams of "an unbounded thirst for ridiculous pomp, foolish adulation, and selfish avarice [greed]."

The Sedition Act was never challenged before the Supreme Court, in part because the Democratic-Republicans feared how the Federalist-dominated Court might rule. The immensely unpopular act contributed to the defeat of the Federalists in 1800 and expired soon thereafter. No other national sedition law was passed until 1917.

**THE CIVIL WAR ERA.** The states, not the national government, were the primary arenas for laws restricting free speech between 1800 and 1917. The most controversial issue was slavery. Slaves, of course, had no free speech rights. And in the antebellum South, free speech on the slavery issue was forbidden to whites as well. In some southern states, for example, the mail was censored to prevent any abolitionist materials from coming in. In the 1830s, proslavery forces even convinced Congress to refuse to receive antislavery petitions. In 1844, Congress reversed its policy after a prolonged outcry against this denial of free speech and petition.

**THE LABOR MOVEMENT.** One of the most critical forces in the battle for free speech was the labor movement in the late nineteenth and early twentieth centuries. The struggle to organize the industrial workforce into unions was often violent, and labor unions faced intense opposition. Streets and public parks were frequently closed to labor speakers under local permit systems. Also, labor unions challenged the boundary between speech and action, claiming that picketing against businesses was protected speech. Business leaders, however, saw pickets as coercive action, and the courts routinely issued injunctions, orders prohibiting a specified action, to prevent union pickets. Members of the International

Close Up Foundation/Renée Bouchard

*Demonstrators march both for abortion rights and against. Demonstrations are a form of speech plus action protected by the First Amendment.*

Workers of the World (IWW), or "Wobblies," were particularly active in challenging local ordinances suppressing speech. A group of middle-class reformers, the Free Speech League, also opposed the restrictive laws.

**THE ESPIONAGE ACT OF 1917.** With the advent of World War I, the national government once again acted to punish speech. To suppress criticism of the war, Congress passed the Espionage Act of 1917. The act made it a crime to interfere with the recruiting of soldiers or the draft and to "willfully utter, print, write, or publish any disloyal, profane, scurrilous, or abusive language about the form of government of the United States."

More than 2,000 people were convicted under the Espionage Act. The law was challenged repeatedly, and for the very first time the Supreme Court heard cases on freedom of speech. Although the Court upheld the law on several occasions, it began developing a doctrine of free speech that would eventually protect the very speech forbidden by the Espionage Act. As of World War I, the Supreme Court became the primary player in defining freedom of speech.

## PRINCIPLES OF FREE SPEECH

In the years since 1917, the Supreme Court has developed some basic principles regarding freedom of speech. The Court incorporated freedom of speech to apply to the states in *Gitlow v. New York* (1925).

**TYPES OF SPEECH.** Freedom of speech is not limited to spoken words alone, but includes several types of speech. Pure speech involves only spoken words, such as debates and public meetings, and has the greatest protection under the First Amendment. Speech-plus is speech combined with action, such as demonstrations and picketing. The speech portion of speech-plus is generally protected, but the action portion may be regulated. The Supreme Court held that peaceful picketing was protected by the First Amendment in *Thornhill v. Alabama* (1940).

Symbolic speech is conduct that conveys a message in itself, without spoken words, and is sometimes known as "expressive conduct." But the Supreme Court has held: "We cannot accept the view that an apparently limitless variety of conduct can be labeled 'speech' whenever the person engaging in the conduct intends thereby to express an idea." Thus, some forms of symbolic speech are protected by the First Amendment, while others are not.

*Burning Draft Cards.* The Supreme Court held in *United States v. O'Brien* (1968) that burning a draft card to protest the Vietnam War was not symbolic speech protected by the First Amendment. Draft cards were necessary to the legitimate government purpose of raising an army, held the Court, and the federal law prohibiting the destruction of draft cards was not designed to suppress dissent.

*Flag Burning.* The Supreme Court held in *Texas v. Johnson* (1989) that burning an American flag was symbolic speech under the First Amendment. Johnson, who burned a flag at the 1984 Republican National Convention, was convicted under a Texas law that made it a crime to "desecrate" a flag in a manner that "the actor knows will seriously offend" others. Said the Court: "If there is a bedrock principle underlying the First Amendment, it is that the government may not prohibit the expression of an idea simply because society finds the idea itself offensive or disagreeable."

Soon after the *Johnson* decision, Congress passed the Flag Protection Act of 1989, which punished flag desecration whether or not it offended onlookers. Protesters burned flags on the steps of the U.S. Capitol in response. In *United States v. Eichman* (1990), the Supreme Court held that the Flag Protection Act was unconstitutional because it punished any person who "knowingly mutilates, defaces, physically defiles, . . . or tramples upon any flag." Each of those terms, said the Court, prohibited a person from showing *disrespect* for the flag, not from the mere act of burning the flag—which was the proper way to destroy a worn or soiled flag. Thus, held the Court, the law punished the content of the message, not the action itself, and violated the First Amendment.

# Case Study: Texas v. Johnson (1989)

*Gregory Lee Johnson burned an American flag as part of a political protest and was convicted of desecrating a flag under Texas law. The Supreme Court held that the Texas law violated the First Amendment.*

UPI/Bettmann

*Police arrest a man who burned an American flag on the steps of the U.S. Capitol to protest the Flag Protection Act.*

### Justice Brennan
delivered the opinion of the Court. . . .

The First Amendment literally forbids the abridgement only of "speech," but we have long recognized that its protection does not end at the spoken or written word. . . .

It remains to consider whether the state's interest in preserving the flag as a symbol of nationhood and national unity justifies Johnson's conviction. . . .

If there is a bedrock principle underlying the First Amendment, it is that the government may not prohibit the expression of an idea simply because society finds the idea itself offensive or disagreeable. . . .

We have not recognized an exception to this principle even where our flag has been involved. . . .

. . . To conclude that the government may permit designated symbols to be used to communicate only a limited set of messages would be to enter territory having no discernible or defensible boundaries. Could the government, on this theory, prohibit the burning of state flags? Of copies of the presidential seal? Of the Constitution? In evaluating these choices under the First Amendment, how would we decide which symbols were sufficiently special to warrant this unique status? To do so, we would be forced to consult our own political preferences, and impose them on the citizenry, in the very way that the First Amendment forbids us to do. . . .

There is, moreover, no indication—either in the text of the Constitution or in our cases interpreting it—that a separate . . .

category exists for the American flag alone. Indeed, we would not be surprised to learn that the persons who framed our Constitution and wrote the [First] Amendment were not known for their reverence for the Union Jack [England's flag]. The First Amendment does not guarantee that other concepts virtually sacred to our Nation as a whole—such as the principle that discrimination on the basis of race is odious and destructive—will go unquestioned in the marketplace of ideas. . . .

We are tempted to say, in fact, that the flag's deservedly cherished place in our community will be strengthened, not weakened, by our holding today. Our decision is a reaffirmation of the principles of freedom and inclusiveness that the flag best reflects, and of the conviction that our toleration of criticism such as Johnson's is a sign and source of our strength. . . .

The way to preserve the flag's special role is not to punish those who feel differently. . . . It is to persuade them that they are wrong. . . . We can imagine no more appropriate response to burning a flag than waving one's own, no better way to counter a flag-burner's message than by saluting the flag that burns, no surer means of preserving the dignity even of the flag that burned than by—as one witness here did—according its remains a respectful burial. We do not consecrate the flag by punishing its desecration, for in doing so we dilute the freedom that this cherished emblem represents. . . .

### Chief Justice Rehnquist,
dissenting. . . .

. . . For more than 200 years, the American flag has occupied a unique

*W*e do not consecrate the flag by punishing its desecration, for in doing so we dilute the freedom that this cherished emblem represents.

position as the symbol of our nation, a uniqueness that justifies a governmental prohibition against flag burning in the way . . . Johnson did here. . . .

The American flag, . . . throughout more than 200 years of our history, has come to be the visible symbol embodying our nation. It does not represent the views of any particular political party, and it does not represent any particular political philosophy. The flag is not simply another "idea" or "point of view" competing for recognition in the marketplace of ideas. Millions and millions of Americans regard it with an almost mythical reverence regardless of what sort of social, political, or philosophical beliefs they may have. I cannot agree that the First Amendment invalidates the act of Congress, and the laws of 48 of the 50 states, which make criminal the public burning of the flag. . . .

. . . The Texas statute deprived Johnson of only one rather inarticulate symbolic form of protest—a form of protest that was profoundly offensive to many—and left him with a full [range] of other symbols and every conceivable form of verbal expression to express his deep disapproval of national policy. Thus, in no way can it be said that Texas is punishing him because his hearers—or any other group of people—were profoundly opposed to the message that he sought to convey. Such opposition is no proper basis for restricting speech or expression under the First Amendment. It was Johnson's use of this particular symbol, and not the idea that he sought to convey by it . . . for which he was punished. . . .

. . . The Court decides that the American flag is just another symbol, about which not only must opinions pro and con be tolerated, but for which the most minimal public respect may not be [required]. The government may [draft] men into the armed forces where they must fight and perhaps die for the flag, but the government may not prohibit the public burning of the banner under which they fight. I would uphold the Texas statute as applied in this case.

**PUBLIC FORUMS.** A basic principle of free speech is the concept of a public forum—a place such as a street or a park that is traditionally used for freedom of speech and other First Amendment rights. Government may not deny free speech rights in a public forum, but it may issue "time, place, and manner" regulations about when, where, and how freedom of speech may be exercised. For instance, the government can forbid speeches on loudspeakers in parks after 9:00 p.m. to regulate noise. In making regulations for a public forum, the government must be content-neutral, meaning that it cannot forbid speech based on its content, on the nature of the message.

As long as it is content-neutral, the government may also restrict free speech in a public forum if it interferes with the exercise of another constitutional right. In *Madsen v. Women's Health Center* (1994), the Supreme Court allowed restrictions on antiabortion protesters that were designed to protect access to abortion clinics. The Court upheld both limits on amplified noise and a buffer zone in which protests were not allowed near the clinic's entrance.

**OVERBREADTH AND VAGUENESS.** The Supreme Court has held that certain laws have a "chilling effect" on speech—that is, they prevent citizens from exercising their First Amendment rights. Overbreadth means that a law restricts protected speech as well as unprotected speech and is not written narrowly to serve the government's legitimate purposes. Vagueness means that a law is not clear and specific, so that reasonable people are not able to understand what kind of expression is forbidden. The Supreme Court will also strike down a law as "void for vagueness" if it gives government officials too much discretion and can be enforced in a discriminatory manner.

One example of overbreadth is an airport regulation stating that the terminal area "is not open for First Amendment activities by any individual or entity." The Supreme Court struck down the regulation in 1987, holding that it could be read to "prohibit even talking and reading or the wearing of campaign buttons or symbolic clothing." "No conceivable government interest," said the Court, "would justify such an absolute prohibition of speech."

**THE RIGHT NOT TO SPEAK.** Government cannot force a person to be silent, but neither can it force a person to speak. This principle was upheld in *West Virginia State Board of Education v. Barnette* (1943), in which the Court ruled that students cannot be forced to say the pledge of allegiance. In *Wooley v. Maynard* (1977), the Court held that government also cannot force citizens to become "mobile billboards." Maynard, a Jehovah's Witness like Barnette, objected to the New Hampshire state motto, "Live Free or Die," on his automobile license plate because it conflicted with his beliefs about eternal life. Maynard was arrested three times for covering the words with tape, but the Supreme Court upheld his right not to speak.

**GOVERNMENT AS SPEAKER.** While government must be content-neutral about citizens' speech, it is not forbidden from communicating its own messages and making value choices. In *Rust v. Sullivan* (1991), the

Supreme Court upheld government regulations forbidding family planning clinics that received federal funds from giving their clients any information about abortion. The clinics claimed that the regulations denied their employees and clients freedom of speech. Lawyers for the government, however, argued that "the government is able to take sides, it is able to have viewpoints, when it is funding." The Court agreed, holding that "when the government appropriates public funds to establish a program it is entitled to define the limits of that program." Critics of the decision charge that, in an era of widespread federal funding, government now has broad authority to limit speech. In the words of one commentator, government can "bribe people to say . . . things that it couldn't bludgeon them into saying."

**SPEECH IN CAMPAIGNS.** In politics, the Supreme Court has held, "money is speech." Therefore, campaign financing laws are subject to the First Amendment. In *Buckley v. Valeo* (1976), the Court upheld laws that restricted direct contributions to a candidate, since large contributions could imply corruption. But the Court struck down laws that limited how much a person could spend independently on behalf of a candidate, since that limited freedom of expression.

The Supreme Court has generally allowed states to regulate speech to ensure the integrity of elections. Thus, in 1992, the Court upheld a Tennessee restriction on campaigning within 100 feet of polling places and a Hawaii ban on write-in voting. But in 1995, the Court struck down an Ohio prohibition of anonymous campaign literature—as applied to a lone pamphleteer on a school tax issue. In such limited situations, said the Court, the First Amendment protected the right to remain anonymous.

## LIMITS ON FREE SPEECH

Freedom of speech has limits. As Justice Oliver Wendell Holmes once wrote: "The most stringent protection of free speech would not protect a man in falsely shouting fire in a theater and causing a panic." Some areas of restricted speech include obscenity, defamation, fighting words, commercial speech, speech in special places, and speech that leads to illegal action.

**OBSCENITY.** Obscene speech is not protected by the First Amendment. Obscenity is generally defined as anything that depicts sex or nudity in a way that violates society's standards of decency. The problem is how to define obscenity legally. As Justice Potter Stewart noted: "I may not be able to define [obscenity], but I know it when I see it."

The Supreme Court set forth a complex three-part test for obscenity in *Miller v. California* (1973). Speech or conduct is obscene if it has all of the following characteristics:

1. "[T]he average person, applying contemporary community standards," would find that the work, taken as a whole, "appeals to the prurient interest"—that is, an obsessive interest in sex.
2. "[T]he work depicts or describes, in a patently offensive way," a type of sexual conduct prohibited by law.
3. "[T]he work, taken as a whole, lacks serious literary, artistic, political, or scientific value."

The *Miller* test gave local communities a great deal of authority in outlawing obscenity. As Chief Justice Warren Burger said: "It is neither realistic nor constitutionally sound to read the First Amendment as requiring that the people of Maine or Mississippi accept public depiction of conduct found tolerable in Las Vegas or New York." Furthermore, obscene material must be taken as a whole: "A quotation from Voltaire on the flyleaf of a book will not redeem an otherwise obscene publication."

The Supreme Court upheld the right of a person to possess obscene materials for private use in his or her home in *Stanley v. Georgia* (1969). "If the First Amendment means anything," said the Court, "it means that the state has no business telling a man, sitting alone in his own home, what books he may read or what films he may watch." But the Court has also upheld laws that forbid sending obscene materials in interstate commerce or importing them. The Court has been most strict with pornography that involves children.

Some speech is considered "indecent" without being technically obscene. The Supreme Court ruled in 1989 that an interstate ban on obscene telephone messages, known as "dial-a-porn," was constitutional, although a ban on indecent telephone services was not. And in *Cohen v. California* (1971), the Court held that some arguably obscene speech could be used in political statements to express intense emotions.

In 1991, the Supreme Court ruled that nude dancing, although it is an expressive activity, does not enjoy full First Amendment protection. States can regulate public nudity, including nude dancing, without violating the First Amendment. Justice Antonin Scalia argued that the Indiana law at issue was not focused solely on nude dancing and was

UPI/Bettmann

*Attorney General Edwin Meese in 1986 announced the findings of his Commission on Pornography, which concluded that pornography is harmful to society. Is the statue behind Meese, entitled* The Spirit of Justice, *obscene?*

legitimate even though the club involved only admitted adults. Wrote Scalia: "The purpose of Indiana's nudity law would be violated, I think, if 60,000 fully consenting adults crowded into the Hoosierdome to display their genitals to one another, even if there were not an offended innocent in the crowd."

**DEFAMATION.** Besides obscenity, the First Amendment also does not protect defamation, damaging another person's reputation through false information. Slander is defamation through the spoken word; libel is defamation through the written word. For instance, if a client told other people that her lawyer was unethical, she could be sued for slander; if she made the accusation in a letter, she could be sued for libel. Truth is always a complete defense in defamation cases.

The Supreme Court has developed very strict standards for slander and libel of public officials and public figures, because defamation lawsuits can create a chilling effect on free speech. These standards are discussed in greater detail under freedom of the press, because most defamation cases involving public figures are libel suits against newspapers, magazines, or books.

**FIGHTING WORDS.** The First Amendment does not protect abusive or insulting language, known as "fighting words." In *Chaplinsky v. New Hampshire* (1942), the Supreme Court held that such words, spoken face-to-face, "have a direct tendency to cause acts of violence" and are not protected speech. Chaplinsky was arrested for calling a city official a "damned Fascist" and a "goddamned racketeer." Fighting words are more like a verbal assault than an exchange of information and opinion.

*Hate speech.* Some people argue that ethnic slurs are like "fighting words" and should not be protected by the First Amendment. Some colleges and cities have even adopted policies and laws that prohibit "hate speech" on the basis of race, religion, gender, or sexual orientation. Supporters of prohibitions on hate speech point out that the First Amendment already has limits; speech that hurts people based on race or religion should be one of those limits—just like defamation or fighting words. They agree with Justice Oliver Wendell Holmes, who wrote that "words can be weapons."

Critics charge that codes against "hate speech" violate freedom of speech by determining what is "politically correct." They also maintain that censorship does not change bigoted attitudes. Furthermore, say such critics, speech codes punish general remarks about groups of people that, while offensive, do not cause the types of direct harm to specific individuals that are currently recognized by the Supreme Court as exceptions to the First Amendment. Otherwise, they say, any speech that hurt someone's feelings would not be protected by the First Amendment.

The Supreme Court has ruled on two cases that deal with hate speech. In *R.A.V. v. St. Paul* (1992), the Court overturned a St. Paul, Minnesota, city ordinance prohibiting the use of symbols, such as a burning cross or a Nazi swastika, on public or private property that "arouses anger, alarm, or resentment in others on the basis of race, color, creed, religion or gender." R.A.V., a white juvenile, was accused of burning a cross in a black family's yard.

The Supreme Court held that the St. Paul law punished speech that could not be regulated purely on the basis of its content. The Court pointed out that the city of St. Paul had other ways of punishing cross-burning—such as laws against arson and "terroristic threats." Said the Court: "Let there be no mistake about our belief that burning a cross in someone's front yard is reprehensible. But St. Paul has sufficient means at its disposal to prevent such behavior without adding the First Amendment to the fire." Indeed, R.A.V. was later jailed for the crime under other criminal statutes.

But in *Wisconsin v. Mitchell* (1993), the Supreme Court upheld a Wisconsin law that increased the penalty for crimes committed because of the victim's race, religion, sexual orientation, or other listed factors. Todd Mitchell, a black man, was accused of leading an attack against a white juvenile after watching the movie *Mississippi Burning*—in which a white man beat a black youth who was praying. Mitchell asked the men in his group, "Do you all feel hyped up to move on some white people?"

This case was not like *R.A.V.,* the Supreme Court said in its *Mitchell* decision: "A physical assault is not by any stretch of the imagination expressive conduct protected by the First Amendment." The Court held that although Mitchell's words and thoughts about the white victim contributed to his sentence, such is often the case in criminal law where differing motives lead to differing punishments. For instance, some states use the death penalty in cases of murder for financial gain but not in other types of murder. Moreover, said the Court, federal laws already prevent discrimination in housing, employment, public accommodations, and other areas. According to the Court, such laws do not violate the First Amendment because they prohibit discriminatory action, not speech.

**COMMERCIAL SPEECH.** Advertising, or commercial speech, is not fully protected by the First Amendment. For instance, government can regulate false advertising, but it cannot regulate false ideas. Government can also prohibit the advertisement of illegal products or services. Moreover, in 1986 the Supreme Court held that government may restrict advertisements for legal products if it has the power to outlaw them altogether. Thus, Congress has passed laws restricting advertisements for alcohol and tobacco products.

Advertising does have some protection under the First Amendment, however. States cannot prohibit abortion clinics from advertising, and professional associations cannot ban all advertising by their members. Lawyers, for example, can advertise their services, and pharmacies can advertise the price of prescription drugs. And in 1993, the Supreme Court overturned a Cincinnati, Ohio, ordinance that prohibited news racks containing free advertising publications.

**SPEECH IN SPECIAL PLACES.** Speech may be restricted in some places, even though it could not be in others. The Supreme Court has upheld restrictions on freedom of speech in military bases, prisons, and schools when the expression interferes with the purpose of the facility. In 1976, for example, the Court ruled that military authorities can prohibit the distribution of political literature on military bases.

*Speech in Schools.* The Supreme Court established the principle that teachers and students do not "shed their constitutional rights to freedom of speech or expression at the schoolhouse gate" in *Tinker v. Des Moines School District* (1969). Mary Beth and John Tinker were suspended from school for wearing black armbands to protest the Vietnam War. While the Court recognized the students' right to use symbolic speech, it warned that free speech could be limited if students' actions would "materially and substantially disrupt" the school's educational purpose.

In *Bethel School District v. Fraser* (1986), the Supreme Court held that the rights of students are not the same as the rights of adults in similar settings. Matthew Fraser, a high school senior, had been suspended for making a sexually suggestive speech at a student assembly. Fraser used no obscene words, but he did make several graphic sexual allusions. Although an adult could not have been punished for the same speech, the Court ruled that "the First Amendment does not prevent the school officials from determining that to permit vulgar and lewd speech such as [Fraser's] would undermine the school's basic educational mission." The Court distinguished between the political speech at issue in *Tinker* and the sexual speech made by Fraser.

The Supreme Court has also upheld the broad power of school officials to censor "school-sponsored expressive activities," such as student

## The Courage of Their Convictions: Mary Beth and John Tinker

*Suspended from school for wearing black armbands to protest the Vietnam War, Mary Beth Tinker and her brother John helped define students' First Amendment rights. Below, Mary Beth—as an adult looking back—describes the price she paid for her actions.*

After all the publicity about what we did, we got a lot of repercussions. People threw red paint at our house, and we got lots of calls. We got all kinds of threats to our family, even death threats. They even threatened my little brother and sisters, which was *really* sick. People called our house on Christmas Eve and said the house would be blown up by morning. There was a radio talk-show host in Des Moines who was a right-wing war hawk, and he would always start in on our family, the Tinker family. My mother used to listen to this all the time. I couldn't stand to listen to it, but she loved to tune in and see what they were saying. One night he said that if anyone wanted to use a shotgun on my father he would pay for the court costs if anything happened.

I was leaving for school one morning, on my way out the door, and the phone rang and I picked it up. This woman said, "Is this Mary Tinker?" And I said yes.

UPI/Bettmann

And she said, "I'm going to *kill* you!" At that time, I started a policy I still have today; it's a habit. When anyone calls, I always find out who it is before I talk to them, because of that happening that one morning. It's made me a lot more hardened in certain ways, when you learn in a personal way what the repercussions are for doing unpopular things.

*Mary Beth and John Tinker*

Reprinted with permission of The Free Press, a division of Macmillan, Inc., from *The Courage of Their Convictions: Sixteen Americans Who Fought Their Way to the Supreme Court* by Peter Irons. Copyright 1988 by Peter Irons.

newspapers and plays. The Court held in *Hazelwood School District v. Kuhlmeier* (1988) that "educators do not offend the First Amendment by exercising editorial control over the style and content of student speech in school-sponsored expressive activities so long as their actions are reasonably related to legitimate pedagogical [educational] concerns."

**SPEECH AND UNLAWFUL ACTION.** At what point does speech that advocates an unlawful action become more action than speech? At what point can such speech be punished?  In the earliest cases under the First Amendment, speech that advocated an unlawful action, even as an abstract doctrine, was not protected.  But under current law, speech must directly incite specific and immediate unlawful acts to be punished.

*Clear and Present Danger.*  Several important First Amendment cases were decided under the Espionage Act of 1917, which made it a crime to obstruct the draft during World War I.  In *Schenck v. United States* (1919), the Supreme Court upheld the conviction of Schenck, an official of the Socialist party, for mailing thousands of pamphlets to young men to persuade them to resist the draft.  The Court ruled that the Espionage Act did not violate freedom of speech.  As Justice Oliver Wendell Holmes wrote for the unanimous Court:

> Words can be weapons. . . . The question in every case is whether the words are used in such circumstances and are of such a nature as to create a clear and present danger that they will bring about the substantive evils that Congress has a right to prevent.

The "clear and present danger" test established that government can punish speech when it creates an immediate threat of criminal action.  While the Court admitted that in peacetime Schenck's speech would have been protected, in wartime it was not.  "The character of every act depends upon the circumstances in which it is done," said the Court.

*Advocacy of Abstract Doctrine.*  During the 1940s and 1950s, Congress passed several laws to prevent the spread of communism.  The Smith Act of 1940 made it a crime to teach or advocate the violent overthrow of the United States.  In *Dennis v. United States* (1951), the Supreme Court upheld the constitutionality of the Smith Act.  But in *Yates v. United States* (1957), the Court interpreted the Smith Act to forbid only advocacy of the actual violent overthrow of the government, rather than advocacy of government overthrow as an abstract doctrine.  Thus, government can punish an action but not a belief.

*Imminent Action.*  The current test for when speech that advocates an illegal action can be punished was developed in *Brandenburg v. Ohio* (1969).  In that case, the Supreme Court overturned the conviction of a Ku Klux Klan leader who at a rally had advocated violence to overturn civil rights laws.  The Court held that speech cannot be punished, even when it advocates illegal action, unless it is "directed to inciting or producing imminent lawless action" and is likely to do so.  For instance, a speaker cannot be punished for saying, "Let's overturn the government," unless she also says, "and let's blow up the courthouse at nine o'clock tonight."

UPI/Bettmann Newsphotos

*These members of the National Socialist Party of America (American Nazis) rallied in Chicago in 1978. The Nazis never marched in Skokie despite their court victory.*

## THE PRICE OF FREE SPEECH

Taken together, the Supreme Court decisions on freedom of speech create a philosophy about its place in American society. Justice Oliver Wendell Holmes argued that the First Amendment should promote "free trade in ideas—that the best test of truth is the power of the thought to get itself accepted in the competition of the market." According to this theory, government should allow speech that promotes offensive ideas because suppressing speech would be even more damaging to society. As Justice Holmes also said, the First Amendment is not designed to protect "free thought for those who agree with us but freedom for the thought that we hate."

Under the "marketplace of ideas" model of free speech, the best way to respond to offensive speech is with more speech, or counterspeech. Thus, some people argue that in 1977 when Nazis sought to march in Skokie, Illinois, a suburb of Chicago with many survivors of the Holocaust, the residents should have held their own anti-Nazi demonstration rather than try to prohibit the Nazi march. But other people say that the "marketplace of ideas" model unfairly penalizes those who have the least power in the market—such as women, racial minorities, and unpopular religions. The most vulnerable people must pay the price of free speech for others. But, advocates of free speech point out, the most vulnerable people also benefit the most from the protection of unpopular ideas. Freedom of speech protects Ku Klux Klan marches, but it also protects civil rights demonstrations. As one civil liberties activist remarked, "that's the price we pay for liberty."

Tribune Media Services

## FREEDOM OF THE PRESS

. . . *or of the* **PRESS**, . . .

Thomas Jefferson believed so strongly in freedom of the press that he once said: "Were it left to me to decide whether we should have a government without newspapers or newspapers without a government, I should not hesitate a moment to prefer the latter." Like freedom of speech, freedom of the press is essential to a democratic government. A free press ensures that citizens have the information they need to make sound decisions—even when the government wishes otherwise.

Traditionally, freedom of the press applied to the printed word, including pamphlets, books, newspapers, and magazines. But today, freedom of the press protects other media, such as radio and television. However, certain media are subject to more restrictions than others.

### ENGLISH ROOTS

In the late fifteenth century, the art of printing spread rapidly across Europe, aided by the invention of movable type by Johann Gutenberg, a German artisan. With printed material more widely available, censorship soon followed. Monarchs and religious leaders were afraid of the political power that came with a free press.

In England, church officials could suppress heretical books by the 1520s, and Henry VIII issued the first list of banned books in 1529. He also created a licensing system for all books in 1538. As of 1559, all new written works had to be submitted for censors' approval under the order of Henry's daughter, Queen Elizabeth I.

In 1644, John Milton, a renowned Puritan poet and writer, criticized England's licensing system in his oft-quoted essay, *Areopagetica:* "[T]hough all the winds of doctrine were let loose to play upon the earth, so Truth be in the field, we do injuriously by licensing and prohibiting to misdoubt her strength. Let her and falsehood grapple; who ever knew Truth put to the worst, in a free and open encounter?" However, Parliament did not abolish the licensing system until 1694.

Another restraint on freedom of the press, developed by the English courts, was the doctrine of seditious libel—"the intentional publication, without lawful excuse or justification, of written blame of any public man, or of the law, or of any institution established by law." The supposed justification for punishing seditious libel was that criticism of the government led to revolution and unrest. Even if writers told the truth, they could be punished, for "the greater the truth, the greater the libel." Truthful criticism would be most likely to provoke the people to take action against the government.

### FREE PRESS IN AMERICA

The colonial press was licensed, just as in England, and Americans were prosecuted for seditious libel as well. But the crown's defeat in a famous seditious libel trial in New York put a halt to such prosecutions.

**THE ZENGER TRIAL.** A German immigrant who knew little English, John Peter Zenger was the printer of a New York newspaper. Zenger acted as a front for several lawyers who anonymously wrote many articles in his newspaper criticizing the royal governor. Zenger refused to reveal the identity of the writers and was prosecuted for seditious libel, which carried a possible death sentence. At Zenger's trial in 1735, his attorney argued that truth should be a defense against the charge. Said the attorney in his closing argument to the jury:

> The question before the Court and you gentlemen of the jury is not of small or private concern; it is not the cause of a poor printer, nor of New York alone, which you are now trying. No! It may in its consequence affect every freeman that lives under a British government on the main of America. . . . [B]y an impartial and uncorrupt verdict, [you will] have laid a noble foundation for securing . . . that to which nature and the laws of our country have given us a right—the liberty—both of exposing and opposing arbitrary power . . . by speaking and writing truth.

The jury acquitted Zenger, and seditious libel prosecutions virtually ended. But colonial legislatures still had licensing powers.

The Bettmann Archive

*Andrew Hamilton defends John Peter Zenger at his trial in 1735 for seditious libel.*

**AFTER THE REVOLUTION.** The Virginia Declaration of Rights was the first state constitutional protection of freedom of the press after the Revolutionary War. Five states listed freedom of the press in their suggested amendments to the U.S. Constitution of 1787, and freedom of the press became part of the First Amendment when the Bill of Rights was ratified in 1791.

## PRIOR RESTRAINT

The most basic principle of a free press is that government may not, except in extraordinary circumstances, exercise prior restraint or censor a work *before* it is published. Government may sometimes punish certain writings after they are published, however.

**NEAR V. MINNESOTA (1931).** In *Near v. Minnesota*, which incorporated freedom of the press to apply to the states, the Supreme Court struck down a state law that authorized prior restraints. The law allowed local courts to issue an injunction to stop publication of any periodical designated as a "nuisance." A weekly newspaper had been enjoined under the law when it ran articles charging that local officials were guilty of corruption. The Court declared that upholding such prior restraint "would be but a step to a complete system of censorship." But the Court also warned that prior restraint might be permissible in certain cases of national security, such as publishing the "sailing dates of transports or the number and location of troops."

**THE PENTAGON PAPERS.** National security was at issue in the famous "Pentagon Papers" case, which involved top-secret documents on the history of the Vietnam War. Daniel Ellsberg, a former Pentagon employee, illegally copied the Pentagon Papers and leaked them to *The New York Times* and *The Washington Post,* which published excerpts from the documents. The U.S. government obtained a court order forbidding further publication of the Pentagon Papers, the first time in American history that the federal government successfully used a prior restraint.

The newspapers appealed to the Supreme Court in the case of *New York Times v. United States* (1971). The Court held that the government had not proven that publishing the Pentagon Papers would jeopardize national security, thus not overcoming the "heavy presumption" against prior restraints. Wrote Justice Hugo Black: "In the First Amendment, the [Founders] gave the free press the protection it must have to fulfill its essential role in our democracy. The press was to serve the governed, not the governors."

UPI/Bettmann

*The chief pressman for* The Washington Post *celebrates the Supreme Court's decision in the "Pentagon Papers" case.*

**FREE PRESS VS. FAIR TRIAL.** Sometimes freedom of the press can conflict with other rights, such as a defendant's right to a fair trial under the Sixth Amendment. Pretrial publicity can prejudice the community so much that it is impossible to find an impartial jury. But even the defendant's right to a fair trial does not justify prior restraint, held the Supreme Court in *Nebraska Press Association v. Stuart* (1976). In that case, a county judge had issued a "gag order" preventing the media from reporting certain inflammatory details of a murder trial. The Supreme Court struck down the gag order, noting that "a prior restraint on expression comes to this Court with a 'heavy presumption' against its constitutionality." Judges may take certain measures to ensure a fair trial, such as keeping the jury in isolation or changing the location of the trial, but they are not allowed to use prior restraints on the media.

**PERMISSIBLE PRIOR RESTRAINTS.** In a few cases, the Supreme Court has upheld prior restraints. In *Snepp v. United States* (1980), for example, the Court upheld a Central Intelligence Agency (CIA) rule that forbade agents from ever publishing information about the CIA without its approval, even when no longer employed by the agency.

## LIBEL

Prior restraint is a way that the government can limit free press. But individuals can also restrict freedom of the press through libel suits, charging that their reputations have been damaged through false information. When laws make libel easy to prove, the press is often reluctant to publish information in fear of potential lawsuits.

In *New York Times v. Sullivan* (1964), the Supreme Court made libel harder to prove when public officials are involved. *The New York Times* had published an ad by a civil rights group that accused the police in Montgomery, Alabama, of conducting a "wave of terror" against blacks. The ad contained some errors about specific details of police action, and the city commissioner in charge of police, L. B. Sullivan, sued the *Times* for libel. A local Alabama jury awarded him $500,000 in damages.

The Supreme Court unanimously overturned the libel judgment. The Court held that in cases where a public official was criticized for official conduct, errors of fact alone were not enough to prove libel, nor was carelessness in printing the error. To win a libel suit, a public official had to prove the error was made with actual malice, "that is, with knowledge that it was false or with reckless disregard of whether it was false or not." Actual malice is very difficult to prove in libel cases. In later decisions, the Court extended the actual malice standard in libel cases to public figures, as well as public officials. In 1991, the Court held that public figures could sue for libel if they were misquoted to such an extent that there was a "material change in the meaning" of what they actually said.

### CONFIDENTIALITY

At least since John Peter Zenger refused to reveal the names of his writers, the press has claimed the right to deny certain information to the government. Today, reporters often claim that freedom of the press guarantees their right to withhold the names of their confidential sources. Without confidentiality, the reporters argue, many sources would not reveal information vital to the public interest.

But the Supreme Court has held that, in criminal cases, reporters have no special privileges under the First Amendment to refuse to testify. The Court held in *Branzburg v. Hayes* (1972) that reporters "like other citizens, [must] respond to relevant questions put to them in the course of a valid grand jury investigation or criminal trial." Many states, however, have enacted shield laws that give reporters some protection against revealing confidential information.

But what if the press breaks its promise of confidentiality to a source? In 1991, the Supreme Court ruled that news organizations can be sued by sources to whom they had promised confidentiality.

Freedom of the press is not limited to the printed word, but applies to all mass media: forms of information such as film, radio, television, and newspapers that affect large numbers of people. However, print media receive more protection under the First Amendment than do films, radio, and television.

At first, the Supreme Court did not consider movies to be protected by freedom of the press. In 1915, the Court ruled that "the exhibition of moving pictures is a business, pure and simple," and "not . . . part of the press of the country." Many states established movie review boards after this decision to judge films acceptable to community standards. But in 1952, the Supreme Court extended First Amendment protection to motion pictures. Today, the film industry has its own rating system for violence and sexual themes.

Radio and television are regulated by the Federal Communications Commission (FCC). As the Supreme Court noted in *Red Lion Broadcasting v. FCC* (1969), "of all forms of communication, it is broadcasting that has received the most limited First Amendment protection." In *Red Lion,* the Court upheld the power of the FCC to regulate broadcasting more than newspapers and other print media, because radio and television use the airwaves, which are public property that may be controlled by the government. While the First Amendment applies to broadcasting, the Court held in *Red Lion,* "it is the right of the viewers and listeners, not the right of the broadcasters, which is paramount."

However, improved technology has increased the availability of channels and thus lessened the government's role in regulating a formerly scarce commodity. In addition, the rise of cable television, which transmits through wires rather than broadcasts over the public airwaves, created a new hybrid of free speech. In 1994, the Supreme Court ruled that, because it does not use the airwaves, cable television is entitled to greater protection than broadcasting, although it still does not receive as much protection as newspapers.

## FREEDOM OF ASSEMBLY AND PETITION

*. . . or the right of the people* **PEACEABLY TO ASSEMBLE,** *and to* **PETITION THE GOVERNMENT** *for a redress of grievances.*

This clause of the First Amendment protects the right of the people to assemble peacefully and to ask the government to solve certain problems.

Traditionally, the rights of assembly and petition were linked, as though citizens had the freedom to assemble *in order to* petition the government. Indeed, freedom of assembly was almost omitted in the early versions of the Bill of Rights as being too trivial. But the right of assembly has overtaken its sibling, petition, so much so that the right to petition has received less analysis by the courts than any other First Amendment right.

### ASSEMBLY AND PETITION BEFORE 1791

Historically, the right of petition was protected far more than the right of assembly. The Magna Carta of 1215 came about when English noblemen petitioned King John, under threat of force, for solutions to their grievances. The English Parliament then developed the practice of restricting funds for the king unless he responded to its petitions about various problems. In 1689, the English Bill of Rights extended the right of petition beyond Parliament to all English subjects, explicitly stating "that it is the right of the subjects to petition the King and all commitments and prosecutions for such petitioning are illegal."

In America, the right to petition the king took on added significance. The Declaration of Independence specifically lists the king's failure to listen to Americans' petitions as a cause of the Revolutionary War. According to the Declaration, "In every stage of these oppressions, we have petitioned for redress in the most humble terms; our repeated petitions have been answered only by repeated injury."

*In 1769, residents of London, England, petitioned the king "with all the humility which is due from free subjects to their lawful sovereign."*

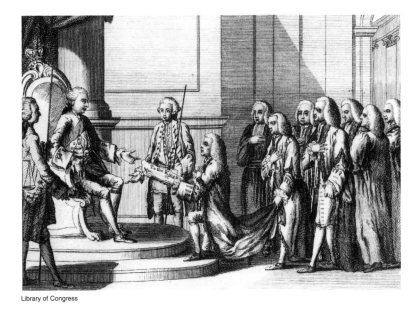

Library of Congress

After the Revolution, four of the newly independent states protected assembly and petition in their bills of rights. Three states recommended that assembly and petition be included in amendments to the U.S. Constitution of 1787. When Congress was considering the proposed Bill of Rights, however, at least one legislator opposed including freedom of assembly on the grounds that it was beneath the dignity of Congress to descend to such trivial details, comparing it to listing the right to put on one's hat. But another representative pointed out that "[i]f the people could be deprived of the power of assembling under any pretext whatsoever, they might be deprived of every other privilege" in the First Amendment. Thus, freedom of assembly stayed in the Bill of Rights.

## FREEDOM OF ASSEMBLY

Far more Supreme Court cases have dealt with assembly than petition. In *DeJonge v. Oregon* (1937), the Supreme Court incorporated freedom of assembly to apply to the states. DeJonge had participated in a public meeting sponsored by the Communist party about alleged police brutality. He was sentenced to seven years in prison under a local law that made advocating violence a crime. The meeting was peaceful and DeJonge himself did not propose violence, but the Communist party, of which he was a member, supported the overthrow of the U.S. government in its platform.

The Supreme Court noted that Oregon's law, like many others at the time, was a reaction to the widespread fear of a Communist takeover of the U.S. government. But, said the Court:

> The greater the importance of safeguarding the community from incitements to the overthrow of our institutions by force and violence, the more imperative is the need to preserve inviolate [untouched] the constitutional rights of free speech, free press, and free assembly in order . . . that changes, if desired, may be obtained by peaceful means. Therein lies the security of the Republic, the very foundation of constitutional government.

The Supreme Court overturned DeJonge's conviction, holding that "peaceable assembly for lawful discussion cannot be made a crime."

## PEACEABLE ASSEMBLY

The First Amendment protects the right of *peaceable* assembly, which means that citizens do not have the right to riot, block public streets, or take over public buildings. As in free speech cases, government may not forbid assemblies based on their content, but it may make reasonable regulations regarding the time, place, and manner of assemblies and demonstrations. The Supreme Court upheld such regulations in *Cox v. New Hampshire* (1941), as long as they were not used to deny freedom of assembly altogether.

**HAGUE V. CIO (1939).** In this case, the Supreme Court found that regulations were being used to deny freedom of assembly. The Committee for Industrial Organization (CIO) applied for a permit to hold union organizing meetings in the streets and parks of Jersey City, New Jersey. The mayor of the town, Frank Hague, opposed unions and denied the permit, which was allowed under city law if officials believed that such action would prevent riots, disturbances, or disorderly meetings.

Hague did not support First Amendment rights in general. As he once said: "You hear about constitutional rights, free speech, and the free press. Every time I hear those words I say to myself, 'That man is a Red, that man is a Communist.' You never hear a real American talk like that."

The Supreme Court struck down the Jersey City permit law, holding that it gave city officials too much arbitrary power. The Court noted that "streets and parks . . . have immemorially been held in trust for the use of the public and, time out of mind, have been used for purposes of assembly." While the privilege to use streets and parks was not absolute, the Court held, "it must not, in the guise of regulation, be abridged or denied."

## ASSEMBLY ON PUBLIC PROPERTY

As a general rule, citizens have the right to use public property, such as streets and parks, for assemblies and demonstrations. In certain cases, however, the Supreme Court has held that freedom of assembly may be denied if it interferes with the purpose of a public building, such as a jail or a courthouse if the demonstration would influence court proceedings.

The Court has also ruled that a city may forbid assemblies near schools that disrupt normal school activities. But the Court struck down a law that banned all demonstrations near schools except in labor disputes, because the law regulated the content of the assemblies, not just their time, place, and manner. And the Court has upheld demonstrations on the grounds of a state capitol, peaceful sit-ins at a public library, and picketing at the Supreme Court building itself.

*More than 200,000 people gathered near the grounds of the Lincoln Memorial in Washington, D.C., to hear the Rev. Martin Luther King's "I Have a Dream" speech in 1963. Public parks are a traditional place to exercise freedom of assembly.*

## ASSEMBLY ON PRIVATE PROPERTY

The Bill of Rights does not apply to private persons, so citizens have no right to assemble on private property under the U.S. Constitution. Property owners can prosecute demonstrators for trespassing, or going on a person's land without permission.

Private shopping malls present a unique First Amendment situation. Because malls are gathering places for large numbers of people, they are—similar to a town square—a natural spot for petitions, demonstrations, and speeches. But because malls are privately owned, the First Amendment does not apply, held the Supreme Court in *Lloyd Corporation v. Tanner* (1972). The Court noted, however, that demonstrators were entitled to use the public streets and sidewalks surrounding shopping malls.

State courts have interpreted their state constitutions to allow freedom of speech and assembly in private shopping malls, even though the U.S. Constitution does not. In *PruneYard Shopping Center v. Robins* (1980), the Supreme Court held that such state action does not deprive the mall owners of their property without just compensation, as required by the Fifth Amendment.

## HOSTILE AUDIENCES

What if the assembly is peaceful but the audience is not? Do the police have an obligation to stop the demonstration or speech? The ability of a hostile onlooker, or heckler, to disrupt an otherwise peaceful assembly or speech is known as a heckler's veto. By jeering or threatening violence, an angry audience can sometimes provoke police to stop the demonstration to protect public safety.

In *Feiner v. New York* (1951), the Supreme Court upheld the conviction of Irving Feiner for "unlawful assembly." In his sidewalk speech, Feiner called the president a "bum" and the American Legion a "Nazi Gestapo," as well as encouraged the predominantly black neighborhood to fight for equal rights. The crowd became angry and restless, and one man threatened to shut Feiner up himself if the police did not. Feiner twice refused to stop speaking, and police arrested him, claiming it was necessary to prevent a fight. The Supreme Court held that "when the speaker passes the bounds of argument and undertakes incitement to riot," police are not "powerless to prevent a breach of the peace."

In *Gregory v. Chicago* (1969), however, the Court overturned the convictions of Dick Gregory and other civil rights activists for disorderly conduct. Gregory had led a march to the home of Chicago Mayor Richard Daley to protest unfair treatment of black students in the city schools. Residents of the all-white neighborhood began throwing rocks and eggs at the protesters and shouting obscenities. The 175 police officers escorting the marchers asked them to leave, but they refused and were arrested. The Supreme Court ruled that the marchers had been acting peacefully and that the angry neighbors were disorderly.

## FREEDOM OF ASSOCIATION

Freedom of association is not specifically mentioned in the First Amendment. Freedom of association involves the ability of people to join together for a common purpose or activity.

The Supreme Court has held that "effective advocacy of both public and private points of view, particularly controversial ones, is undeniably enhanced by group association." For that reason, the Court has ruled that freedom of association is protected by the First Amendment. The Court first recognized freedom of association in *NAACP v. Alabama* (1958). The Court struck down an Alabama law that required organizations to disclose their membership lists, because the harassment of NAACP members that would likely result (during the civil rights era) would impinge on freedom of association.

In 1967, the Supreme Court struck down state loyalty oaths requiring school teachers to swear they were not members of the Communist party or any other subversive organization. But in 1987 and 1988, the Supreme Court ruled that state laws requiring civic organizations and private clubs to include women and minorities did not violate freedom of association because of the state's "compelling interest in eliminating discrimination."

In 1989, the Supreme Court held that freedom of association did not include a general right of "social association." The Court upheld a city law that created special teen dance halls where teenagers were not allowed to socialize with adults. The teenagers were not involved in discussions on public issues, said the Court, and the First Amendment did not protect "chance encounters in dance halls."

®Rotary International

*The Supreme Court ruled in 1987 that state law could require the admission of women to the all-male Rotary Club without violating freedom of association.*

## FIRST AMENDMENT FREEDOMS

The First Amendment protects those freedoms fundamental to a democratic society. Without freedom of expression—including speech, press, assembly, petition, and association—citizens would not have the free exchange of ideas and information necessary to make sound political decisions. And without freedom of religion, a democracy can be torn by religious strife and deny some citizens their basic rights to participate in government, as was done in colonial America. The rights protected by the First Amendment help ensure that democracy is not just majority rule by uninformed bigots, but rather a government run by well-informed citizens who respect each other's differences.

# The **SECOND** *Amendment*

**A WELL-REGULATED MILITIA,** *being necessary to the security of a free state, the right of the people to* **KEEP AND BEAR ARMS** *shall not be infringed.*

The Second Amendment protects the "right of the people to keep and bear arms." But the amendment also begins with a phrase explaining its purpose. This phrase states that a "well-regulated militia" is "necessary to the security of a free state." Does this phrase mean that the people are only allowed to bear arms if they are part of a militia or defending their country? Can guns be used for national defense but not for self-defense?

These questions are part of the ongoing debate over gun control and the Second Amendment. One critical question is the definition of a militia, a group of citizens who defend their community as emergencies arise. In 1791, the militia was composed of all free male citizens—armed with muskets, bayonets, and rifles. Today, the official militia consists of volunteer National Guard units in every state—armed with tanks, automatic weapons, and grenades. Is a militia in the 1990s the same as a militia in the 1790s? How does that affect the meaning of the Second Amendment?

Some Americans believe they have a right to bear arms in private groups and call themselves a militia—despite Supreme Court rulings to the contrary. Whether or not the people have a right to bear arms as individuals, rather than just as part of an official militia, is the central controversy surrounding the meaning of the Second Amendment.

## ENGLISH ROOTS

The right to bear arms was recognized by English courts before the invasion of William the Conqueror in 1066. In fact, English subjects were required to keep weapons to be part of the militia. Although militiamen were trained in the use of arms, they were everyday people—butchers, peasants, farmers, carpenters—not full-time professional soldiers.

But the right to bear arms in England was limited. Laws restricting the use and ownership of private arms dated to the fourteenth century. Guns could not be carried in public, and in the sixteenth and seventeenth centuries, Parliament limited gun ownership to the wealthy. By 1671, the property ownership requirement for keeping guns was fifty times the amount of land required for voting. Consequently, less than one percent of English subjects had the legal right to bear arms.

Some English kings used these restrictions on gun ownership to weaken the militia system, because the militia was under local control. Instead of relying on a militia, these kings preferred a standing army, professional troops hired by the crown and subject only to royal authority. Under Charles II, gunsmiths were required to keep strict records of gun sales, and people needed licenses to carry guns.

James II, a Catholic, succeeded his brother Charles II. James used the arms restrictions to persecute his Protestant subjects during a time of great strife between Catholics and Protestants. After the Glorious Revolution, when James was driven from England in 1688, Parliament included a right for Protestants to bear arms in the English Bill of Rights, which William and Mary of Orange had to sign before taking the throne. Even though the English Bill of Rights thus recognized a right to bear arms, it was only "as allowed by law" and not an absolute right. Furthermore, Parliament did not prohibit a standing army, although it required the king to have Parliament's consent when raising an army during peacetime.

## THE CITIZEN-SOLDIER IN AMERICA

To many political theorists at the time of the American Revolution, the militia represented the perfect alternative to the potential tyranny of a standing army. Adam Smith, a Scottish philosopher, described the difference between a militia and a standing army in his book *The Wealth of Nations* (1776):

> Men of republican principles have been jealous of a standing army as dangerous to liberty. . . . In a militia, the character of the laborer, artificer, or tradesman, predominates over that of the soldier: in a standing army, that of the soldier predominates over every other character. . . .

*The "minutemen" of the American Revolution were typical examples of the militia system's citizen-soldiers.*

In other words, a part-time citizen-soldier would represent the values of the community, and would be less likely to become an instrument of oppression than a full-time professional soldier whose sole identity lay in the use of arms at the king's command.

In the American colonies, the citizen-soldier idea and the militia system flourished. Bearing arms to defend the community was considered a duty of property-owning men. Colonial laws required that all free adult males possess arms and ammunition—or else be fined or disciplined by the community. Periodically, the militia was required to "muster," or assemble for training.

## THE REVOLUTIONARY ERA

British monarchs used the standing army to suppress liberties in America, just as in England. British troops kept the colonists in line when Americans rebelled against acts of the British government they saw as unjust. These actions of the British troops increased Americans' resolve against standing armies.

Nonetheless, to fight the prolonged war of independence against England, America had to rely on more than just the militia system. The famous "minutemen" of the New England militias—ready to fight "at a minute's warning in case of alarm"—also had to be disciplined enough to sustain years, not just minutes, of battle. They had to acquire the traits of professional soldiers, at least for the duration of the revolution.

After the war, however, the newly independent states were still wary of keeping a standing army. When the states wrote constitutions, several

Nancy Hart captures British soldiers during the American Revolution.

The Bettmann Archive

included a right to bear arms, tied to the importance of a "well-regulated militia." Some states included in this right an exemption to militia service for conscientious objectors—pacifists who had religious or moral scruples about using weapons.

## BEARING ARMS AND THE CONSTITUTION

When the new U.S. Constitution was written in 1787, it gave Congress the power in Article I to "raise and support armies" as well as "calling forth the militia." The Constitution forbade states, however, from keeping "troops, or ships of war in time of peace." Many opponents of the Constitution feared that these provisions endangered the state militia system—the only safe defense, they thought, against a standing army of the national government.

At the Virginia ratifying convention, George Mason warned that "the militia may be here destroyed by rendering them useless, by disarming them." Mason reminded the convention that England had many years before "disarm[ed] the people . . . by totally diffusing and neglecting the militia" and creating a standing army to take the militia's place. Five states, including Virginia, recommended that a right to bear arms be included in amendments to the Constitution.

In his proposed amendments submitted to Congress, James Madison included the right to bear arms, as well as an exemption for conscientious objectors. As reported by a committee of the House of Representatives, the original language of the Second Amendment read: "A well-regulated militia, composed of the body of the people, being the best security of a free state, the right of the people to keep and bear arms shall not be infringed," but "no person religiously scrupulous shall be compelled to bear arms." The Senate changed this wording somewhat and deleted the exemption for conscientious objectors. The precise meaning of those final words of the Second Amendment was to prove controversial for years to come.

## COLLECTIVE RIGHTS VS. INDIVIDUAL RIGHTS

Some constitutional scholars argue that the Second Amendment was designed only to protect the rights of states to have militias, not the right of individuals to bear arms for their own self-defense. These experts note that the right to bear arms is the only one in the Bill of Rights whose purpose is explained in the text itself. The right to bear arms, they maintain, is limited to the needs of a "well-regulated militia" and the "security of a free state." Consequently, they argue, the Second Amendment guarantees the collective right of the militia to be armed for the defense of the community—not an individual's right to carry weapons for whatever purpose, including hunting or self-defense.

Those who maintain that the Second Amendment protects an individual right to bear arms point to the historical definition of the militia as "the body of the people." Under this definition, the militia includes everyone in the community. Furthermore, these people point out, the Second Amendment does not specifically protect the rights of the *states,* as does the Tenth Amendment. Rather, the Second Amendment uses the phrase "right of the *people,*" just as the First, Fourth, and Ninth amendments do. These rights of the people—such as freedom of religion, speech, and press—are meant to protect individuals, not the states. The right to bear arms is no different, say these advocates of an individual rights approach.

## THE SECOND AMENDMENT AND THE COURTS

In *Presser v. Illinois* (1886), the Supreme Court held that the Second Amendment applied only to acts of the national government. Unlike other provisions of the Bill of Rights, the Second Amendment has not since been applied to the states. The Supreme Court in *Presser* upheld an Illinois law that prohibited the "drill or parade with arms" of any group "other than the regular organized volunteer militia of this state."

The only modern Supreme Court case dealing with the Second Amendment is *United States v. Miller* (1939). In that case, the Court ruled that the National Firearms Act of 1934, which required registration of

Maryland National Guard

*The Maryland National Guard is part of today's militia system, along with other state units. These "weekend warriors" serve in state crises and natural disasters, and may be ordered by the U.S. president to serve overseas—as in the Persian Gulf War of 1991.*

# Firing Line

*The essays below are adapted from two contributions to the op-ed page (so named because it is usually located opposite the editorial page) of* **The Washington Post.** *A newspaper's op-ed page often contains heated disputes about legislation before Congress—in this case, the regulation of military-style assault weapons.*

*N*ever in history has a federal court invalidated a law regulating the private ownership of firearms on Second Amendment grounds.

## Phantom Second Amendment "Rights"

By Erwin N. Griswold
Former Dean of Harvard Law School

In the recent congressional debate over crime control, there was much talk about the Constitution. The constitutionality of the laws is certainly a legitimate issue to be considered on the floor of Congress. It is not legitimate, however, to manufacture a constitutional issue when the courts have agreed for years that the "issue" in question does not exist. This is what has happened in the recent debate about control of military-style assault weapons, where reasoned debate was overcome by the unsupportable claim that restrictions would violate the Second Amendment's right to keep and bear arms. All rhetoric aside, these lawmakers and their mentors in the National Rifle Association should recognize the undeniable fact that the Second Amendment has never been an impediment to laws limiting the private ownership of firearms.

The full text of the Second Amendment reads: "A well regulated Militia, being necessary to the security of a free State, the right of the people to keep and bear Arms, shall not be infringed." The amendment is unique among the guarantees of the Bill of Rights because its purpose is clearly expressed in its text. This was explicitly recognized by the Supreme Court in its 1939 opinion in *United States v. Miller*, where it said that the "obvious purpose" of the amendment was "to assure the continuation and render possible the effectiveness" of state militias and that it "must be interpreted and applied with that end in view."

The clear meaning of *Miller* is that the Constitution does not guarantee a right to be armed for private purposes unrelated to the organized state militia, whether they be hunting, recreation, or even self-protection. The fact is that no American today owns an AK-47 or any other kind of firearm for reasons even remotely related to the organized militia or the "security of a free State." The days when militiamen were required by law to muster for military exercises in the town square—complete with their own guns and well-groomed horses—are long gone.

Following the Supreme Court's lead, the lower federal courts have shown a remarkable unanimity in applying the Second Amendment. Never in history has a federal court invalidated a law regulating the private ownership of firearms on Second Amendment grounds. Indeed, that the Second Amendment poses no barrier to strong gun laws is perhaps the most well-settled proposition in American constitutional law. Yet the incantation of this phantom right continues to pervade congressional debate.

## Taking Exception: The Right to Keep Firearms

By Michael K. McCabe
General Counsel, National Rifle Association

Erwin Griswold dismisses the Second Amendment's right to keep and bear arms as a "phantom right" posing "no barrier to strong gun laws." History clearly dictates a contrary conclusion. William Blackstone, in his classic treatise on the common law, recognized that the right to keep arms for the purpose of self-defense was a "primary law of nature" that could not be "taken away by the law of society." The right to keep arms for this purpose was considered basic by the drafters of the Bill of Rights.

The Second Amendment served two purposes. First, the militia, in addition to its utility for purposes of defense, would also serve as a counterbalance to the distrusted standing army. What was the "militia"? George Mason, one of the fathers of the Bill of Rights, reflected the common contemporary understanding of the term when he said that it consisted simply of "the whole people."

The Second Amendment also served the higher purpose of ensuring that the people would remain armed and resistant to tyranny. Thomas Jefferson's famous observation that the "tree of liberty must be refreshed from time to time with the blood of patriots and tyrants" merely suggests a commonly held belief.

The one case in this century squarely decided on the Second Amendment, the 1939 Supreme Court case of *United States v. Miller,* certainly does not support Griswold's theory. The court in *Miller,* refusing to hold that a short-barreled shotgun had "some reasonable relationship to the preservation or efficiency of a well-regulated militia," merely concluded that that particular firearm did not warrant Second Amendment protection. Does *Miller* then mean that the only militia that may have guns is the "organized" militia?

Decidedly not. There is increasing recognition that the Second Amendment may actually mean what it says—that the "right of the people to keep and bear Arms, shall not be infringed." Professor Sanford Levinson, in a 1989 *Yale Law Journal* article titled "The Embarrassing Second Amendment," suggests that the drafters did indeed recognize the Second Amendment as conveying individual, not collective, rights. Also, the Supreme Court in 1990 noted that the term "the people" has the same meaning in the First, Second, Fourth, Ninth, and Tenth Amendments.

The Bill of Rights was created as an inalienable and perpetual shield against government abuse. If it is possible to convert the Second Amendment into a "phantom," then there is no reason to expect that any other fundamental guarantee of liberty stands on stronger ground.

sawed-off shotguns, did not violate the Second Amendment. The Court declared that the amendment's "obvious purpose" was to "assure the continuation and render possible the effectiveness" of the militia and that the amendment "must be interpreted and applied with that end in view." Since a sawed-off shotgun had no "reasonable relationship" to a well-regulated militia, the Court concluded, the right to keep and bear such a weapon was not protected by the Second Amendment.

Advocates of gun control argue that *Miller* clearly ties the right to bear arms to the militia, refuting once and for all an individual right to bear arms for recreation or self-defense. Opponents of gun control state that *Miller* only held that a particular type of weapon, a sawed-off shotgun, was not related to the militia and therefore not protected. Although the debate about the meaning of *Miller* continues, no federal court has ever struck down gun control legislation as a violation of the Second Amendment.

Similarly, when a U.S. Court of Appeals reaffirmed that the Second Amendment did not apply to the states in *Quilici v. Morton Grove* (1982),

International Association of Chiefs of Police

*Handguns account for about half of all homicides committed in the United States, almost three times the number of homicides committed with all other firearms combined. As of 1994, about 222 million firearms were in circulation among U.S. civilians.*

the Supreme Court let the decision stand without reviewing it. The village of Morton Grove, Illinois, was the first town in America to ban the possession of handguns in the home. Morton Grove's gun control ordinance required any person who owned a handgun to turn it in to the police department—with certain exceptions for police officers, members of the armed forces, security guards, and others. Guns for recreational shooting had to be stored at gun clubs. Morton Grove's law was upheld because the Second Amendment only applied to the national government, not states and local communities.

## THE FUTURE OF GUN CONTROL

The debate over gun control continues in the courts and in the legislatures. Opponents of gun control, led by the National Rifle Association, argue that if Second Amendment rights are threatened, no other constitutional rights are safe either. As one commentator has written, the Second Amendment "is not a deer-hunting or duck-hunting amendment. It affords us some protection against wanna-be tyrants."

Opponents of gun control point out that in the case of free speech, society is willing to accept that some degree of harm comes to others through hurtful speech—such as Nazis marching through a Jewish community—without prohibiting the right to free speech. Similarly, just because criminals use guns does not mean that law-abiding citizens should be denied their constitutional right to bear arms.

Advocates of gun control counter by saying that—even if the Second Amendment does grant an individual right, not a collective right to a militia—no right is absolute. Therefore, the Second Amendment is not a total ban on gun control. Like any other right in the Constitution, the right to bear arms must be weighed against the potential harm it can cause society. In the case of guns, that harm can be more deadly than speech.

These arguments are used to persuade legislators to vote for or against gun control measures. But until the Supreme Court incorporates it, the Second Amendment does not restrict gun control laws passed by states and local communities. And until the Court updates the *Miller* ruling, federal gun control laws will probably withstand legal challenge as well. James Madison wrote in *Federalist* 46 about "the advantage of being armed, which the Americans possess over the people of almost every other nation." Whether Madison was talking about an individual right or a collective right is the real question.

# The **THIRD** *Amendment*

**NO SOLDIER** *shall, in time of peace be* **QUARTERED IN ANY HOUSE**, *without the* **CONSENT OF THE OWNER**, *nor in time of war, but in a manner to be prescribed by law.*

What if the U.S. Army, to save money, ordered local citizens to house and feed its troops?  According to the Third Amendment, such action is unconstitutional, at least during peacetime.

The Third Amendment has two parts.  First, it absolutely prohibits the government during peacetime from forcing private citizens to quarter, or provide room and board for, government soldiers without the property owner's permission.  Second, if the government needs to quarter troops in private property during wartime, it must do so according to legal procedures.

Although the Third Amendment has never been the subject of a Supreme Court decision, it has been cited in cases involving the right to privacy, which is not specifically mentioned in the Constitution.  The Supreme Court has said that the Third Amendment, among others, supports the principle that government cannot interfere with individual privacy in general.  So even though most Americans, unlike their colonial ancestors, no longer worry about having to feed and shelter armed soldiers, the Third Amendment continues to play an important role in the Bill of Rights.

## ENGLISH BEGINNINGS

The prohibition against quartering troops in *private* homes without the owner's consent traces its roots to early England. The right was first protected in the Petition of Right of 1628. It was also guaranteed by the English Bill of Rights in 1689. English law, however, did provide that troops could be quartered in *public* establishments like inns, at government expense.

The actual words of the Third Amendment do not distinguish between a "house" that is used by the public, like an inn, or a "house" that is used as a private home. The amendment just says that "any house" cannot be used to quarter troops in peacetime without the consent of the owner.

## THE FRENCH AND INDIAN WAR

The issue of quartering troops in private homes first arose in America during the French and Indian War (1754-1763), which was fought by the English colonies against rival French colonies who were allied with many American Indian tribes. British troops arriving to fight the war were quartered in both public and private houses in the American colonies, if barracks were not available. This action was taken under the military authority of Lord Loudoun, the commander in chief of the British Army in North America. Local government officials were responsible for getting the colonial legislatures to reimburse homeowners for quartering expenses.

Only occasionally did colonists challenge the British authority to quarter troops in their homes during the French and Indian War, probably because they depended on the soldiers for protection. But in Albany, New York, a center of military operations against the French, a major confrontation flared up in the summer of 1756. Lord Loudoun ordered the citizens of Albany to quarter officers and soldiers in their homes until barracks were built. When the townspeople refused, Loudoun took the homes by force, seizing a church as well in which to store gunpowder.

Perhaps the Albany uprising was not surprising, since New York had in its 1683 Charter of Liberties and Privileges prohibited the quartering of troops in private homes during peacetime—the first American colony to do so. Yet during all of the colonial period, the Albany incident was the only major occasion in which British troops actually used force to be quartered in private homes.

## STANDING ARMIES IN THE COLONIES

After the French and Indian War, the British army did not go home. The British government decided to keep a standing, or permanent, army in the colonies—even during peacetime. While the main purpose of the army was to protect the colonists from attacks by hostile American Indians, it also acted as a police force against the colonists themselves, making sure they obeyed the commands of the British government. Therefore, colonists saw the British soldiers as not just protectors, but also enforcers.

The presence of a standing army upset many colonists. Keeping an organized army during peacetime, they believed, only meant that it would be used against civilians. Americans knew that standing armies had been often used in England to suppress the liberties of the English people. And in 1765, Americans would not only be forced to tolerate a standing army, but to pay for it as well.

## THE QUARTERING ACT OF 1765

In 1765, the British Parliament passed the first Quartering Act, which required the American assemblies, or legislatures, to pay the costs of feeding and housing British troops in the colonies. In addition, if regular barracks did not have enough room for the soldiers, the act directed colonial governments to hire alehouses, livery stables, and inns as quarters. Furthermore, colonial governments were instructed to provide the soldiers with bedding, candles, firewood, salt, and cooking equipment, as well as a daily ration of rum, beer, or hard cider. The act also authorized innkeepers to feed British troops at the colonies' expense.

Benjamin Franklin decried the Quartering Act. "Let [England] first try the effects of quartering soldiers on butchers, bakers, or other private houses [in Britain] and then transport the measure to America," he wrote. Other colonists realized that the Quartering Act was in fact a tax, forcing them to pay for a standing army many did not want in the first place.

New York protested against the quartering of troops once again, just as it had in 1756. The New York assembly refused to comply with the Quartering Act. In 1767, however, the British Parliament suspended the assembly until it obeyed the act. Finally, the New York legislature gave in.

*Paul Revere's famous engraving of the Boston Massacre depicts one consequence of the Quartering Act of 1765.*

Library of Congress

## THE BOSTON MASSACRE

Like New York, Massachusetts resisted the Quartering Act. In Boston, a hotbed of rebellion, several thousand additional British troops arrived in 1768 to enforce British customs duties, or taxes, on imports into Boston Harbor. These new troops created a quartering crisis. The Massachusetts Council, composed of delegates from the colonial legislature, refused to quarter the troops in the town itself. Instead, the Council wanted the troops kept on an island in Boston Harbor—a safe distance of three miles away. In response, the British camped on Boston Common, the public park in the center of town, and occupied the town hall. Nonetheless, the Massachusetts Council refused to comply with the Quartering Act and did not provide supplies and housing for the British soldiers.

Tensions between the townspeople and the British soldiers mounted over time. Fights broke out, children threw stones at the troops, and soldiers shouted drunken obscenities at passers-by. Local rowdies and the British redcoats clashed repeatedly, resulting in sporadic street warfare.

The conflict came to a head on March 5, 1770, when a crowd hurled rocks and snowballs at a patrol of British soldiers outside the Customs House, where the hated customs officials had their offices. Details of the incident are unclear, but it appears that the soldiers either panicked or were goaded by the crowd into shooting. Five Americans were killed, and outraged colonists called the event the "Boston Massacre."

One prominent Bostonian, Dr. Joseph Warren, saw the Boston Massacre as the inevitable result of standing armies:

> The ruinous consequences of standing armies to free communities may be seen in the histories of Syracuse [a city-state in ancient Greece], Rome, and many other once flourishing states. . . . And this will be more especially the case when the troops are informed that the intention of their being stationed in any city is to overawe the inhabitants. That this was the avowed design of stationing an armed force in this town is sufficiently known; and we, my fellow citizens, have seen, we have felt the tragical effects! The fatal fifth of March 1770, can never be forgotten. The horrors of that dreadful night are but too deeply impressed in our hearts.

## QUARTERING AND REVOLUTION

After the Boston Massacre, British troops were removed from the city to reduce tension. But the quartering crisis did not end for good, because the fires of rebellion continued to burn. In the Boston Tea Party of 1773, colonists protested a tax on tea by dressing up as American Indians and dumping more than 300 chests of valuable British tea into Boston Harbor. In response, British troops returned to Boston, and in 1774 Parliament passed a series of restrictive laws that Americans called the "Intolerable Acts." Included among these laws was a new Quartering Act, which allowed royal troops to be housed in private *homes,* not just public buildings.

Finally, the colonies decided to sever their ties with England. The Declaration of Independence lists quartering of troops as one of the specific reasons justifying the colonists' revolution against Britain's King George III. The Declaration stated that the king "has kept among us, in time of peace, standing armies, without the consent of our legislatures" and agreed to Parliament's laws "quartering large bodies of armed troops among us." Ironically, however, colonial troops were quartered among private citizens during the Revolutionary War.

## QUARTERING AND THE CONSTITUTION

Quartering of troops was still an issue in America even after the Revolutionary War, when the hated British soldiers had finally gone home. A significant objection to the new U.S. Constitution of 1787 was that it provided for a peacetime, or standing, army. And as Patrick Henry of Virginia noted, there was no protection in the Constitution against quartering of that army's troops upon the people. During the Virginia convention on the ratification of the new U.S. Constitution in 1788, Henry declared: "One of our first complaints, under the former government, was the quartering of troops among us. This was one of the principal reasons for dissolving the connection with Great Britain. Here [under the Constitution] we may have troops in time of peace. They may be billeted [quartered] in any manner—to tyrannize, oppress, and crush us."

Five of the eight states that suggested amendments when they ratified the Constitution included on their lists a protection against the quartering of troops. Several state bills of rights already banned quartering. When James Madison submitted his proposals for the Bill of Rights in Congress, the quartering provision passed with little debate. It became the Third Amendment.

## THE THIRD AMENDMENT AND THE COURTS

The Third Amendment has never been the subject of a Supreme Court decision. It has also never been incorporated by the Supreme Court to apply to the states. The only major case to interpret the Third Amendment's ban on quartering troops is *Engblom v. Carey* (1982), which was decided by the U.S. Court of Appeals—a court one level lower than the Supreme Court. But the Supreme Court has referred to the Third Amendment in cases upholding the right to privacy in general, rather than specifically regarding the quartering of troops. Privacy is where the Third Amendment's real constitutional importance lies today.

### ENGBLOM V. CAREY

*Engblom v. Carey* is not the final authority on the meaning of the Third Amendment's ban on quartering of troops, because it was not decided by the Supreme Court. Nonetheless, the case is an interesting story of a modern-day application of the seemingly outdated Third Amendment. *Engblom* involved a strike by prison guards in New York state. Some of the guards in the Mid-Orange Correctional Facility lived in dormitory-style housing on the grounds of the prison itself, for which they paid a small rent. For some guards, those rooms were their only homes. When the prison guards went on strike, Governor Hugh Carey ordered the

*Government-owned barracks provide quarters for most modern U.S. troops, rather than privately owned hotels, saloons, or civilian homes—as was the British practice in colonial America.*

state's National Guard to provide security at the prisons. During the three-week emergency that followed, the striking guards were locked out of their living quarters at Mid-Orange, and National Guard soldiers were housed there instead.

Marianne E. Engblom, one of the guards locked out, filed suit in federal court under the Third Amendment, claiming that soldiers had been quartered in her home without her consent. The U.S. Court of Appeals for the Second Circuit (which includes New York) ruled that the Third Amendment did apply to the states—at least those states in the Second Circuit.

The appeals court then analyzed the language of the Third Amendment as it applied to Engblom's case. The court determined that members of the National Guard were indeed "soldiers" within the meaning of the Third Amendment. But was Engblom's dwelling a "house" and was she its "owner"? The court concluded that even a dormitory-style room on the grounds of a state prison deserved the protection of the Third Amendment. And despite the fact that Engblom rented the room and did not technically own it, she still was entitled to privacy within it— which is what the court believed was safeguarded by the Third Amendment. Although Engblom eventually lost her case on other grounds, for the first time since it was ratified, the federal courts had finally interpreted the Third Amendment.

## THE THIRD AMENDMENT AND PRIVACY

The most significant role the Third Amendment has played in constitutional law is as support for a general right to privacy, which is not specifically mentioned in the Constitution. As early as 1833, Justice Joseph Story noted that privacy was the underlying principle of the Third Amendment. Story wrote that the Third Amendment's "plain object is to secure the perfect enjoyment of that great right of the common law, that a man's house shall be his own castle, privileged against all civil and military intrusion."

Modern Supreme Court justices have agreed with Story—and even gone further to include rights of privacy beyond the home itself, such as privacy in marital relations. Justice William Douglas wrote in 1961: "Can there be any doubt that a Bill of Rights that in time of peace bars soldiers from being quartered in a home 'without the consent of the owner' should also bar the police from investigating the intimacies of the marriage relation?" In *Griswold v. Connecticut* (1965), the Supreme Court held in an opinion by Justice Douglas that the Third Amendment, together with the First, Fourth, Fifth, and Ninth amendments, created "zones of privacy" that protected the right of married couples to use contraceptives.

Today, the Supreme Court continues to recognize a general right to privacy, although more commonly under the Fourteenth Amendment. Nonetheless, the Third Amendment remains an important reminder that there are limits to government's power to intrude upon its citizens, that there are places it may not go. Citizens can bar the doors to their "castles"—and even the king's soldiers may not enter. As William Pitt the Elder, a famous English statesman, noted in an oft-quoted speech to Parliament in 1766:

> The poorest man may in his cottage bid defiance to all the forces of the Crown. It may be frail—its roof may shake—the wind may blow through it—the storm may enter—the rain may enter—but the King of England cannot enter—all his force dares not cross the threshold of the ruined tenement!

# The **FOURTH** *Amendment*

*The right of the people to be secure* **IN THEIR PERSONS, HOUSES, PAPERS, AND EFFECTS,** *against* **UNREASONABLE SEARCHES AND SEIZURES,** *shall not be violated; and no* **WARRANTS** *shall issue, but upon* **PROBABLE CAUSE,** *supported by oath or affirmation, and* **PARTICULARLY DESCRIBING** *the place to be searched, and the persons or things to be seized.*

A knock at the door in the middle of the night. This fear was familiar to colonial Americans—it could mean a ransacked house or an arrest without cause. The Fourth Amendment was drafted to protect citizens from such arbitrary government invasions of their privacy. According to Justice Louis Brandeis, the Fourth Amendment guarantees the "right to be left alone—the most comprehensive of rights and the right most valued by civilized men."

The Fourth Amendment states that the people and their belongings shall be free from "unreasonable searches and seizures" and that warrants authorizing searches or arrests shall be based on "probable cause," not solely on the whim of a police officer. Also, the warrants must be specific, not broad and general. But the enforcement of the Fourth Amendment's language by the Supreme Court has often been confusing. Not all searches and seizures require warrants, and some do not even require "probable cause." The Court tends to rule on a case-by-case basis, balancing two competing values: protecting privacy and catching criminals. The most recent Supreme Court cases tend to give more weight to the latter.

## GENERAL WARRANTS AND THE FOURTH AMENDMENT

Since the fourteenth century, England allowed the use of general warrants, which authorized government agents to search wherever they wanted and to seize whatever or whomever they wished. Because the general warrant did not expire until the king's death, it could remain in effect for years. None of the great English documents of liberty, such as the Magna Carta or the English Bill of Rights, forbade general warrants, although English courts restricted their use in the mid-eighteenth century. Nonetheless, the British government widely used general warrants in colonial America.

As Justice William Brennan wrote two hundred years later, "the evil of the general warrant is often regarded as the single immediate cause of the American Revolution." A type of general warrant known as a writ of assistance allowed British customs officials to search colonial homes and businesses at will, without any restrictions, to look for smuggled goods on which import duties had not been paid. The warrant did not specify particular persons suspected of illegal activity or houses to be searched. The general warrant permitted totally arbitrary acts of government. Boston colonists, in somewhat exaggerated terms, decried such behavior:

> Our houses and even our bed chambers, are exposed to be ransacked, our boxes, chests, and trunks broke open, ravaged, and plundered by wretches, whom no prudent man would venture to employ even as menial servants; whenever they are pleased to say they suspect there are in the house wares, etc., for which the duties have not been paid. Flagrant instances of the wanton exercise of this power, have frequently happened in this and other sea port towns. By this we are cut off from that domestic security which renders the lives of the most unhappy in some measure agreeable.

Perhaps the most famous American protest against general warrants occurred in 1761 in the Massachusetts Superior Court. A group of Boston merchants challenged the new writs of assistance to be issued to British customs officials after the death of King George II in 1760. James Otis represented the Boston merchants, resigning his prestigious post as the king's principal lawyer in Boston to do so. In his argument before the court, Otis condemned writs of assistance as a violation of the right of privacy:

> Now one of the most essential branches of English liberty, is the freedom of one's house. A man's house is his castle; and whilst he is quiet he is as well guarded as a prince in his castle. This writ, if it should be declared legal, would totally annihilate this privilege.

Otis lost the case, but won the ultimate battle. John Adams, who would become president of the United States, later wrote about Otis's argument: "Then and there was the first scene of the first act of opposition to the arbitrary claims of Great Britain. Then and there the child Independence was born."

Colonial Americans agreed with James Otis that "a man's house is his castle" and that government officials should not be able to invade that domain at will. After the Revolutionary War, eight states included a protection against general warrants in their new constitutions. And during the ratification of the U.S. Constitution, five states proposed adding an amendment restricting searches and seizures. In 1789, James Madison's version of what became the Fourth Amendment passed with little debate in Congress.

That amendment had two parts. The first part protected the people against "unreasonable searches and seizures." The second part, the Warrant Clause, required that a warrant, or court order, for an arrest or search specifically describe the "place to be searched, and the persons or things to be seized." Also, warrants had to be based on probable cause, that is, reasonable grounds—not just the whim of a government official. The Fourth Amendment did not define an "unreasonable" search or seizure, however, nor was it clear whether *all* searches and seizures required a warrant and probable cause.

## UNREASONABLE SEARCHES AND SEIZURES

*The right of the people to be secure* **IN THEIR PERSONS, HOUSES, PAPERS, AND EFFECTS,** *against* **UNREASONABLE SEARCHES AND SEIZURES,** *shall not be violated; . . .*

This first part of the Fourth Amendment sets forth the conditions under which it applies. The amendment protects the people's right to be secure "in their persons, houses, papers, and effects." Does this phrase mean that the Fourth Amendment only applies within a home or office, not to telephone conversations in a public phone booth? Also, the Fourth Amendment prohibits only *unreasonable* searches and seizures. How does the Supreme Court define an unreasonable search or seizure?

### REASONABLE EXPECTATIONS OF PRIVACY

At first, the Supreme Court interpreted the Fourth Amendment to apply only to actual physical intrusions into "a constitutionally protected area"—such as a home, office, or a physical body. On these grounds, for instance, the Court in *Olmstead v. United States* (1928) held that wiretapping without a warrant did not violate the Fourth Amendment if the bugs were planted *outside* the home. The federal agents in that case had not committed an "actual physical invasion" of the home or office of Olmstead, a suspected bootlegger.

In *Katz v. United States* (1967), the Supreme Court expressly overruled *Olmstead*. Katz was convicted of sending betting information across state lines, based on police wiretaps of a public phone booth. Even though the bug was placed on the *outside* of the booth, the Supreme Court overturned Katz's conviction. As Justice Potter Stewart, on behalf of the Court's majority, wrote:

> [T]he Fourth Amendment protects people, not places. What a person knowingly exposes to the public, even in his own home or office, is not a subject of Fourth Amendment protection. . . . But what he seeks to preserve as private, even in an area accessible to the public, may be constitutionally protected. . . .
>
> What [Katz] sought to exclude when he entered the booth was not the intruding eye—it was the uninvited ear. He did not shed his right to do so simply because he made his calls from a place where he might be seen.

The *Katz* decision established that the Fourth Amendment applied wherever a person had "a reasonable expectation of privacy," not just in a home or an office. This phrase has become the critical test for what the Fourth Amendment protects.

The expectation of privacy is ordinarily very high for the home and its curtilage, the area immediately surrounding it, but the Court has found exceptions. For instance, in *California v. Ciraolo* (1986), the Supreme Court ruled that aerial photographs of marijuana plants growing in the backyard of a house, surrounded by two fences, did not violate the Fourth Amendment. The Court noted that the surveillance occurred "from a public vantage point"—above 1,000 feet—where the officer was entitled to be and "which renders the activities clearly visible." Any expectation of privacy at that altitude was unreasonable, the Court ruled, despite two fences. In 1987, however, the Supreme Court held that an expectation of privacy against low-altitude hovering was reasonable. The Court struck down a search warrant based on a police officer's sighting of marijuana plants in a greenhouse while hovering in a helicopter at 400 feet.

Outside the curtilage, the expectation of privacy can sometimes be diminished. As a rule, sealed containers are protected by the Fourth

# Case Study: California v. Greenwood (1988)

*Are sealed garbage bags protected by the Fourth Amendment? The majority opinion in* Greenwood *said no, because the garbage had been exposed to the public by being placed on the curb for collection. The minority opinion maintained that sealed garbage bags, like any other sealed containers, were entitled to Fourth Amendment protection. Both opinions cited* Katz *to support their views.*

Close Up Foundation/Renée Bouchard

*Would the dissenting opinion in* Greenwood *have been different for this clear trash bag?*

**Justice White** delivered the opinion of the Court. . . .

The issue here is whether the Fourth Amendment prohibits the warrantless search and seizure of garbage left for collection outside the curtilage of a home. We conclude . . . that it does not. . . .

The warrantless search and seizure of the garbage bags left at the curb outside the Greenwood house would violate the Fourth Amendment only if respondents manifested a subjective expectation of privacy in their garbage that society accepts as objectively reasonable. . . .

. . . It is common knowledge that plastic garbage bags left on or at the side of a public street are readily accessible to animals, children, scavengers, snoops, and other members of the public. Moreover, respondents placed their refuse at the curb for the express purpose of conveying it to a third party, the trash collector, who might himself have sorted through respondents' trash or permitted others, such as the police, to do so. Accordingly, having deposited their garbage "in an area particularly suited for public inspection and, in a manner of speaking, public consumption, for the express purpose of having strangers take it," . . . respondents could have had no reasonable expectation of privacy in the inculpatory items they discarded.

. . . Hence, "[w]hat a person knowingly exposes to the public, even in his own home or office, is not a subject of Fourth Amendment protection." . . .

**Justice Brennan,** dissenting. . . .

"A container which can support a reasonable expectation of privacy may not be searched, even on probable cause, without a warrant." . . . Thus, as the Court observes, if Greenwood had a reasonable expectation that the contents of the bags he placed on the curb would remain private, the warrantless search of those bags violated the Fourth Amendment. . . .

. . . So far as Fourth Amendment protection is concerned, opaque plastic bags are every bit as worthy as "packages wrapped in green opaque plastic" and "double-locked footlocker[s]." . . .

. . . [A]ll that Greenwood "exposed . . . to the public" were the exteriors of several opaque, sealed containers. Until the bags were opened by police, they hid their contents from the public's view. . . .

The mere *possibility* that unwelcome meddlers *might* open and rummage through the containers does not negate the expectation of privacy in its contents any more than the possibility of a burglary negates an expectation of privacy in the home; or the possibility of a private intrusion negates an expectation of privacy in an unopened package; or the possibility that an operator will listen in on a telephone conversation negates an expectation of privacy in the words spoken on the telephone. "What a person . . . seeks to preserve as private, *even in an area accessible to the public,* may be constitutionally protected."

Amendment because they carry a high expectation of privacy, even when outside the home. But in *California v. Greenwood* (1988), the Court ruled that the occupants of a house who left opaque, sealed garbage bags on the curb for the trash collectors had "exposed their garbage to the public sufficiently to defeat their claim to Fourth Amendment protection." Consequently, the Court upheld narcotics convictions based on evidence found in the garbage bags.

## WHAT ARE UNREASONABLE SEARCHES AND SEIZURES?

The Fourth Amendment only applies to "unreasonable searches and seizures." The Supreme Court's definition of each of these three main words helps determine whether or not a specific situation is covered by the Fourth Amendment. In *Terry v. Ohio* (1968), the Court defined all three of these terms.

**WHAT ARE SEARCHES AND SEIZURES?** In *Terry,* the Court recognized that searches and seizures vary in degree. At issue in *Terry* was the police practice of "stop and frisk," where an officer stops persons on the street and pats them down for weapons. The Court agreed that a "stop" was not the same thing as an arrest, where the accused was taken into police custody, nor was a "frisk" of a person's outer clothing the same thing as a search of that person's pockets. Nonetheless, the Court held that a "stop and frisk" was a search and seizure within the meaning of the Fourth Amendment:

> It is quite plain that the Fourth Amendment governs "seizures" of the person which do not [result] in a trip to the station house and prosecution for a crime—"arrests" in traditional terminology. It must be recognized that whenever a police officer accosts an individual and restrains his freedom to walk away, he has "seized" that person. And it is nothing less than sheer torture of the English language to suggest that a careful exploration of the outer surfaces of a person's clothing all over his or her body in an attempt to find weapons is not a "search." . . .

> . . . We therefore reject the notions that the Fourth Amendment does not come into play at all as a limitation upon police conduct if the officers stop short of something called a "technical arrest" or a "full-blown search."

**WHAT IS UNREASONABLE?** Having ruled that a "stop and frisk" was indeed a "search and seizure" within the meaning of the Fourth Amendment, the Court in *Terry* then had to determine whether that search and seizure was "unreasonable." In general, the Supreme Court has ruled that while the Fourth Amendment expresses a preference for warrants based on probable cause, it does not always require them. (These types of "warrantless" cases are discussed more fully later under the second part of the Fourth Amendment, the Warrant Clause.) As a rule, however, the Court has held that warrantless searches or seizures without probable cause are inherently "unreasonable."

But in *Terry* the Supreme Court created an exception to that rule. The Court said that probable cause is not required for every "search and seizure" under the Fourth Amendment. Some searches can be "reasonable" without probable cause, depending on the circumstances. In *Terry,* the Court emphasized the specific facts of the case. Officer McFadden, a policeman with thirty-nine years of experience, noticed three men in downtown Cleveland, two of whom walked back and forth around a store window about a dozen times. He suspected the men of "casing a job, a stick up," and decided to investigate. He also feared "they may have a gun."

Officer McFadden had no concrete information giving him probable cause to stop the men or search them—he just had a generalized "hunch" based on his experience. Nonetheless, Officer McFadden "approached the men, identified himself as a police officer, and asked for their names." When the men gave mumbled answers, the officer grabbed defendant Terry, patted him down and found a gun, then discovered another revolver when patting down the other two suspects.

The Court ruled that Officer McFadden's actions, while certainly searches and seizures, were not "unreasonable" under the Fourth Amendment. On behalf of the Court's majority, Chief Justice Earl Warren wrote:

> . . . Each case of this sort will, of course, have to be decided on its own facts. We merely hold today that where a police officer observes unusual conduct which leads him reasonably to conclude in light of his experience that criminal activity may be afoot and that the persons with whom he is dealing may be armed and presently dangerous, where in the course of investigating this behavior he identifies himself as a policeman and makes reasonable inquiries, and where nothing in the initial stages of the encounter serves to dispel his reasonable fear for his own or others' safety, he is entitled for the protection of himself and others in the area to conduct a carefully limited search of the outer clothing of such persons in an attempt to discover weapons which might be used to assault him.

The *Terry* decision was issued in 1968, a time when America's high crime rate was a major issue, by a Court that had been strongly criticized for its rulings supporting defendants' rights. Justice William O. Douglas recognized these pressures on the Warren Court in his dissenting opinion, but he still believed that probable cause was a minimum standard under the Constitution:

> There have been powerful hydraulic pressures throughout our history that bear heavily on the Court to water down constitutional guarantees and give the police the upper hand. That hydraulic pressure has probably never been greater than it is today.

> Yet if the individual is no longer to be sovereign, if the police can pick him up whenever they do not like the cut of his jib [the way he looks], if they can "seize" and "search" him in their discretion, we enter a new regime. The decision to enter it should be made only after a full debate by the people of this country.

The majority of the Court, however, believed that a "stop and frisk" was a reasonable police practice to prevent crime. As Justice William Rehnquist wrote in a later "stop and frisk" case: "[t]he Fourth Amendment does not require a policeman who lacks the precise level of information necessary for probable cause to arrest to simply shrug his shoulders and allow a crime to occur or a criminal to escape."

In *Minnesota v. Dickerson* (1993), the Supreme Court widened the *Terry* decision's scope for warrantless searches and seizures. The Court held that during a "pat down," a police officer may seize not only weapons, but also nonthreatening contraband. However, the contraband must be immediately recognizable through the suspect's clothing, which the officer may not manipulate to make a better identification.

**OTHER "REASONABLE" SEARCHES AND SEIZURES.** The *Terry* decision made way for other exceptions to the probable cause requirement besides a "stop and frisk." Ordinarily, probable cause would require that a particular person was reasonably likely to have committed a particular offense. But the Court has found certain searches and seizures to be "reasonable" even without probable cause in cases where the intrusion was believed to be slight or in special situations—such as schools. Under current Fourth Amendment law, searches and seizures without probable cause are "reasonable" in circumstances such as the following:

*Sobriety Checkpoints.* Even without probable cause that a specific driver has been drinking and driving, police may routinely stop all motorists in roadblocks. Such "seizures" are not "unreasonable" because the states have a strong interest in deterring drunk driving and the intrusion on the drivers stopped is "slight." However, random "spot checks" of individual motorists without probable cause violates the Fourth Amendment.

Supreme Court of the United States

*Earl Warren, former governor of California, was chief justice of the United States from 1953 to 1969. The Warren Court was noted for its rulings upholding defendants' rights.*

U.S. Customs Service

*Border searches of all passengers are not a violation of the Fourth Amendment, even without probable cause that a specific passenger has committed a particular offense.*

*Border Crossings.* Probable cause is not required for customs agents to search automobiles, luggage, wallets, or other belongings at permanent checkpoints between nations or at airports with international flights.

*Airport Searches.* In view of the danger of airplane hijacking, searches without probable cause of all carry-on luggage and, using a metal detector, of all passengers are "reasonable."

*Drug Testing.* Federal law can require drug and alcohol tests of railroad workers after major accidents without probable cause to believe a person was using drugs or alcohol, because of the government's interest in safety. Also, certain federal customs employees who might be investigating drug crimes can be required to undergo mandatory drug testing without probable cause.

*Student Searches.* The Supreme Court ruled in *New Jersey v. T.L.O.* (1985) that probable cause is not required when students are searched by school officials. In that case, a teacher accused T.L.O., a high school student, of smoking in the bathroom in violation of school rules. When questioned by the assistant principal, the girl denied that she smoked at all. The assistant principal then demanded to see the contents of her purse, which upon a thorough search revealed marijuana and drug-related paraphernalia. As a result, the state brought delinquency charges against the student in juvenile court.

The Supreme Court ruled that while the Fourth Amendment applies to public school officials and teachers, a student's expectation of privacy

## The Thin Blue Line: One Police Officer's Point of View

*The Supreme Court has ruled that excessive use of force when making an arrest is an "unreasonable" seizure. In March 1991, Los Angeles police officers were videotaped beating motorist Rodney King after a car chase. The officers' acquittal a year later triggered the worst urban riot in modern American history. In the excerpt below, Sr. Sgt. Russell Schmidt—himself twice suspended for excessive force—describes a viewpoint from "the thin blue line."*

*S*chmidt has a saying about police work: "The dirt rubs both ways."

Schmidt has been involved in several high-speed chases during his career. He says they scare him every time. And often change his behavior. He sees a connection between his last chase [in which the suspect's car crashed and Schmidt rescued him from the exploding wreckage], all chases, and what happened in Los Angeles.

"You get real, real frightened in the chase. And it's like you gotta vent that, and either you're at a level where you can vent it without hurting somebody—or you hurt somebody. Somebody gives you an excuse, you know, he'll swing at you, won't do what you tell him to do, he'll reach for something and do something he shouldn't do. He gets hurt.

"People don't understand that. I mean, here you are, you've got a wife and kids, and they're paying you to do a job, and this guy's making you drive faster than you should. . . . And you get out and the guy's there and he wants to confront you. And when he does, you just take all the stops out. I've seen that happen."

Schmidt has a saying about police work: "The dirt rubs both ways." By that he means that police mirror their environment. He believes that no human being, no matter how sensitive or fair, can patrol the streets of an American city without undergoing a period where they change for the worse. He struggles with conflicting feelings about that transformation, who is to blame for it, and how it can be avoided.

"It upsets me that we get a bad deal some of the time when we don't deserve it," he said. "But then again we do deserve it. We do some things we shouldn't do and I'm not quite sure there's an excuse for it. Like the L.A. thing, a lot of people want an excuse for this and an excuse for that—those guys were mean. They were just mean. Whether it is the environment or their training or whatever it is, I don't know, but you see people kill each other and ignore each other and let them die and abuse themselves and the whole system, and it hurts you. It's psychologically impossible to stay the way you should stay."

Bette Mayfield Photography

*Sr. Sgt. Russell Schmidt*

must be weighed against the school's need to preserve a sound learning environment. School officials do not need warrants or probable cause to conduct in-school searches, the Court ruled, as long as they meet the test of "reasonableness under all circumstances." Police officers who conduct searches on school premises, however, must still have probable cause.

The Supreme Court further restricted students' Fourth Amendment rights in *Vernonia School District 47J v. Acton* (1995). The Court held that schools may require all student athletes to take drug tests, whether or not any of them was suspected of actual drug use.

*Consent Searches.* Police do not need probable cause when a person consents to a search. However, consent must be given by someone authorized to do so. Parents may allow the police to search their child's room, for instance, but a landlord may not permit a search of a tenant's dwelling—although the tenant's roommate could.

The consent must also be voluntary, not coerced. In *Florida v. Bostick* (1991), the Supreme Court considered whether consent is voluntary when police officers, as part of the "war on drugs," routinely board buses, request passengers' tickets and identification, and ask to search their luggage. The Supreme Court ruled that consent under such circumstances is voluntary, despite the lower court's finding that the police presence on the buses was inherently coercive.

Taken together, these cases indicate that "unreasonable" is the controlling word in the Fourth Amendment. Not all searches and seizures require warrants, or even probable cause. But they all must be "reasonable." How the Supreme Court defines "reasonable" varies from case to case.

## THE WARRANT CLAUSE

*. . . and no **WARRANTS** shall issue, but upon **PROBABLE CAUSE**, supported by oath or affirmation, and **PARTICULARLY DESCRIBING** the place to be searched, and the persons or things to be seized.*

This second part of the Fourth Amendment is known as the Warrant Clause. It states that all warrants, or court orders, for searches and seizures must be based on probable cause—not just the arbitrary whim of a police officer. Furthermore, a warrant must specifically describe the place that will be searched and the persons or evidence that will be seized, which is known as the particularity requirement. The warrant clause does not say that *all* searches and *all* seizures require warrants—it only says what is required to get a warrant, not when a warrant is necessary. The Supreme Court has ruled that, while a warrant is a general "preference" under the Fourth Amendment, there are certain exceptions.

## PROBABLE CAUSE

To get a warrant, a police officer must first have probable cause. Probable cause is more than just a "hunch" that a crime has been committed, but less proof than is required to convict a person at trial "beyond a reasonable doubt." The Supreme Court has explained probable cause as follows:

> In dealing with probable cause . . . we deal with probabilities. These are not technical; they are the factual and practical considerations of everyday life on which reasonable and prudent men, not legal technicians, act. . . . Probable cause exists where the facts and circumstances within [the officers'] knowledge, and of which they had reasonably trustworthy information, [are] sufficient in themselves to warrant a man of reasonable caution in the belief that an offense has been or is being committed.

To require more proof than that "would unduly hamper law enforcement," said the Court; "[t]o allow less would be to leave law-abiding citizens at the mercy of the officers' whim or caprice."

Furthermore, a "neutral and detached magistrate," or court official, must determine whether probable cause exists for a warrant. The warrant must describe in detail the place to be searched and the person or things to be seized. This requirement helps establish probable cause that a specific person or a specific place is linked to criminal activity. It also prevents "dragnet" operations in which large numbers of people are arrested, as well as "fishing expeditions" in which police search a wide area without a clear idea of what they want to find.

## WHEN IS A WARRANT NEEDED?

Not all searches and seizures require a warrant. The day-to-day realities of police work mean that it is not always possible to get a warrant before making an arrest or conducting a search. Listed below are some examples of when warrants are and are not required. In all instances, the search or seizure must be based on probable cause, whether or not a warrant is used—unlike the cases discussed under "reasonable" searches and seizures.

**ARRESTS.** If police see a suspect in the act of committing a crime, they do not have to go before a judge to get a warrant before making an arrest. If

Renée Bouchard Photography

*Police officers always need probable cause to make an arrest, whether or not they have a warrant.*

a suspect is wanted for a previous crime, police *always* need a warrant to make an arrest in that person's home, but not in a public place. All arrests require probable cause, which must be proven to a magistrate within a reasonable time after the arrest is made, if a warrant has not been issued. The Supreme Court ruled in 1991 that forty-eight hours, including weekends and holidays, is the maximum time a suspect can be kept in custody before a probable cause hearing is held.

**SEARCHES.** As one expert on the Fourth Amendment has noted, the "great majority" of police searches are made and upheld without a warrant. Some of the major exceptions to the warrant requirement are:

*Search Incident to a Lawful Arrest.* Most warrantless searches fit under this category. The Supreme Court ruled in *Chimel v. California* (1969) that police may search a lawfully arrested person and the area immediately surrounding the suspect for hidden weapons or evidence that could be destroyed. Police may do so even after the suspect has been handcuffed and removed from the area.

*Plain View.* If an officer is in a place where he or she has a right to be, then evidence of a crime in plain view may be seized without a warrant. For instance, an officer may seize a gun that is visible on the car seat while citing a driver for a traffic violation.

*Hot Pursuit.* If police are in hot pursuit of a suspect, then they may follow a suspect into a building without first obtaining a search warrant. Also, they may seize any evidence they find.

*Automobiles.* Police may search automobiles without a warrant because they are likely to be removed before a warrant can be obtained. Also, the Supreme Court has ruled that there is a "diminished expectation of privacy" in automobiles.

*Exigent Circumstances.* In emergency situations, the police do not need a search warrant. For example, no warrant is required to search a building for explosives after a bomb threat or to enter a house after seeing flames in the windows or hearing screams.

## THE EXCLUSIONARY RULE

What happens when police violate any of the Fourth Amendment rules for searches? How should the Fourth Amendment be enforced by the courts? Some legal experts have suggested that victims of improper searches could sue the police for damages. But the Supreme Court decided in *Weeks v. United States* (1914) that the best remedy for Fourth Amendment violations was the exclusionary rule, which prohibited illegally seized evidence from being admitted at trial. The exclusionary rule was controversial from the beginning, however. Justice Benjamin Cardozo criticized the rule before he joined the Court in 1932, saying that under the exclusionary rule "the criminal is to go free because the constable has blundered."

At first, the exclusionary rule applied only to the federal government. Even when the Supreme Court incorporated the Fourth Amendment to apply to the states in *Wolf v. Colorado* (1949), it did not require the states to use the exclusionary rule. But in *Mapp v. Ohio* (1961), the Supreme Court changed its mind and applied the exclusionary rule to the states.

### MAPP V. OHIO (1961)

On May 23, 1957, city police officers arrived at the home of Dollree Mapp in Cleveland, Ohio. They had received a tip that "a person [was] hiding out in the home, who was wanted for questioning in connection with a recent bombing, and that there was a large amount of [left-wing] paraphernalia being hidden in the home." Mapp and her daughter lived on the top floor of the two-family house. When the police officers knocked on her door and demanded to be let in, Mapp telephoned her attorney and refused to let the police in without a search warrant. The police officers then notified their headquarters of the situation and began a surveillance of the home.

When reinforcements arrived about three hours later, the officers again tried to enter the home. Mapp did not answer the door immediately, and the police forcibly entered the house. Mapp's attorney arrived in the meantime, but the officers refused to let him see his client or enter the house. Mapp was on her way to the front door when the officers broke into her hall. One of the officers held up a paper, claiming it was a warrant. Mapp grabbed the "warrant" and placed it in her blouse. A struggle followed, during which the police retrieved the paper. They then handcuffed Mapp because she had been "belligerent" in resisting attempts to recover the "warrant."

Mapp was then forced upstairs to her bedroom where the police searched a closet, a dresser, some suitcases, and a chest of drawers. They then searched the kitchen, dinette, living room, and the child's bedroom. The police also searched a trunk in the basement, where they found some obscene materials, which Ms. Mapp was convicted of possessing.

At trial, no search warrant was ever produced or accounted for. On appeal, the Ohio Supreme Court stated that there was "considerable doubt as to whether there ever was any warrant." But it upheld Dollree Mapp's conviction, because the exclusionary rule did not apply to the states.

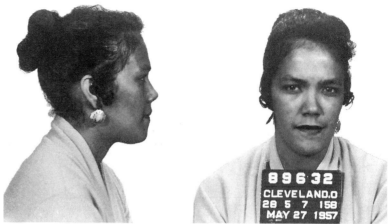

*The Plain Dealer*, Cleveland, Ohio

*Dollree Mapp, shown in a police mug shot, eventually had her conviction overturned by the Supreme Court in* Mapp v. Ohio *(1961).*

The U.S. Supreme Court ruled in *Mapp* that denying the exclusionary rule to enforce the Fourth Amendment "is to grant the right but in reality to withhold the privilege and enjoyment." The Court held that the exclusionary rule was essential to "judicial integrity," so that the courts would not be used to uphold crimes by the government. In *Mapp* the Court stated: "The criminal goes free, if he must, but it is the law that sets him free. Nothing can destroy a government more quickly than its failure to observe its laws."

### TAKING EXCEPTION TO THE RULE

The exclusionary rule continues to be one of the most controversial areas of Fourth Amendment law. For one reason, the rule punishes society and prosecutors for the errors of the police. Also, the people who benefit from the exclusionary rule most directly are seeking to exclude incriminating evidence. However, advocates of the exclusionary rule note that it has caused police departments to better train their officers about the guarantees of the Fourth Amendment—thus protecting *all* citizens, not just alleged criminals. But opponents of the rule have not been convinced. Chief Justice Warren Burger wrote in 1971: "Suppressing unchallenged truth has set guilty criminals free but demonstrably has neither deterred deliberate violations of the Fourth Amendment nor decreased those errors in judgment that will inevitably occur given the pressures inherent in police work."

In the 1980s, the Supreme Court recognized several exceptions to the exclusionary rule. The Court held in *United States v. Leon* (1984) that when police act in "good faith," that is, they have good reason to believe that a search warrant is valid, evidence may be used even if the warrant is later found to be technically invalid. In another 1984 case, the Supreme Court ruled that illegally obtained evidence is admissible if it would have been "inevitably" discovered by lawful means. And in 1987 the Court held that evidence seized improperly as a result of "honest mistakes" by police may be used at trial.

In a 1990 case, however, the Supreme Court began to backtrack somewhat on its exceptions to the exclusionary rule. "So long as we are committed to protecting the people from the disregard of their constitutional rights during the course of criminal investigations," said the Court, "inadmissibility of illegally obtained evidence must remain the rule, not the exception."

## MORE EXCEPTIONS THAN RULES?

Justice Lewis Powell has even admitted that certain parts of Fourth Amendment law are "intolerably confusing." It is no wonder that average citizens and police officers can be perplexed as well. Although there are a few clear principles under the Fourth Amendment, almost every rule has an exception. Whether or not the exceptions swallow the rules is the major question about the Fourth Amendment.

For instance, are there so many exceptions to the Fourth Amendment's requirement of probable cause that citizens are too often subject to the arbitrary whims of government officials—the very evil the Fourth Amendment was designed to prevent? Or are these exceptions necessary for police officers to catch criminals?

Justice Robert Jackson, who had prosecuted Nazi war criminals at the Nuremberg trials after World War II, resisted exceptions to the requirements of a warrant and probable cause. Jackson warned that Fourth Amendment rights "are not mere second-class rights but belong in the catalog of indispensable freedoms. Among deprivations of rights, none is so effective in cowing a population, crushing the spirit of the individual and putting terror in every heart. Uncontrolled search and seizure is one of the first and most effective weapons in the arsenal of every arbitrary government."

The conflict between preventing government tyranny and protecting citizens' security is at the heart of the Fourth Amendment. On a case-by-case basis, the Supreme Court—and each individual citizen—must continue to weigh the balance between law and order and individual privacy under the Fourth Amendment.

# The **FIFTH** Amendment

*No person shall be held to answer for a capital, or otherwise infamous crime, unless on a presentment or indictment of a* **GRAND JURY**, *except in cases arising in the land or naval forces, or in the Militia, when in actual service in time of War or public danger; nor shall any person be subject* **FOR THE SAME OFFENSE TO BE TWICE PUT IN JEOPARDY** *of life or limb; nor shall be compelled in any criminal case,* **TO BE A WITNESS AGAINST HIMSELF**, *nor be deprived of life, liberty, or property, without* **DUE PROCESS OF LAW**; *nor shall private property be taken for public use without* **JUST COMPENSATION**.

The Fifth Amendment is the longest and most diverse amendment in the Bill of Rights. It is a constitutional hodgepodge, guaranteeing five rights—some criminal, some civil. Among the rights protecting criminal defendants is the right to a grand jury indictment. This right means that a group of citizens—not just government officials—determines whether there is enough evidence to bring the accused to trial. The Fifth Amendment also prohibits double jeopardy: a defendant cannot be tried twice for the same offense. Perhaps the most well-known right in the Fifth Amendment is the right against self-incrimination, popularly known as "taking the Fifth." A defendant cannot be forced to testify against herself.

The Fifth Amendment also ensures due process of law, a guarantee that the government must be fair in its actions—both in criminal and civil cases. Finally, this amendment requires that the government give just compensation, or fair payment, when it takes private property for public use. Taken together, the rights guaranteed by the Fifth Amendment have the most diverse scope of any amendment in the Bill of Rights.

## GRAND JURY INDICTMENT

*No person shall be held to answer for a capital, or otherwise infamous crime, unless on a presentment or indictment of a* **GRAND JURY**, *except in cases arising in the land or naval forces, or in the Militia, when in actual service in time of War or public danger;* . . .

This first clause gives civilian defendants accused of serious crimes the right to a grand jury. A grand jury (French for "large jury") is a group of citizens, usually twenty-three, that investigates the evidence of a crime and decides whether or not the accused should be prosecuted. A grand jury is different from a petit jury (French for "small jury"), or trial jury, which usually consists of six to twelve persons and decides whether the accused is guilty of the crime.

An indictment, or formal criminal charge, is issued when the grand jury believes the prosecutor has presented enough evidence to justify a trial. In that case, the grand jury returns a "true bill of indictment." If the grand jury believes the prosecutor lacks sufficient evidence, then it issues a "no true bill." A grand jury can also make its own formal charges, called a presentment, without going through the prosecutor.

## HISTORY OF THE GRAND JURY

The grand jury was the first type of jury, preceding the petit jury. It developed in England during the twelfth century. Originally, the grand jury was made up of local landowners with direct knowledge of the disputes in their community. Because of this knowledge, the king's traveling judges used the grand jury to help decide which crimes to prosecute. In the beginning, the grand jury also determined the guilt or innocence of the accused. But many people felt it was unfair to have a person's innocence depend on the same people who had made the accusation in the first place. Eventually the process was split, so that the grand jury filed charges and the petit jury determined guilt.

The grand jury became a barrier to the arbitrary power of the king. Prosecutors could not make random accusations and haul people into court without first securing the approval of a neutral body of citizens. The grand jury took on added significance in America, where it was one of the colonists' few means of restricting the power of colonial prosecutors, most of whom represented the king. Grand jury indictment was protected by the New York Charter of Liberties (1683), and three states included it in their recommended amendments to the 1787 Constitution.

## GRAND JURY VS. INFORMATION

Despite its history of protecting individual liberty, the grand jury has come under increasing criticism. Indeed, in 1933 it was abolished in England, where it began. And a grand jury indictment is one of rights of criminal defendants that have *not* been incorporated by the Supreme Court to apply to the states, as held in *Hurtado v. California* (1884). Thus, a grand jury indictment is only required of the federal government.

While many states require grand juries, more than half do not. Those states allow prosecution by information, a sworn statement by the prosecutor that there is sufficient evidence for a trial. But a judge must first hold a preliminary hearing to decide if the prosecutor has enough evidence for an information to be filed.

There are several major differences between a grand jury investigation and a preliminary hearing. The grand jury is an *ex parte* proceeding, involving only one party—the prosecutor, not the defendant. Grand jury witnesses are not allowed to have their lawyers present, and the grand jury's sessions are secret. Grand juries are also allowed to consider evidence that may not be admissible at trial. At a preliminary hearing, however, both prosecuting and defense attorneys present their cases to the judge in open court.

Defenders of the grand jury argue that its secrecy is necessary to get witnesses to testify freely and to protect the reputations of people whom the grand jury may not actually indict. Critics say that the grand jury, despite its original purpose, is too much under the influence of the prosecutor. They point out that grand juries return indictments about 95 percent of the time. One judge even argued that a prosecutor could make a grand jury "indict a ham sandwich." But supporters note that grand juries have the power to act according to the spirit, not just the letter, of the law. At times grand juries refuse to indict a person despite the evidence, believing that justice will not be served otherwise. That is a power, say some, worth keeping.

## DOUBLE JEOPARDY

*. . . nor shall any person be subject* **FOR THE SAME OFFENSE TO BE TWICE PUT IN JEOPARDY** *of life or limb; . . .*

This part of the Fifth Amendment prohibits double jeopardy, or retrying a case in which the accused has been acquitted. The actual language of the Double Jeopardy Clause forbids putting someone in jeopardy, or danger, "of life or limb"—referring to the early English practice of cutting off an ear or other "limb" as punishment. But the Supreme Court has interpreted these words to include prison terms as well. The Double Jeopardy Clause was incorporated to apply to states in *Benton v. Maryland* (1969).

## HISTORICAL BACKGROUND

Double jeopardy is an ancient right, tracing its roots to Greek and Roman law. It was recognized by English common law as well. In America, the right was first protected by the Massachusetts Body of Liberties (1641), and it was included in several state bills of rights. Only two states recommended that double jeopardy be part of the amendments to the Constitution, but Madison kept it in his draft of the Bill of Rights.

## DOUBLE JEOPARDY AND THE COURTS

Justice Hugo Black explained the purpose of the guarantee against double jeopardy in *Green v. United States* (1957):

> The underlying idea, one that is deeply ingrained in at least the Anglo-American system of jurisprudence, is that the State with all its resources and power should not be allowed to make repeated attempts to convict an individual for an alleged offense, thereby subjecting him to embarrassment, expense, and ordeal and compelling him to live in a continuing state of anxiety and insecurity, as well as enhancing the possibility that even though innocent he may be found guilty.

The government may not use its vast resources to retry a defendant who is found innocent. If the jury cannot reach a verdict, however, a mistrial is declared and the accused may be tried again. Also, double jeopardy is not involved when a case is appealed to a higher court, even if the prosecution is appealing for a stiffer sentence. Similarly, double jeopardy does not apply if the appeals court grants the defendant a new trial.

But a single criminal act may result in several criminal charges. For instance, a person who breaks into a record store, steals merchandise, and then sells it on the street can be prosecuted for breaking and entering, theft, and selling stolen goods. Also, a person may be prosecuted under both state and federal law for the same offense, such as selling narcotics.

## SELF-INCRIMINATION

*. . . nor shall be compelled in any criminal case,* **TO BE A WITNESS AGAINST HIMSELF,** *. . .*

This clause of the Fifth Amendment prohibits self-incrimination: forcing a defendant to testify against herself. This right was incorporated to apply to the states in *Malloy v. Hogan* (1964). In popular language, the right against self-incrimination is known as "taking the Fifth." This right has often been controversial because some see it as an admission of guilt. During the 1950s, for instance, Senator Joseph McCarthy applied the term "Fifth Amendment Communists" to people who "took the Fifth" when testifying before Congress about communists in the U.S. government. But historically the right against self-incrimination evolved as one of the great protections against the coercive power of the state.

### HISTORICAL BACKGROUND

The right against self-incrimination was first recognized in England during the sixteenth and seventeenth centuries. At this time, the English rulers created special royal courts—most famous among them the Star Chamber, which heard criminal cases, and the High Commission, which tried offenses against the Church of England. Both these courts used a system of inquisition, or questioning the accused under oath to determine if defendants were guilty. For religious dissenters in particular, the oaths presented a dilemma. If they lied about their beliefs, then their souls were in jeopardy. But if they told the truth, they could lose their freedom or their lives.

In 1637, John Lilburne, a Puritan printer, was accused of distributing treasonous pamphlets. Lilburne refused to take the oath required by the Star Chamber. Lilburne accused the Chamber of trying to "ensnare" him—that lacking proof of his offenses, the Chamber was trying to get new charges against him through its questions. Lilburne's assertion of the right against self-incrimination led Parliament to abolish the Star Chamber and the High Commission and to forbid any oath forcing a person "to confess or to accuse himself or herself of any crime."

In America, many colonial courts—often controlled by the king's officials—also used inquisitorial tactics. By the end of the seventeenth century, the right against self-incrimination was recognized in some colonies. In 1776, the right was guaranteed for the first time in a written constitution by the Virginia Declaration of Rights. Three states

recommended that the prohibition against self-incrimination be included in amendments to the U.S. Constitution.

### INQUISITION VS. ACCUSATION

In an inquisitional system, the accused may be forced to be a witness against himself or even tortured to obtain a confession. But the United States operates under a system of accusation, in which the government must find evidence to prove its case. In some ways, an accusatory system is less efficient than an inquisitional system. As one English legal commentator noted in the nineteenth century, "it is far pleasanter to sit comfortably in the shade rubbing red pepper into a poor devil's eyes than to go about in the sun hunting up evidence."

In America, however, the defendant is presumed innocent until proven guilty, and the government has the burden of proving otherwise. As the Supreme Court has said: "Our accusatory system of criminal justice demands that the government seeking to punish an individual produce the evidence against him by its own independent labors, rather than by the cruel, simple [means] of compelling it from his own mouth." Also, coerced confessions are untrustworthy; a tortured defendant will say anything just to stop the pain.

### VOLUNTARY CONFESSIONS

The Supreme Court will allow confessions to be admitted into evidence only if they are voluntary and not coerced. For instance, in *Ashcraft v. Tennessee* (1944), the Supreme Court overturned the conviction of a man who had confessed to hiring someone to murder his wife. The man had confessed only after thirty-six straight hours of abusive and threatening interrogation under high-powered lights. The police officers had to

Phoenix Newspapers, Inc.

*Ernesto Miranda was retried and convicted, on the basis of other evidence, after his confession was struck down by the Supreme Court. Years later, Miranda was found murdered near a courthouse, his pockets stuffed with Miranda warning cards that he sold to defendants.*

work in shifts so they could rest. Such "third-degree" tactics are always unconstitutional under the Fifth Amendment.

But what if police do not actually beat or threaten the suspect? Under what other circumstances can a confession be coerced? In the landmark case of *Miranda v. Arizona,* the Supreme Court held that coercion is inherent when police question a suspect in custody, unless the accused has been informed of her constitutional rights.

**MIRANDA V. ARIZONA (1966).** Ernesto Miranda, who was mentally disabled, confessed to kidnapping and rape after two hours of police questioning. The police did not tell Miranda that, among other things, he had the right to an attorney during questioning. The Supreme Court overturned Miranda's conviction, on the grounds that his confession was not voluntary. Previously, confessions were struck down only if they were the result of threats or physical violence.

But in *Miranda,* the Court noted the inherently coercive atmosphere of police interrogation. As Chief Justice Earl Warren wrote: "Even without employing brutality . . . the very fact of custodial interrogation exacts a heavy toll on individual liberty and trades on the weaknesses of individuals." Warren added, "it is obvious that such an interrogation environment is created for no other purpose than to subjugate the individual to the will of the examiner. This atmosphere carries its own badge of intimidation."

Part of a truly voluntary confession, said the Court, is that the defendant knows his rights before he gives them up. In *Miranda,* the Supreme Court announced that it would no longer uphold confessions as voluntary unless the accused had been advised by the police of the following rights:

1. You have the right to remain silent.
2. Anything you say can be used against you in court.
3. You have the right to an attorney and to have the attorney present while you are being questioned.
4. If you cannot afford an attorney, one will be appointed for you before any questioning begins.

These "Miranda warnings" must be given at the time of arrest, before any questioning begins. Statements made by the accused without these warnings are inadmissible at trial. Furthermore, any evidence that police discover as the result of an illegal confession is also inadmissible under the "fruit of the poisonous tree" doctrine, unless the police can prove they would have found the evidence independent of the confession. Also, once the defendant has invoked the right to remain silent, police may not make repeated attempts to get the accused to talk.

**AFTER MIRANDA.** Since the *Miranda* decision was issued, the Supreme Court has considered many types of cases to determine if the Miranda warnings were violated. Key issues have been whether the defendant was in custody and whether police were interrogating the suspect. If the defendant is not in custody or being questioned, the Miranda warnings are not necessary. But interrogations do not have to be formal to be covered by the *Miranda* decision.

In *Brewer v. Williams* (1977), for instance, the Court struck down the confession of a man accused of murdering a 10-year-old girl, even though he was not formally questioned. When arrested, Williams was given the Miranda warnings, and his attorney advised him to keep quiet. Williams told the police he would not discuss the case. While riding with Williams to a jail in another city, a police officer commented that the girl's body had not been found. "I wish we could stop and locate the body," the officer said, "because this little girl's parents are entitled to give her a Christian burial." Williams then agreed to show the police where the body was located. The Supreme Court ruled that the officer's remarks were "subtle coercion" because he took advantage of Williams's mental illness and religious beliefs.

In *Illinois v. Perkins* (1990), however, the Supreme Court upheld a jailed suspect's confession obtained without Miranda warnings by a police officer posing as a fellow inmate. The suspect had bragged to the officer about committing the alleged murder. The Court said that the *Miranda* decision "forbids coercion, not mere strategic deception by taking advantage of a suspect's misplaced trust in one he supposes to be a fellow prisoner."

But in *Arizona v. Fulminante* (1991), the Supreme Court struck down a confession given to a fellow inmate who was an FBI informer, when the informer promised the suspect protection from the other inmates in exchange for the confession. In that same case, however, the Supreme Court reversed a longstanding rule that involuntary confessions always result in a new trial on appeal. The Court held that such confessions can be "harmless error" if the appeals court finds that, beyond a reasonable doubt, the jury would have convicted the defendant anyway, even without the confession.

**EXCEPTIONS TO MIRANDA.** The Supreme Court has recognized one clear exception to the *Miranda* ruling, known as the "public safety" exception.

In *New York v. Quarles* (1984), the Court ruled that police may ask the suspect questions before giving Miranda warnings if public safety is jeopardized. In that case, police chased a rape suspect, whom they believed to be armed, into a grocery store. When arresting the accused, the police asked where his gun was, and the defendant pointed it out. Despite the lack of Miranda warnings, the Court said that the gun was admissible evidence, because the police's questions were necessary to ensure public safety.

Many people criticize the *Miranda* ruling because they believe it "puts criminals back on the street." They applaud the Supreme Court's 1991 ruling that a coerced confession may be a "harmless error." But others contend that without *Miranda,* police would be able to force confessions out of people—including the innocent—who did not know their constitutional rights. Such a result, say supporters of *Miranda,* is never "harmless."

*Lt. Col. Oliver North initially "took the Fifth" in his 1987 testimony before Congress about the Iran/contra affair, but Congress granted him "use" immunity to testify.*

## NONTESTIMONIAL EVIDENCE

The Fifth Amendment applies to any government proceeding, criminal or civil, in which a person is forced to answer questions. But it does not prohibit the government from requiring a defendant to provide nontestimonial evidence—such as fingerprints, handwriting samples, fingernail clippings, and blood specimens. This type of evidence is considered physical evidence, rather than testimony. In *Schmerber v. California* (1966), for instance, the Supreme Court upheld a drunk driving conviction based on a blood sample taken without the defendant's permission. And in 1990 the Supreme Court held that videotaped sobriety tests, when asking routine booking questions (name, address, height, weight, etc.), can be used without Miranda warnings because they are physical evidence. A defendant may also be required to appear in a police line-up and repeat words that help the victim make an identification without violating the Fifth Amendment. A defendant cannot be forced to take a lie-detector test, because that is considered testimonial evidence.

## IMMUNITY

The government may force a witness to testify or produce incriminating evidence only if it grants that person immunity from prosecution. As Justice Felix Frankfurter noted: "Immunity displaces the danger. Once the reason for the privilege [against self-incrimination] ceases, the privilege ceases." The government may grant total immunity from prosecution or limited immunity. Under limited, or "use," immunity, the government agrees not to use the witness's testimony against him or her, but may still prosecute the witness based on independent evidence. The Supreme Court has held that "use" immunity does not violate the Fifth Amendment.

## DUE PROCESS

*. . . nor be deprived of life, liberty, or property, without* **DUE PROCESS OF LAW**; *. . .*

This part of the Fifth Amendment is known as the Due Process Clause. The Constitution has two Due Process Clauses—one in the Fifth Amendment, which applies only to the federal government, and one in the Fourteenth Amendment, which applies only to the states. Due process of law means that the government must be fair in its actions— both in criminal and civil cases. While due process of law has no exact definition, it generally means that government must follow established rules and not act arbitrarily or unreasonably. There are two types of due process, procedural and substantive. Procedural due process means that the way laws are carried out must be fair; substantive due process means that the laws themselves must be fair.

### THE ROOTS OF DUE PROCESS

The concept of due process of law had its beginnings in the Magna Carta of 1215. Chapter Thirty-nine of that document stated: "No freeman shall be captured or imprisoned . . . or in any way destroyed . . . , except by . . . the law of the land." Over the years, "law of the land" evolved into "due process of law."

In America, due process of law was first guaranteed by the Maryland Act for the Liberties of the People in 1639. Other colonies protected due process in their charters. The Virginia Declaration of Rights (1776) was the first constitutional guarantee of due process. The first use in America of the actual words "due process of law" was in New York's suggested amendments to the U.S. Constitution. Three other states also recommended that due process be included.

*"What's so great about due process? Due
process got me ten years."*

## PROCEDURAL DUE PROCESS

"The history of American freedom is, in no small measure, the history of procedure," said Justice Felix Frankfurter. Procedure refers to the rules and regulations that carry out the laws. If the government did not have to follow certain rules, individuals would be at the government's mercy. The government must treat individuals fairly in both criminal and civil cases.

**CRIMINAL CASES.** The Bill of Rights is full of rules that the government must follow in criminal cases, such as trial by jury and notice of the charges. But the Due Process Clause also requires the government to follow certain rules not specifically mentioned in the Bill of Rights. For instance, the Supreme Court has ruled that the Due Process Clause includes the right to be presumed innocent until proven guilty and to have the state prove its case beyond a reasonable doubt.

*Shocking Police Conduct.* The Supreme Court has also held in *Rochin v. California* (1952) that police methods that "shock the conscience" violate the Due Process Clause. Three Los Angeles County deputies, suspecting Rochin of dealing narcotics, went to his rooming house. Finding the door open, they entered and forced their way into his room. Rochin was sitting on the bed, with two capsules on the nightstand beside him. One of the deputies asked, "Whose stuff is this?" Rochin grabbed the capsules and swallowed them, despite the officers' efforts to stop him. The officers then took Rochin to the hospital to have his stomach pumped—revealing that the capsules contained morphine. Rochin was convicted of violating the state narcotics laws.

The Supreme Court reversed Rochin's conviction on appeal, holding that the deputies had violated the Due Process Clause of the Fourteenth Amendment. Said the Court:

> This is conduct that shocks the conscience. Illegally breaking into the privacy of the petitioner, the struggle to open his mouth and remove what was there, the forcible extraction of his stomach's contents—this course of proceeding by agents of government to obtain evidence is bound to offend even hardened sensibilities. They are methods too close to the rack and the screw.

*Due Process for Juveniles.* The Supreme Court has extended many of the due process rights of adults in criminal trials to young people in juvenile court proceedings. Juvenile courts try young people accused of breaking the law. These courts are based on the principle of *parens patriae*—that the court is acting as a "benevolent parent," not a prosecutor, and is trying to rehabilitate instead of punish. In the process, however, juveniles were often denied many of the trial rights of adults—until the case of *In re Gault* (1967).

Fifteen-year-old Gerald Gault was on six-months' probation when a neighbor accused him of making an obscene phone call. Gault was arrested when his parents were not at home, and they were not notified of the arrest. At his hearing the next day, Gault was not represented by a lawyer nor could he challenge the neighbor, who did not testify. Not warned of his right against self-incrimination, Gault admitted he dialed the neighbor's number, but insisted that a friend made the obscene remarks. The judge found that Gault was a "juvenile delinquent" and committed him to a state reformatory until he was 21, a sentence of six years. The same offense had a maximum penalty for adults of fifty dollars or two months in jail.

Gault's parents appealed his sentence to the Supreme Court. The Court asserted that "the Bill of Rights is [not] for adults alone." "Under our Constitution," said the Court, "the condition of being a boy does not justify a kangaroo court." The Court held that juveniles were entitled to the following rights: (1) to receive notice of the charges far enough in advance to prepare an adequate defense; (2) to have a lawyer, appointed by the state if necessary; (3) to be warned about the right against self-incrimination; and (4) to confront their accusers and question witnesses. As a result of *Gault,* juveniles acquired many, but not all, rights of adult defendants. Juveniles are still not guaranteed the right to trial by jury.

**CIVIL CASES.** In civil cases, the government cannot take away "liberty or property without due process of law." While due process does not guarantee that citizens will always *like* the government's actions, it does ensure that those actions must be taken according to fair procedures. In civil due process cases, the courts first determine whether or not a "liberty" or "property" interest has been affected, and then they decide "what process is due"—or what procedures are necessary to protect the interest.

*What Process Is Due?* The basic elements of due process are notice and a hearing: a person must be warned that a liberty or property interest will be affected and must have an opportunity to be heard. As a general rule, the government may not take away a benefit without notice and a hearing. For instance, in *Goldberg v. Kelly* (1970), the Supreme Court held that welfare benefits are a "property" interest that the government cannot take away without notifying the person and giving him or her an opportunity to be heard. Due process is also required if the government fires someone from a government job, revokes a prisoner's parole, or cuts off a person's social security payments.

However, different types of liberty and property interests receive different levels of due process protection. For some rights, notice and a hearing must come *before* the right is taken away; for others, notice and a hearing can come afterwards. Sometimes due process will include a hearing before a neutral magistrate, the right to have an attorney and to call witnesses, and the chance to appeal the decision. In *Mathews v. Eldridge* (1976), the Supreme Court set guidelines for determining what process is due. According to *Mathews,* the specific procedures required depend on: (1) how seriously a citizen might be harmed; (2) how much the procedures would cost the government in time and money; and (3) how likely the government would be to make a mistake without the procedures.

*Student Suspensions.* A good example of a civil due process case is *Goss v. Lopez* (1975), which involved the rights of students who are suspended from school. In 1971, many students were suspended for participating in, or being present at, widespread demonstrations in the schools of Columbus, Ohio. Many suspensions lasted ten days, and the students were not given a hearing before they were suspended. The Supreme Court held that the right to a public education was a "property" interest. Therefore, the students were entitled to certain rights before their suspension, including: (1) either oral or written notice of the charges; (2) if students deny the charges, an explanation of the evidence against them; and (3) a chance to tell their side of the story. But in an emergency, said the Court, these rights could be provided after the suspension. The Supreme Court held that the students were not entitled to a lawyer, to call witnesses, or to have a hearing before a neutral magistrate.

## SUBSTANTIVE DUE PROCESS

"That's not fair!" is a common complaint on the playground. Even small children have a sense that some things are not fair. Substantive due process means that the laws themselves, not just the procedures that carry them out, must be fair. Many legal experts criticize substantive due process because they believe it depends too much on judges' individual ideas of what is fair. Perhaps for this reason, the Supreme Court has often been reluctant to uphold rights under substantive due process.

Most substantive due process cases arise under the Fourteenth Amendment, so they are discussed in more detail in that chapter. However, one example of substantive due process under the Fifth Amendment is *Bolling v. Sharpe* (1954). In that case, the Supreme Court struck down a law enacted by Congress that required segregated schools in the District of Columbia. Such schools, said the Court, deprived black children of their "liberty" in violation of the Due Process Clause. In similar cases, segregated schools in the states were also struck down on the basis of the Equal Protection Clause of the Fourteenth Amendment, which prohibits unreasonable discrimination. But since the Fourteenth Amendment applies only to the states, and not the federal government, the Court had to use the Fifth Amendment's guarantee of due process to overturn a federal law authorizing segregation.

## JUST COMPENSATION

*. . . nor shall private property be taken for public use without* **JUST COMPENSATION.**

This phrase in the Fifth Amendment is known as the Just Compensation Clause. It restricts eminent domain, the government's power to take private property for public use, by requiring the government to pay a fair price for property it takes. The Just Compensation Clause was the first part of the Bill of Rights to be incorporated to apply to the states, in *Chicago, Burlington, & Quincy Railroad Co. v. Chicago* (1897).

The case in which the Supreme Court first declared that the Bill of Rights did *not* apply to the states, *Barron v. Baltimore* (1833), also involved the Just Compensation Clause. John Barron sued the City of Baltimore because it had diverted several streams while paving its streets, drying up Barron's wharf in the process. The Supreme Court, led by Chief Justice John Marshall, held that the Fifth Amendment and the rest of the Bill of Rights did not apply to the states. Only after the Fourteenth Amendment was ratified did the Supreme Court begin applying the Bill of Rights to the states.

The fact that a just compensation claim was the first part of the Bill of Rights to be tested against the states, both before and after the Fourteenth Amendment, indicates the importance of property rights to Americans. The three major issues that have arisen under the Just Compensation Clause are what action by the government is in fact a "taking," what purposes of the government qualify as "public use," and how much compensation is "just."

### HISTORICAL ORIGINS

The roots of the Just Compensation Clause are in the Magna Carta, which addressed royal officials' abuse of taking private property without compensation. The right was first protected in America in the Massachusetts Body of Liberties (1641). The first guarantee of just compensation in a written constitution was in the Virginia Declaration of Rights (1776). But no states included just compensation in their recommended amendments to the U.S. Constitution. Nonetheless, Madison included it in his proposed amendments.

Department of Transportation

*This historic house is being moved to make way for highway construction, an example of eminent domain in action.*

## TAKINGS

Usually, when the government wishes to "take" private property, it goes through procedures to condemn the property, or appropriate it for public use. In the 1800s, government often condemned private property to make way for railroads, canals, and bridges. A common public use today is to take property and tear down homes to build new highways.

But more recently, one of the biggest questions about "takings" is how much government can regulate the use of private property without in effect taking the property away, and thus requiring just compensation. Under its police powers, a state has the authority to pass laws regulating the health, safety, and welfare of its citizens. However, Justice Oliver Wendell Holmes decried state regulations as the "petty larceny of the police power," when they impinged too much on citizens' enjoyment of their private property.

The Supreme Court has not developed a general rule to determine when regulations of property amount to a taking. Instead, they use a case-by-case approach. The Court has upheld zoning laws, which allow some property to be used for businesses and some only for residences, without requiring just compensation. Similarly, landmark preservation laws that restrict owners of historic buildings do not require just compensation, as long as the building remains at all usable. In *PruneYard Shopping Center v. Robins* (1980), the Supreme Court said that a California court ruling allowing free speech rights in private shopping malls was not a "taking" that required just compensation.

But the Supreme Court said that just compensation was necessary when a New York law required owners of apartment buildings to let cable television companies install cables on top of the building. And the Court struck down the Environmental Protection Agency's requirement that a chemical company reveal its trade secrets to the public before licensing certain pesticides. The Court held that such secrets were property that would have to be compensated.

During the 1990s, the Supreme Court decided two significant cases that upheld property owners' rights. The case of *Lucas v. South Carolina Coastal Commission* (1992) involved beachfront property that was later rezoned by local government to forbid building, thus making it worthless to the owner, a developer. The Court said that when government regulation totally eliminates the value of the property, the owner must be compensated—unless the property is a public nuisance. In *Dolan v. City of Tigard* (1994), the Court held that a city may not force a property owner to donate land for public use in order to get a permit to develop the land, unless the city demonstrates that such a requirement is related to the "extent and nature" of that development. Many experts believe these cases indicate a renewed concern by the Supreme Court to protect property rights.

## PUBLIC USE

The Fifth Amendment also requires that any taking of private property by the government be for "public use." If government takes property to build a highway, it is clearly for public use, since many citizens will actually use the highway. But what if government takes property from one private citizen and gives it to another private citizen? Is that a "public use"?

In *Hawaii Housing Authority v. Midkiff* (1984), the Supreme Court upheld as a "public use" a Hawaii law that redistributed land from one group of private citizens to another. The law's stated purpose was to prevent a land oligopoly, a concentration of land ownership in which 47 percent of the state's land was held by only 72 landholders. Consequently, most homeowners rented the land their homes were on, instead of owning it.

The Supreme Court held in *Midkiff* that ending a land oligopoly was a legitimate public purpose, even though the means of achieving it involved taking land from one private citizen and giving it to another. The "public use" requirement is satisfied, said the Court, if the government offers a legitimate public *purpose* for the taking, even if the government or the general public never physically "uses" the land. Generally, the courts defer to the legislature in defining a legitimate public purpose.

### JUST COMPENSATION

If a taking has occurred, what compensation is just? The general rule established by the Supreme Court is that owners are "entitled to receive what a willing buyer would pay in cash to a willing seller at the time of the taking." This standard is known as "fair market value." Property owners are not entitled to moving expenses or replacement costs. Although a house may be much more expensive to rebuild in another neighborhood, the government is only required to pay the fair market value of the original home.

### THE FIFTH AMENDMENT'S FIVE RIGHTS

The five rights of the Fifth Amendment are very diverse. Most of them deal with criminal law. The grand jury gives the people, not just the government, a role in deciding who is prosecuted for crimes. Double jeopardy prevents the government from using its enormous resources to try a defendant twice for the same crime. The right against self-incrimination makes the government prove its case, rather than relying on coerced confessions. Due process requires that the government be fair in its actions, both in criminal and civil cases. And just compensation means that the government cannot take private property without paying a fair price. These five rights have a very wide scope, including many stages of the criminal process as well as civil issues. Thus, although the right against self-incrimination is the most well known, "taking the Fifth" means much more than just not having to testify against oneself.

# The **SIXTH** *Amendment*

**IN ALL CRIMINAL PROSECUTIONS**, *the accused shall enjoy the right to a* **SPEEDY AND PUBLIC TRIAL**, *by an* **IMPARTIAL JURY** *of the State and district* **WHEREIN THE CRIME SHALL HAVE BEEN COMMITTED**; *which district shall have been previously ascertained by law, and to be* **INFORMED OF THE NATURE AND CAUSE OF THE ACCUSATION**; *to be* **CONFRONTED WITH THE WITNESSES AGAINST HIM**; *to have* **COMPULSORY PROCESS** *for obtaining witnesses in his favor, and to have the* **ASSISTANCE OF COUNSEL** *for his defense.*

Article III of the U.S. Constitution requires that "the trial of all crimes, except in cases of impeachment, shall be by jury." But what if the government could postpone a trial for years, or prosecute the accused in secret, or exclude women from the jury, or refuse to tell the accused the charges, or allow witnesses to make accusations secretly? What if only the government could force witnesses to testify or use lawyers?

The Sixth Amendment goes beyond the right to a jury trial by guaranteeing a fair trial, although it does not use those exact words. Rather, the Sixth Amendment lists many parts of a fair trial: that it be speedy and public; that it be conducted by an impartial and local jury; that the accused be informed of the charges; and that defendants have some of the same tools to prove their innocence as the state has to prove their guilt. The Sixth Amendment attempts to give the defendant a fair chance when going against the enormous resources of the government—which has both police and prosecutors on its payroll. Under the Sixth Amendment, a fair trial is an essential part of a fair society.

# TRIAL RIGHTS BEFORE THE SIXTH AMENDMENT

The Sixth Amendment protects many rights of criminal defendants at trial. These rights evolved over hundreds of years, in both England and America. While defendants' rights had their beginnings in England, they became written guarantees in America.

## IN ENGLAND

Trial by jury had been established in criminal trials by the thirteenth century in England. Trial by jury was used in civil trials first, however, so much of its history relates to civil trials. This history is discussed in the chapter on the Seventh Amendment, which guarantees trial by jury in civil cases.

Trial by jury was not used in all criminal cases in England, however. During the sixteenth and seventeenth centuries, the English rulers created special courts, called prerogative courts, which did not use juries. The most notorious prerogative court was the Star Chamber, which held its proceedings in secret. For most of their history, the Star Chamber and other prerogative courts were quite popular among the English people as sources of cheap and speedy justice. During the 1630s, however, Charles I used these courts to suppress dissent from royal policies—making the Star Chamber a symbol of secret and arbitrary court proceedings.

Even after the prerogative courts were abolished in 1641, the rights of the accused still received little protection. The English common law courts, like the prerogative courts, recognized few rights for defendants. Judges were appointed by the king, and they could imprison or fine jurors who gave a verdict against the judge's instructions. The English Bill of Rights of 1689 did protect some rights for defendants before and after trial, but it did not guarantee them many rights during the trial itself. Eventually, English judges did recognize some trial rights for defendants.

## IN AMERICA

Colonial Americans protected defendants' trial rights in written codes and laws. The Massachusetts Body of Liberties (1641), for example, guaranteed a speedy trial, trial by jury, the right to counsel, and the right to challenge jurors for bias. But defendants' rights varied from colony to colony.

During the 1760s and 1770s, Americans' awareness of the importance of defendants' rights increased when more of them became defendants themselves. Among other new English laws restricting the colonists, the Stamp Act of 1765 gave special vice-admiralty courts power over violations of the act. These courts, which operated without juries, outraged the colonists. Furthermore, defendants could be sent back to England for trial, where an English jury would likely be less sympathetic than an American one.

The Declaration of Independence in 1776 listed the violation of Americans' trial rights as justification for the revolution against England. The Declaration noted that the king had "made judges dependent on his will alone." The Declaration criticized the king "for depriving us, in many cases, of the benefit of trial by jury" and "for transporting us beyond seas to be tried for pretended offences."

After the Revolutionary War, many of the newly independent states protected defendants' trial rights in their constitutions. Virginia's Declaration of Rights, for example, guaranteed the right of trial by a local jury, a speedy trial, confrontation of accusers and witnesses, the power to compel witnesses to appear for the defendant, and unanimous verdicts.

But the new U.S. Constitution of 1787 did not give extensive protection to defendants' trial rights. The Constitution guaranteed trial by jury in criminal cases other than impeachment, but no more than that. Several states included defendants' rights in their proposed amendments to the Constitution.

## SPEEDY AND PUBLIC TRIAL

**IN ALL CRIMINAL PROSECUTIONS,** *the accused shall enjoy the right to a* **SPEEDY AND PUBLIC TRIAL,** . . .

This first part of the Sixth Amendment states that "in all criminal prosecutions" the accused has certain rights. But the amendment does not apply to *every* criminal charge, such as a speeding ticket. Rather, it is designed to protect defendants' rights in more serious charges, even including misdemeanors if the defendant could be imprisoned as a result. Among the rights the Sixth Amendment protects is a "speedy and public trial."

### SPEEDY TRIAL

Many legal scholars say that "justice delayed is justice denied." This means that even if a just decision is eventually made, too long a time in reaching that decision can cause other injustices. Therefore, the Sixth Amendment guarantees the right to a speedy trial.

One of the most important reasons for a speedy trial is that a person is presumed innocent until proven guilty. The defendant deserves to have the question of guilt or innocence resolved as soon as possible, to avoid long periods of uncertainty and damage to his or her reputation. Also, some defendants are kept in jail while awaiting trial—even though they have not been convicted of a crime. A speedy trial prevents defendants from spending a long time in jail before trial. A speedy trial also helps guarantee a more accurate verdict. Witnesses to a crime are likely to forget details after too much time has passed.

Sometimes, however, defendants waive their right to a speedy trial. They may need more time to prepare their cases or to locate witnesses. And a delay can work in *favor* of the defendant, because prosecution witnesses may become unavailable or their memories may fade.

**DEFINING A SPEEDY TRIAL.** How long is too long for a defendant to wait for trial? The courts have had trouble answering this question precisely. In *Barker v. Wingo* (1972), the Supreme Court upheld Barker's conviction, even though his trial had been delayed seventeen times over a period of five years. Barker had not objected to the first eleven delays. In the *Barker* case, the Court rejected specific timetables for a speedy trial. Instead, the Court issued some general factors to be examined on a case-by-case basis: (1) length of delay; (2) the prosecution's reasons for the delay; (3) whether the defendant claimed the right to a speedy trial; and (4) actual harm to the defendant because of the delay. If a trial is not speedy, then the charges against the defendant must be dropped.

Congress has required a stricter standard than *Barker* for speedy trial in federal cases. In the Speedy Trial Act of 1974, Congress set fixed time limits for the federal government to begin criminal prosecutions. As of 1984, federal trials must begin no more than 100 days after an arrest. The Supreme Court in 1992 decided a case in which the federal government, because of its own negligence in locating the defendant rather than an intent to delay prosecution, waited eight years before bringing a defendant to trial. Nonetheless, said the Court, such a delay denied the defendant's right to a speedy trial.

The right to a speedy trial was applied to the states in *Klopfer v. North Carolina* (1967). Some states have also enacted laws setting time limits in which a defendant must be brought to trial. But these laws only have to meet the general guidelines of *Barker* to be upheld—one case took eleven years to come to trial without violating the Sixth Amendment.

## PUBLIC TRIAL

The Sixth Amendment also protects the defendant's right to a public trial. This right was applied to the states in the case of *In re Oliver* (1948). In this case, the Supreme Court held that a public trial "has always been recognized as a safeguard against any attempts to employ our courts as instruments of persecution." The Sixth Amendment prohibits American courts from becoming modern versions of the Star Chamber.

**TOO PUBLIC?** But what happens when a trial becomes *too* public, when the community knows all the details of a crime before the trial? What if the defendant has been "convicted in the media" before even appearing in the courtroom? Can the defendant still get a fair trial?

In *Sheppard v. Maxwell* (1966), the Supreme Court ruled that too much pretrial publicity can deny the defendant a fair trial. At the murder trial of Dr. Sam Sheppard in Cleveland, the Supreme Court noted, "bedlam reigned at the courthouse during the trial and newsmen took over practically the entire courtroom, hounding most of the participants in the trial, especially Sheppard." The case had become a "'Roman holiday' for the news media," said the Court, that "inflamed and prejudiced the public." In such cases, the local trial court must take measures to ensure that the jury is impartial. Such measures include changing the location, or venue, of the trial and sequestering the jury—isolating jurors from the community and the news media.

**WHOSE RIGHT?** The right to a public trial is for the benefit of the *defendant*. If the defendant agrees, the prosecution and the judge can close the courtroom. Under the Sixth Amendment, the news media and the American people have no right to attend *all* trials, ruled the Supreme Court in *Gannett Co. v. De Pasquale* (1979).

But the Supreme Court has held that under the First Amendment, the public has a right to attend criminal trials. In *Richmond Newspapers, Inc. v. Virginia* (1980), the Court said that the public has this right, except in cases that require secrecy, such as those involving national security.

**CONFLICTING RIGHTS.** The issue of a public trial thus creates a conflict between the defendant's Sixth Amendment right to a fair trial and the public's First Amendment rights to speak about and attend criminal trials. The Supreme Court has tried to balance these conflicting rights by denying trial courts a broad power to forbid pretrial publicity or close the courtroom, but at the same time forcing trial courts to do everything possible to isolate the jury from prejudicial news coverage.

## IMPARTIAL AND LOCAL JURY

*. . . by an* **IMPARTIAL JURY** *of the State and district* **WHEREIN THE CRIME**

**SHALL HAVE BEEN COMMITTED**; *which district shall have been previously*

*ascertained by law, . . .*

This part of the Sixth Amendment guarantees trial by jury in criminal cases, just as the original Constitution does in Article III. In fact, trial by jury in criminal cases is the only right mentioned in both the Bill of Rights and the original Constitution. But the Sixth Amendment also provides that the jury must be impartial and not prejudiced against the defendant. Also, it requires that the jury be local, of the "district wherein the crime shall have been committed."

### TRIAL BY JURY IN CRIMINAL CASES

There are many elements to a trial by jury. How big does a jury have to be under the Constitution? Do all the jurors have to agree on the verdict, or is a majority vote enough? Can a person be convicted of a crime on a five-to-one vote of a six-person jury?

The Supreme Court applied trial by jury to the states in *Duncan v. Louisiana* (1968). For all other rights, the Supreme Court has required that, once a right is incorporated, it must be protected to the same degree by the states as by the federal government. But trial by jury has a double standard. The federal government is required to have twelve-person juries and unanimous verdicts. Yet in *Williams v. Florida* (1970), the Supreme Court ruled that twelve-person juries are not mandated in state courts. And in *Apodaca v. Oregon* (1972), the Court held that unanimous verdicts are not required in state courts for noncapital cases, which do not involve the death penalty.

The Supreme Court has set some limits on the states regarding trial by jury. The Court has held that a state criminal jury must have at least six members, and that if a state jury has only six members, the verdict must be unanimous.

### WHAT IS AN IMPARTIAL JURY?

The Sixth Amendment requires that a jury be impartial. This right was incorporated to apply to the states in *Parker v. Gladden* (1966). At a minimum, no juror should be prejudiced against the defendant. To select

*In the movie* Twelve Angry Men *(1957), one juror convinces the other eleven to change their initial verdicts of guilty in a murder case. Would a woman or a black person be likely to regard this jury as impartial?*

an impartial jury, the prosecuting and defense attorneys and the judge conduct a voir dire, in which potential jurors are questioned about their knowledge of the case and their personal biases. Potential jurors are formed into groups called venires, from which the jury is selected.

During the voir dire, a possible juror may be challenged for cause by either the prosecuting or defense attorney. The juror will be excluded if the attorneys can convince the judge that the juror is likely to be biased. The attorneys can also exclude a certain number of potential jurors without giving any reason at all, by using a peremptory challenge.

What if prosecutors use their peremptory challenges to exclude all blacks from a jury? Would that deny a black person the right to an impartial jury? A white person? And what if a state allowed all women to be excluded from jury duty? Would an all-male jury be impartial?

**A FAIR CROSS-SECTION.** Under the Sixth Amendment's mandate of an impartial jury, the defendant is entitled to have the jury selected from a "fair cross-section" of the community. The Supreme Court has defined the "fair cross-section" requirement as prohibiting the "systematic exclusion" of identifiable groups. Thus, the Court has held that blacks and women may not be excluded from the jury pool.

In *Taylor v. Louisiana* (1975), for example, the Court struck down a state law that excluded women from jury duty unless they asked to serve.

Despite the state's claim that the law helped maintain a stable family life, the Supreme Court held that women were an essential element of the community that must be represented in the jury pool. Said the Court:

> The thought is that the factors which tend to influence the action of women are the same as those which influence the action of men—personality, background, economic status—and not sex. . . . But, if the shoe were on the other foot, who would claim that a jury was truly representative of the community if all men were intentionally and systematically excluded from the panel?

The Supreme Court has also held that, in capital cases, excusing all potential jurors who have moral scruples against the death penalty violates the Sixth Amendment's guarantee of an impartial jury. However, the state may exclude jurors who automatically refuse to impose the death penalty in all cases, because they cannot fairly apply the law—even though doing so may exclude a significant segment of the community.

The Sixth Amendment requires only that the jury pool—not the final trial jury—be representative of the community. Thus, depending on the voir dire and the attorneys' challenges, individual juries may not actually reflect the racial and sexual composition of their communities.

**DISCRIMINATION AND JURY SELECTION.** The Sixth Amendment does not forbid lawyers to use peremptory challenges in a discriminatory way, but the Fourteenth Amendment does. The Supreme Court has ruled that using peremptory challenges to exclude racial groups and women from a jury violates the Equal Protection Clause of the Fourteenth Amendment, which prohibits unreasonable discrimination.

In *Batson v. Kentucky* (1986), a black defendant had been convicted by an all-white jury, because the prosecutor used his peremptory challenges to exclude all four black persons in the venire. The Supreme Court stated that the Equal Protection Clause "forbids the prosecutor to challenge potential jurors on account of race or on the assumption that black jurors as a group will be unable impartially to consider the State's case against a black defendant." The Court also argued that in a multiracial nation, "the rule of law will be strengthened if we ensure that no citizen is disqualified from jury service because of his race." In *Powers v. Ohio* (1991), the Court forbade racial discrimination in jury selection when the defendant is white as well. And in *J.E.B. v. Alabama* (1994), the Court also prohibited gender discrimination in jury selection.

## LOCAL JURIES

Besides an impartial jury, the Sixth Amendment also guarantees a local jury. The jury must be from "the State and district wherein the crime shall have been committed; which district shall have been previously ascertained by law." This requirement was designed to prevent the British practice of sending American colonists overseas to England to be tried by English juries, who were less sympathetic than American juries. The Declaration of Independence specifically protested such tactics by the British.

Today, however, some defendants would rather *not* have a local trial. Sometimes the local community can be prejudiced against the defendant because of pretrial publicity about the crime. In such cases, the defendant may ask the judge to grant a change of venue, or location, to move the trial to another district. The judge can order a change of venue because the guarantee of a local trial, like all others in the Sixth Amendment, works on the defendant's behalf and can be waived by the defendant.

## KNOWING THE CHARGES

*. . . and to be* **INFORMED OF THE NATURE AND CAUSE OF THE ACCUSATION;** *. . .*

Under the Sixth Amendment, the defendant has the right to know the charges against him or her. Otherwise, the defendant would be unable to prepare an adequate defense. Typically, the defendant is informed of the charges at the initial appearance before a judge after arrest. For misdemeanors, minor crimes punishable by small fines or short jail terms, the judge informs the defendant of the charges as part of the arraignment, at which the defendant enters a plea of guilty or innocent. For felonies, serious crimes punishable by prison sentences of more than one year, a grand jury often must return an indictment before the arraignment.

The defendant must be told of the charges in enough detail to prepare a proper defense. For instance, the state cannot accuse a defendant of burglary without specifying the time and place where the crime was allegedly committed. Otherwise, the defendant would be unable to present an alibi for the crime. Not all the specific details of a crime have to be included in the grand jury's indictment, but they must be provided to the defense by the prosecution.

The Sixth Amendment right to know the charges has never been formally incorporated by the Supreme Court to apply to the states. However, notice of the charges is a fundamental part of due process of law, so it applies to the states under the Due Process Clause of the Fourteenth Amendment.

## RIGHT TO CONFRONT

*. . . to be* **CONFRONTED WITH THE WITNESSES AGAINST HIM;** *. . .*

This part of the Sixth Amendment is known as the Confrontation Clause. It states that witnesses must confront the defendant in court, rather than testifying in secret. Defendants also have the right to cross-examine witnesses, and ask questions challenging their testimony. The Confrontation Clause was incorporated to apply to the states in *Pointer v. Texas* (1965).

Normally the defendant has the right to be in the courtroom at all times during the trial, but the Supreme Court has ruled that judges may limit this right if the defendant is unruly or disruptive. In such cases, a judge may remove the defendant from the courtroom.

### HEARSAY AND CROSS-EXAMINATION

Many of the Supreme Court cases concerning the Confrontation Clause have involved hearsay testimony, in which one person testifies about something someone else said, rather than something that person actually experienced. Sam testifies, "Joe told me that Sue forged the check," although Sam never *saw* Sue forge the check, and Joe is not in court to testify directly. How can a defendant adequately cross-examine Joe?

As a general rule, hearsay testimony cannot be used as evidence against the defendant. But there are many exceptions to the rule. What if Joe is dead, or is also accused of the crime? Should Sam's testimony be allowed then? The Supreme Court has allowed hearsay testimony in certain cases despite the Confrontation Clause.

The Court has also made exceptions to the defendant's right to cross-examine witnesses. Sometimes a defendant is not allowed to fully cross-examine a witness because he or she invokes a privilege, such as doctor-patient confidentiality. Or a witness will claim a memory loss, making cross-examination impossible. In such cases, the Supreme Court has held, the Sixth Amendment only requires that the defendant have the *opportunity* for cross-examination, not that it be successful.

### FACE TO FACE?

Perhaps the most fundamental question under the Confrontation Clause is whether the witnesses must confront the defendant face to face when testifying. This question has arisen most frequently in child abuse cases, where many state laws allow children to testify without actually seeing the defendant.

In *Coy v. Iowa* (1988), the Supreme Court struck down an Iowa law that required the defendant to be hidden behind a screen during the testimony of a child witness in abuse cases. Justice Antonin Scalia, writing for the Court's majority, emphasized the importance of face-to-face confrontation:

> [T]here is something deep in human nature that regards face-to-face confrontation between accused and accuser as "essential to a fair trial in a criminal prosecution." . . . In this country, if someone dislikes you, or accuses you, he must come up in front. He cannot hide behind the shadow. . . . The phrase still persists, "Look me in the eye and say that."

The Court pointed out the reasons why confrontation is essential to a fair trial. Witnesses may change their minds when they see the actual human being who will suffer greatly if they distort or mistake the facts. Witnesses may also find it harder to lie about a defendant "to his face" rather than "behind his back," and the lie might be told less convincingly. All these factors affect the truth of witnesses' testimony, held the Court, and thus are critical for a judge or jury to consider.

The Court noted "the profound effect upon a witness of standing in the presence of the person the witness accuses," both for good and ill. The Court conceded "that face-to-face presence may, unfortunately, upset the truthful rape victim or abused child; but by the same token it may confound and undo the false accuser, or reveal the child coached by a malevolent adult." But, concluded the Court, "it is a truism that constitutional protections have costs."

In *Coy,* the trial judge had not made a specific finding that the screen was necessary to protect the particular child witnesses in that case. Justice Sandra Day O'Connor noted this fact in her concurring opinion, adding that some of the thirty-three state laws protecting child witnesses might be permissible under the Sixth Amendment. Only two years after *Coy,* the Supreme Court upheld a Maryland law that allowed children to testify in child abuse cases on closed-circuit television.

In *Maryland v. Craig* (1990), Justice O'Connor wrote for the Court's majority that "the Confrontation Clause reflects a *preference* . . . for face-to-face confrontation at trial . . . a preference that must occasionally give way to considerations of public policy and the necessities of the case." Just as there were exceptions for hearsay under the Confrontation Clause, said the Court, so must there be exceptions for child witnesses. Justice Scalia dissented vigorously, arguing that nothing less than face-to-face confrontation should be allowed under the Sixth Amendment.

## RIGHT TO COMPULSORY PROCESS

*. . . to have* **COMPULSORY PROCESS** *for obtaining witnesses in his favor, . . .*

The right to compulsory process means that a defendant can force witnesses to appear in court on her behalf. To do this, the defendant asks the trial court to issue a subpoena (Latin for "under penalty"), a court order requiring a witness to testify and/or turn over relevant documents to the court. The right of compulsory process was incorporated to apply to the states in *Washington v. Texas* (1967).

### UNITED STATES V. NIXON (1974)

Perhaps the most famous case involving the Sixth Amendment right to compulsory process is *United States v. Nixon*. After seven high-ranking White House officials were indicted in the Watergate scandal, President Richard Nixon was subpoenaed to turn over to the trial judge tape recordings and memoranda of certain conversations held in the White House.

Nixon complied with part of the subpoena, but withheld other tapes and papers, claiming executive privilege. Under this doctrine, the president may refuse to testify before Congress or appear in court because doing so would violate the separation of powers. The president of the United States, Nixon argued, was entitled to confidentiality in his communications to carry out his duties under Article II of the Constitution. "No president could function," said Nixon, "if the private papers of his office, prepared by his personal staff, were open to public scrutiny."

But the Supreme Court disagreed. It ruled unanimously that Nixon must surrender the tapes. Executive privilege, held the Court, could not be used to withhold evidence needed in a criminal trial. Not even the president of the United States was above the Sixth Amendment.

### RIGHT TO COUNSEL

*. . . and to have the* **ASSISTANCE OF COUNSEL** *for his defense.*

The last right guaranteed by the Sixth Amendment is the most important. As the Supreme Court has noted, "of all the rights that an accused person has, the right to be represented by counsel is by far the most pervasive for it affects his ability to assert any other rights he may have." Often only a

# Case Study: United States v. Nixon (1974)

*The Sixth Amendment right to compulsory process in criminal trials outweighs the president's general claim of executive privilege.*

Nixon Archive

*President Richard Nixon*

**Chief Justice Burger** delivered the opinion of the Court. . . .

. . . [Executive] privilege must be considered in light of our historic commitment to the rule of law. This is nowhere more profoundly manifest than in our view that "the twofold aim of criminal justice is that guilt shall not escape or innocence suffer." We have elected to employ an adversary system of criminal justice in which the parties contest issues before a court of law. The need to develop all relevant facts in the adversary system is both fundamental and comprehensive. The ends of criminal justice would be defeated if judgments were to be founded on a partial or speculative presentation of the facts. The very integrity of the judicial system and public confidence in the system depend on full disclosure of all the facts, within the framework of the rules of evidence. To ensure that justice is done, it is imperative to the function of courts that compulsory process be available for the production of evidence needed either by the prosecution or by the defense.

In this case the President challenges a subpoena served on him as a third party requiring the production of materials for use in a criminal prosecution on the claim that he has a privilege against disclosure of confidential communications. He does not place his claim of privilege on the ground they are military or diplomatic secrets. As to these areas of Article II duties, the courts have traditionally shown the utmost deference to presidential responsibilities. . . . No case of the Court . . . has extended this high degree of deference to a President's generalized interest in confidentiality. Nowhere in the Constitution . . . is there any explicit reference to a privilege of confidentiality, yet to the extent this interest relates to the effective discharge of a President's powers, it is constitutionally based.

The right to the production of all evidence at a criminal trial similarly has constitutional dimensions. The Sixth Amendment explicitly confers upon every defendant in a criminal trial the right "to be confronted with the witnesses against him" and "to have compulsory process for obtaining witnesses in his favor." Moreover, the Fifth Amendment also guarantees that no person shall be deprived of liberty without due process of law. It is the manifest duty of the courts to vindicate those guarantees and to accomplish that it is essential that all relevant and admissible evidence be produced. . . .

. . . A President's acknowledged need for confidentiality in the communications of his office is general in nature, whereas the constitutional need for production of relevant evidence in a criminal proceeding is specific and central to the fair adjudication of a particular criminal case in the administration of justice. . . .

We conclude that when the ground for asserting privilege as to subpoenaed materials sought for use in a criminal trial is based only on the generalized interest in confidentiality, it cannot prevail over the fundamental demands of due process of law in the fair administration of criminal justice. The generalized assertion of privilege must yield to the demonstrated, specific need for evidence in a pending criminal trial. . . .

UPI/Bettmann

*The Alabama National Guard was called out to protect the "Scottsboro Boys" from threatened mass lynchings in 1931. Ozie Powell, the named plaintiff in* Powell v. Alabama *(1932), is on the far left.*

lawyer knows the defendant's rights; without a lawyer, the defendant is virtually without rights.

Originally, the right to counsel under the Sixth Amendment only meant the right to have a lawyer present. In England, a defendant accused of a felony had no right to counsel, because a neutral judge protected the defendant's rights, at least in theory. But under the Sixth Amendment, the defendant was entitled to have a lawyer represent him in all criminal cases—at least if he could pay for it.

Many of the modern cases involving the right to counsel concern when the government is required to appoint a lawyer for a defendant too poor to pay for one. In *Johnson v. Zerbst* (1938), the Supreme Court held that in federal cases anyone accused of a felony is entitled to an attorney appointed by the court if he cannot afford one. But the Court was reluctant to require the same standard of the states.

### POWELL V. ALABAMA (1932)

The first step toward requiring the states to appoint counsel for poor defendants came in *Powell v. Alabama*. That case involved the infamous story of the "Scottsboro Boys," nine young black men accused of raping two white women on a freight train passing through Scottsboro, Alabama. At trial, the local judge appointed "all the members of the bar" to represent the defendants, who were poor and uneducated, but no one appeared on their behalf until after the trial was over. The defendants were divided into three groups, and their trials each lasted only one day. The defendants were all found guilty and sentenced to death.

The Supreme Court ruled that the defendants had been denied their right to counsel. At least in capital cases, the Court held, the states were required under the Due Process Clause of the Fourteenth Amendment to appoint counsel for poor defendants. Said the Court:

> The right to be heard would be, in many cases, of little avail if it did not comprehend the right to be heard by counsel. Even the intelligent and educated layman has small and sometimes no skill in the science of law. . . . He requires the guiding hand of counsel at every step in the proceedings against him. Without it, though he be not guilty, he faces the danger of conviction because he does not know how to establish his innocence.

*Powell* began the piecemeal incorporation of the right to counsel. However, in *Betts v. Brady* (1942), the Supreme Court held that the states had to appoint counsel for poor defendants only in "special circumstances," such as when the defendant was mentally retarded. In *Betts,* the Court refused to extend a general right to counsel for noncapital defendants in state courts. But Clarence Earl Gideon did not know that.

### GIDEON V. WAINWRIGHT (1963)

Clarence Earl Gideon was a middle-aged, uneducated ex-convict and drifter. In 1961, he was convicted of breaking into a poolroom in Panama City, Florida, and stealing some beverages and about $65 in change from a cigarette machine and a jukebox. This offense was a felony under Florida law, and Gideon was sentenced to five years in prison. At trial, Gideon asked to have the court appoint him a lawyer, since he had no money to pay for one. The judge refused, stating that Florida only allowed lawyers to be appointed in capital cases. Gideon replied, "the United States Supreme Court says I am entitled to be represented by counsel."

Gideon was wrong. He did not meet any of the "special circumstances" in the *Betts* decision, so he was not entitled to a lawyer, according to the current law. But the Supreme Court was prepared to overturn *Betts,* and it agreed to hear Gideon's case when he appealed his conviction from prison.

In *Gideon v. Wainwright* (1963), the Supreme Court applied the right to counsel in all felony cases to the states. The Court held that "the right . . . to counsel may not be deemed fundamental and essential to fair trials in some countries, but it is in ours." The Court noted that the United States uses an adversary system of justice, which relies on a battle between two opposing parties—the defense and the prosecution—to determine the truth. But if that battle is unequal, if one side has a lawyer and the other does not, then the trial is unfair. Thus, said the Court, "lawyers in criminal courts are necessities, not luxuries."

Gideon was granted a new trial, before the same judge. But this time, when the court offered to appoint two lawyers from the Miami office of the American Civil Liberties Union (ACLU) to represent him, Gideon refused—despite the fact that he had been working closely with the ACLU attorneys. Instead, Gideon insisted on a local lawyer.

One of the ACLU lawyers later wrote:

> It has become almost axiomatic that the great rights which are secured for all of us by the Bill of Rights are constantly tested and retested in the courts by the people who live in the bottom of society's barrel. . . .
>
> In the future the name "Gideon" will stand for the great principle that the poor are entitled to the same type of justice as are those who are able to afford counsel. It is probably a good thing that it is immaterial and unimportant that Gideon is something of a "nut," that his maniacal distrust and suspicion lead him to the very borders of insanity. Upon the shoulders of such persons are our great rights carried.

## The Courage of Their Convictions: Clarence Earl Gideon

*Clarence Earl Gideon, an uneducated ex-convict and drifter, petitioned the Supreme Court from prison to overturn his conviction for petty theft because he had been denied a lawyer. The Court agreed to accept Gideon's case and appointed Abe Fortas—a prominent attorney who later served on the Supreme Court—to argue his appeal. In a letter to Fortas, Gideon told his life story. It is reprinted here exactly as he wrote it.*

Miami Herald

*Clarence Earl Gideon*

I suppose, I am what is called individualist a person who will not conform. Anyway my parents where always quarreling and I would be the scapegoat of those quarrels. My life was miserable. I was never allow to do the things of a ordinary boy.

At the age of fourteen year, I ran away from home, I accepted the life of a hobo and tramp in preference to my home. In a month or so I made it to California. At this time I begin to learn the facts of life. How good people can be and how bad they can be I wandered around over the west for all most a year and came back to Missouri. When to my mother's brother and started living with him until my mother found out where I was at and she came and got me. Had me place in the jail at Hannibal [Gideon's hometown] which I excaped from the next day and went back to the country to hide out at this time it was extremely cold weather and a short time later I burglarist a country store for some clothes which I was caught the next day by the store owner with all the clothes on. I was tried in juvnile court in Ralls County Missouri. My mother ask the court to send me to the reformatory which they did for a term of three years. Off all the prisons I

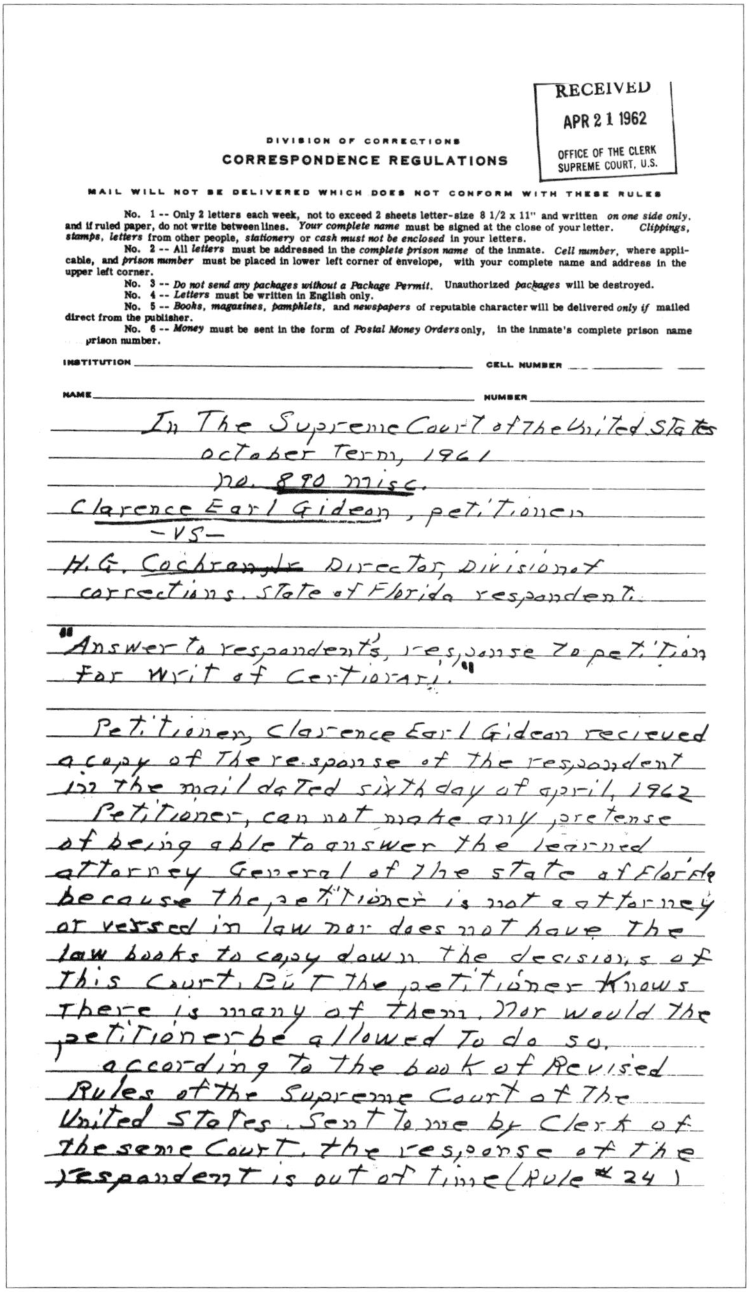

RECEIVED
APR 2 1 1962
OFFICE OF THE CLERK
SUPREME COURT, U.S.

DIVISION OF CORRECTIONS

CORRESPONDENCE REGULATIONS

MAIL WILL NOT BE DELIVERED WHICH DOES NOT CONFORM WITH THESE RULES

No. 1 -- Only 2 letters each week, not to exceed 2 sheets letter-size 8 1/2 x 11" and written *on one side only*, and if ruled paper, do not write between lines. *Your complete name* must be signed at the close of your letter. *Clippings, stamps, letters* from other people, *stationery* or *cash must not be enclosed* in your letters.

No. 2 -- All *letters* must be addressed in the *complete prison name* of the inmate. *Cell number*, where applicable, and *prison number* must be placed in lower left corner of envelope, with your complete name and address in the upper left corner.

No. 3 -- *Do not send any packages without a Package Permit.* Unauthorized *packages* will be destroyed.

No. 4 -- *Letters* must be written in English only.

No. 5 -- *Books, magazines, pamphlets,* and *newspapers* of reputable character will be delivered *only if* mailed direct from the publisher.

No. 6 -- *Money* must be sent in the form of *Postal Money Orders* only, in the inmate's complete prison name prison number.

INSTITUTION ______ CELL NUMBER ______

NAME ______ NUMBER ______

In The Supreme Court of The United States
october Term, 1961
no. 890 misc.
Clarence Earl Gideon, petitioner
-VS-
H.G. Cochran, Jr. Director, Divisions of corrections. State of Florida respondent.

"Answer to respondents, response to petition For writ of Certiorari."

Petitioner, Clarence Earl Gideon recieved a copy of The response of the respondent in the mail dated sixth day of april, 1962

Petitioner, can not make any pretense of being able to answer the learned attorney General of the state of Florida because the petitioner is not a attorney or versed in law nor does not have the law books to copy down the decisions of this Court. But The petitioner Knows there is many of them. Nor would the petitioner be allowed To do so.

according to the book of Revised Rules of the Supreme Court of The United States. Sent To me by Clerk of the same Court. the response of the respondent is out of time (Rule # 24)

National Archives

have been in that was the worst I still have scar on my body from the whippings I received there. . . .

[Gideon then describes five other imprisonments as an adult for burglary over a period of twenty-four years.]

Outside of numerous times of arrest some for investagation, others for compromised convictions, all of the foregoing statements have been true and can stand the any kind of investegation. I am not proud of this biography. I hope that it may help you in preparing this case, I am sorry I could not write better I have done the best I could.

I have no illusions about law and courts or the people who are involved in them. I have read the complete history of law ever since the Romans first started writing them down and before of the laws of religions. I believe that each era finds a improvement in law each year brings something new for the benefit of mankind. Maybe this will be one of those small steps forward. . . .

From *Gideon's Trumpet* by Anthony Lewis. Copyright 1964 by Anthony Lewis. Reprinted by permission of Random House, Inc.

*Clarence Earl Gideon's handwritten response on prison stationery to the attorney general of Florida in the Supreme Court case that became* Gideon v. Wainwright.

Close Up Foundation/Peter

But perhaps Gideon was not such a "nut" after all. The local lawyer Gideon had insisted on used his knowledge of the community to accuse the chief witness against Gideon of committing the crime. The jury acquitted Gideon. After spending two years in prison for a crime of which he was eventually found innocent, Clarence Earl Gideon was at last a free man.

### AFTER GIDEON

The *Gideon* decision limited the right to counsel in state courts to felony cases. But in *Argersinger v. Hamlin* (1972), the Supreme Court extended the right to counsel to misdemeanor cases in the states if the defendant was imprisoned when convicted. However, the Supreme Court ruled in 1994 that a previous misdemeanor conviction—even if the defendant did not have a lawyer—could be used to lengthen a new prison sentence.

## HOW GOOD A LAWYER?

While *Gideon* and other cases established that the state must appoint counsel for poor defendants, the Supreme Court did not say how good the lawyer had to be. Can there be a fair trial if the prosecution has a well-paid and experienced criminal attorney, but the defense has a court-appointed attorney fresh out of law school who specializes in real estate law?

The Supreme Court has held that a defendant is entitled to *effective* assistance of counsel under the Sixth Amendment. But that does not mean the defendant is entitled to an error-free defense. In *Strickland v. Washington* (1984), the Supreme Court set guidelines for effective assistance of counsel. Under *Strickland,* the defendant must show that the lawyer's specific mistakes, not just a lack of experience in general, denied him or her a fair trial.

## WHEN DOES THE RIGHT TO COUNSEL APPLY?

Even if a defendant can pay for his own lawyer, when is the defendant entitled to consult with his lawyer? Only at trial, but not during police questioning? The Supreme Court answered these questions in *Escobedo v. Illinois* (1964).

Danny Escobedo was arrested for murder. When interrogated by police, he repeatedly asked to speak to his lawyer, but was denied permission. The police also did not tell him he had the right to remain silent and refuse to answer their questions. At trial, some of Escobedo's statements were used against him, and he was convicted. Escobedo appealed the conviction on the grounds that, among other things, his right to counsel had been violated.

The Supreme Court held in *Escobedo* that a defendant was entitled to consult with his lawyer during police questioning, despite the fact that a lawyer would probably advise the defendant to remain silent. Wrote Justice Arthur Goldberg for the Court's majority:

> No system worth preserving should have to *fear* that if an accused is permitted to consult with a lawyer, he will become aware of, and exercise, [his] rights. If the exercise of constitutional rights will thwart the effectiveness of a system of law enforcement, then there is something very wrong with that system.

## "DEFENDANTS' LAW"?

The Sixth Amendment guarantees many rights to defendants. Some legal experts argue that American law is "defendants' law" because it gives defendants so many rights. Indeed, one commentator has said that "in no other modern government have so many safeguards been assigned to the rights of persons accused of crimes." Does the Sixth Amendment go too far in protecting defendants' rights? Were Americans in 1791 too concerned with defendants' rights because they had often been defendants themselves? Or does the Sixth Amendment just correct the inherent imbalance between the power of the state and the power of the individual?

# The **SEVENTH** *Amendment*

*In* **SUITS AT COMMON LAW**, *where the value in controversy shall exceed twenty dollars, the right of* **TRIAL BY JURY** *shall be preserved, and* **NO FACT TRIED BY A JURY SHALL BE OTHERWISE RE-EXAMINED** *in any Court of the United States, than according to the rules of the common law.*

Early Americans considered the right of trial by jury so important that it is guaranteed three times in the Constitution. Both the original Constitution of 1787 and the Sixth Amendment protect the right to a jury trial in criminal cases, in which the government punishes an individual for a crime. The Seventh Amendment guarantees the right of trial by jury in civil cases, in which private parties contest noncriminal claims—such as disputes about contracts or injuries to people and property.

The Seventh Amendment also states that no fact tried by a jury shall be reexamined in any U.S. court of law. This means that when a jury decides the facts of the case, no judge can overrule the jury except in certain instances provided for by law. Otherwise, if a judge were free to override the jury, the right to trial by jury would be meaningless. The Seventh Amendment thus guarantees the right of trial by jury in reality, not just in form.

## THE CIVIL JURY

In **SUITS AT COMMON LAW**, *where the value in controversy shall exceed twenty dollars, the right of* **TRIAL BY JURY** *shall be preserved, . . .*

This first part of the Seventh Amendment guarantees the right to trial by jury in civil cases. Historically, juries were used in civil cases even before they were used in criminal cases. Thus, much of the history of civil trial by jury is also the history of criminal trial by jury. But the Supreme Court has used different standards for what is required of civil juries and of criminal juries.

### THE EVOLUTION OF TRIAL BY JURY

Trial by jury developed in England during the Middle Ages as a way to settle disputes. Before trial by jury, people attempted to discover the truth by using various religious practices that were believed to reveal the will of God. In trial by ordeal, for instance, a person accused of a crime or who disputed the civil claims of another had to pass a physical test—such as carrying hot metal for a certain distance. If the person's hand healed after a short time, then that was supposedly a sign from God of innocence.

In trial by battle, the winner of an armed struggle would "prove by his body" that he was innocent or telling the truth. And in trial by oath-giving, the parties to a lawsuit would engage their neighbors to swear oaths on their behalf. The party who could get the most people to swear oaths before God, thus risking their salvation, won the lawsuit.

After the Norman Conquest of England in 1066, however, trial by jury became the preferred method of determining the truth in disputes. Originally, members of the jury were people who had probably witnessed the actual events at issue—unlike today's jurors, who are chosen specifically because they are unfamiliar with the facts of the case. The royal judges in England, who traveled around the country hearing disputes, used juries of local citizens to help decide cases. Historically, the jury was always composed of twelve citizens, who were expected to use their personal knowledge to reach a "declaration of truth," or verdict.

The right of trial by jury was first used in civil cases, not criminal cases. By the end of the twelfth century, a defendant in a civil lawsuit had the right to "put himself upon his country," or request a jury to decide the facts in the case. By the end of the thirteenth century, trial by jury was established in criminal cases as well.

One early root of the right to trial by jury was the Magna Carta of 1215. It protected an English aristocrat's right to be free from punishment "except by lawful judgment of his peers"—that is, his equals in social standing. This section of Magna Carta led to the phrase "judgment by a jury of one's peers," or fellow citizens, but it did not protect a broad right to trial by jury.

England eventually abolished trial by jury in civil cases during the nineteenth century, in a move to make the court system more efficient. But England retained trial by jury in criminal cases. In America, however, the right to trial by jury in both civil and criminal cases flourished.

## JURY TRIAL IN AMERICA

Americans had special reason to support the right of trial by jury. In colonial times, judges were often associated with the king and his interests. Americans preferred to be judged by their fellow colonists, who would be more sympathetic to their claims. Consequently, Americans have since colonial days much preferred a trial by a jury to a trial by a judge alone.

All thirteen colonies protected the right to trial by jury in civil cases in some form by 1776. In fact, as Alexander Hamilton noted in *Federalist* 83, one of the biggest objections to the Constitution of 1787 was that, while it protected the trial by jury in criminal cases, it did not guarantee the same right in civil cases. Seven of the eight states proposing amendments to the Constitution demanded that jury trial in civil cases be added.

## THE SEVENTH AMENDMENT AND THE COURTS

Since the Seventh Amendment was ratified in 1791, the Supreme Court has issued several decisions interpreting the right to trial by jury in civil cases. This right has never been incorporated by the Supreme Court to apply to the states, so jury trials in civil cases are only guaranteed in the federal courts.

The Supreme Court allows different standards for trial by jury in civil cases than in criminal cases. For example, all criminal cases in federal courts require a twelve-person jury. But in *Colgrove v. Battin* (1973), the Supreme Court upheld six-person juries in civil cases. The Court said that six-person juries are more efficient than larger ones and that no proof existed that twelve-person juries reached different verdicts than six-person juries. As a general rule, unanimous verdicts are required in civil trials, just as in federal criminal trials, unless the parties to the lawsuit agree otherwise.

## THE JURY'S POWER

*. . . and* **NO FACT TRIED BY A JURY SHALL BE OTHERWISE RE-EXAMINED** *in any Court of the United States, than according to the rules of the common law.*

This second part of the Seventh Amendment ensures that the right of trial by jury in civil cases is not just an empty promise. It states that no fact tried by a jury shall be reexamined in any U.S. court. Otherwise, judges might be free to ignore the jury's findings and make their own decisions—which would in effect deny the right of trial by jury by making the jury powerless. The Seventh Amendment guarantees that, except in certain instances provided for by law, the jury has the final say about the facts of a case.

## JUST THE FACTS

The roles of the judge and the jury in a trial are clearly defined in the great majority of cases. The jury decides the facts of the case—what actually happened in the issue being disputed. The judge decides what law applies to the case—which statutes and court decisions are relevant and what verdict is required under certain facts. The judge advises the jury on the law before the jury reaches its verdict. The judge tells the jury that, if it finds certain facts to be true, then the law requires one verdict; if it finds other facts to be true, then the law requires another verdict. The Supreme Court emphasized these principles in one of its most important cases on the Seventh Amendment, *Baltimore and Carolina Line v. Redman* (1935).

What if a judge could force a jury to make a certain decision about the facts of a case? That is the very evil the Seventh Amendment was designed to prevent—and for good reason. James Madison and other members of Congress who helped draft the Bill of Rights were very familiar with a famous English case in which the judge had imprisoned the jury for not reaching the verdict he demanded. That case, known as *Bushell's Case,* established clearly that a jury could not be punished for reaching a verdict different from the one that the judge demanded.

### BUSHELL'S CASE (1670)

Edward Bushell was a member of the jury that tried the case of William Penn in England in 1670. Bushell was later charged for misconduct as a juryman for failing to convict Penn as the judge ordered. But telling the story of Edward Bushell means first telling the story of William Penn.

Penn, who would found the colony of Pennsylvania in 1681, was prosecuted for unlawful and tumultuous assembly. A Quaker who criticized the established Church of England, Penn had been forbidden to preach inside any building. Instead, he delivered a sermon to a peaceful assembly of Quakers on Gracechurch Street in London. Penn and a bystander unknown to him, William Mead, were arrested and tried together. They later wrote an account of their trial that became one of the most popular pamphlets of the seventeenth century.

When Penn asked the court to tell him "upon what law you ground my indictment," he received only vague and abusive answers. Penn replied, "You have not answered me; though the rights and privileges of every Englishman be concerned in it." Outraged, one court official said to the chief judge, "My Lord, if you take not some course with this pestilent fellow, to stop his mouth, we shall not be able to do anything tonight." The judge ordered Penn taken away to the bale-dock, a corner of the courtroom walled-off with partitions that did not touch the ceiling. Penn cried out to the jury as he was being led away: "Must I therefore be taken away because I plead for the fundamental laws of England? However, this I leave upon your consciences, who are of the jury (and my sole judges) that if these ancient fundamental laws, which relate to liberty and property . . . must not be indispensably maintained and observed, who can say he hath right to the coat upon his back?"

William Mead then testified before the jury that he was a peaceful person, but stood accused of rioting. According to the law, said Mead, a riot or unlawful assembly was when three or more people beat a person or entered private property by force—which neither Penn nor Mead had done.  A court official sarcastically thanked Mead for telling him "what the law is," and one judge added, "You deserve to have your tongue cut out."  Mead was sent to join Penn in the bale-dock.

The court then gave the jurors their charge, or advised them about the law of the case, in the absence of the defendants—a clear violation of English law.  The court ordered the jury to find Penn and Mead guilty if the jurors decided that Penn had indeed preached in the street.  If instead they decided that Penn's preaching did not violate the riot law, then the jurors would be punished.

Outraged, William Penn climbed above the bale-dock wall and cried: "I appeal to the jurors who are my judges, and this great assembly, whether the proceedings of the court are not most arbitrary, and void of all law, in offering to give the jury their charge in the absence of the prisoners."  Added Mead, also raising himself above the wall: "Are these according to the rights and privileges of Englishmen, that we should not be heard, but turned into the bale-dock, for making our defense?"

After deliberating about two hours, the jurors were divided, and the judges sent for them.  One juror, Edward Bushell, was accused of forcing his opinions on the others.  Bushell replied that he would have willingly avoided jury duty (as had sixty other prospective jurors before him), but could not—at which point one judge threatened to strike him.  The jury went out to deliberate again and soon returned with a verdict that Penn was guilty of speaking on Gracechurch Street, but not of unlawful assembly.  Refusing to accept the verdict, the court told the jury: "You shall be locked up, without meat, drink, fire, and tobacco; . . . we will have a verdict, by the help of God, or you shall starve for it."

Penn protested that "my jury, who are my judges, ought not to be menaced; their verdict should be free, and not compelled."  While a court official threatened to eject Penn from the courtroom, Penn turned to the jury and said, "You are Englishmen, mind your privilege, give not away your right."  Bushell and others responded, "nor will we ever do it."

The jurors kept their word, even though starved for three days and kept without heat or chamberpots.  Several times the court tried to force the jury to change its verdict, but without success.  Bushell was accused of being a "factious fellow," to which he responded that he had only acted according to his conscience.  Said the chief judge, "That conscience of yours would cut my throat. . . . I will cut yours so soon as I can."  The chief judge then ridiculed the jury by referring to Bushell: "Have you no more wit than to be led by such a pitiful fellow?  I will cut his nose."  Penn declared: "It is intolerable that my jury should be

*William Penn addresses the court and the jury at his trial for unlawful assembly in 1670.*

thus menaced. Is this according to the fundamental laws? Are not they my proper judges by the Great Charter [Magna Carta] of England?"

When the jury still refused to change its verdict, the court fined and imprisoned each juror. Edward Bushell filed an appeal from prison to the Court of Common Pleas. At the appeal, the trial court accused Bushell and the other jurors of acquitting Penn and Mead "against full and manifest evidence and against the direction of the court in matter of law." But in *Bushell's Case*, the Court of Common Pleas declared that judges could not hear the evidence in a case and then decide that the facts were on the side of the plaintiff, or of the defendant, and force the jury to find accordingly. Otherwise, said Chief Justice John Vaughan, "the jury is but a troublesome delay, great [expense], and of no use in determining right and wrong." Rather, the jury was to decide what the facts of a case were, and the judge was to give suggestions of what the verdict should be under the law if the jury found certain facts to be true. No more could a judge demand that a jury deliver a particular verdict.

Today, under the Seventh Amendment, a judge is entitled to overturn a jury's decision only if, as a matter of law, the verdict was based on insufficient evidence. This means that in the judge's legal opinion, the evidence did not support the verdict—even considering that reasonable people often disagree about the same set of facts. But a judge overrules a jury's verdict very rarely, because the Seventh Amendment gives such weight to the jury's decision.

## CIVIL JURIES TODAY

The jury is often regarded as an essential part of democratic government. The jury involves ordinary citizens, who have no legal training, in making judicial decisions. Thus, a wide range of citizens participates in the crucial decisions of their government—which some say is what democracy is all about. Critics of the jury system, however, argue that using one decisionmaker—a judge—rather than twelve would save both time and money. One historian wrote that "trial by jury [is] inherently absurd—so much so that no lawyer, judge, scholar, prescription-clerk, cook, or mechanic in a garage would ever think for a moment of employing that method for determining the facts in any situation that concerned him." Civil juries, in particular, have come under intense criticism.

### THE COMPLEXITY EXCEPTION

Some legal experts maintain that civil cases are becoming increasingly long and complex, making trial by jury not only less efficient but also less fair—that the right to a civil jury has become "the right to an irrational verdict." They argue that it is unreasonable to expect the average citizen to follow all the details in trials that can sometimes involve more than 1,000 plaintiffs and last up to two years. These critics of the civil jury propose a complexity exception to the Seventh Amendment: in complicated civil cases, the right to jury trial should be limited to recognize "the practical abilities and limitations of juries."

This argument is not a new one. Alexander Hamilton made the same point about civil juries in *Federalist* 83:

> The circumstances that constitute cases proper for [civil courts] are in many instances so nice and intricate that they are incompatible with the genius of trial by jury. They require often such long, deliberate, and critical investigation as would be impracticable to men called from their occupations, and obliged to decide before they were permitted to return to them.

But one judge has argued that the complexity exception "unnecessarily and improperly demeans the intelligence of the citizens of this nation." Another judge wrote that the jury deciding a complicated case about the breakup of a massive telecommunications company "includes an engineer, a hearing system designer, an accountant, a purchasing agent, an aircraft mechanic, a chemist, a bank loan officer, a secretary, a housewife, a clerk, and a college employee. . . . It is at least doubtful that the experiential background of any judge could match that of this particular jury." Supporters of civil juries argue that if the complexity exception applies to juries, it should apply to judges as well—that some judges do not have the ability to follow complex litigation.

While the Supreme Court has never ruled on the complexity exception, some federal appeals courts just below the Supreme Court have. The U.S. Court of Appeals for the Third Circuit held that a case involving a thirty-year conspiracy and about 100 businesses worldwide met the complexity exception. The court said that using a jury in such a complicated case would violate due process of law under the Fifth Amendment. In this case, said the court, the Fifth Amendment outweighed the Seventh Amendment. "There is a danger that jury verdicts will be erratic and completely unpredictable, which would be inconsistent with even-handed justice," held the court. But it warned that "due process should allow denials of jury trials only in exceptional cases."

The U.S. Court of Appeals for the Ninth Circuit, however, rejected the complexity argument—even in a case that was scheduled to last two years and involved more than 100,000 pages of documents. Said the court: "Such practical considerations diminish in importance when they come in conflict with the constitutional right to a jury in civil cases." And the court added: "Jurors, if properly instructed and treated with deserved respect, bring collective intelligence, wisdom, and dedication to their tasks, which is rarely equalled in other areas of public service."

Until the U.S. Supreme Court rules on the complexity issue, the right to a civil jury even in complicated cases remains protected in most federal courts. As of the Seventh Amendment's bicentennial, most courts are still unwilling to make exceptions to its guarantees.

## JURY DUTY: BURDEN OR BLESSING?

Another objection to civil juries besides the complexity argument is the burden that jury duty places on citizens. Even if jurors are all geniuses, is it fair to make citizens give up their work—and their pay—and totally disrupt their lives for months, and sometimes years? Judges are full-time employees of the government paid to decide cases, but jurors receive only token compensation. In addition, some judges will sequester jurors in notorious cases, keeping them isolated from their friends and family for long periods of time.

Are the burdens on individual jurors worth the benefits society receives as a whole? Some critics of the jury system will concede that in criminal cases a jury is necessary, because of the impact criminal convictions have on the public. But civil cases also involve important issues, such as injuries to thousands of consumers from defective products, say advocates of the jury system. Furthermore, supporters of juries argue, the burden of jury duty is a small price to pay for a government in which citizens participate in the most important decisions—a small price to pay for the blessings of democracy.

# The EIGHTH Amendment

**EXCESSIVE BAIL** *shall not be required, nor* **EXCESSIVE FINES** *imposed, nor* **CRUEL AND UNUSUAL PUNISHMENTS** *inflicted.*

The Eighth Amendment protects three rights, one of which applies before trial and the other two after a person has been convicted of a crime. Bail allows the accused to be freed from jail pending trial by putting up either a money bond or property as security for the court. If the accused does not appear in court on the date scheduled, he or she forfeits the bail. Bail prevents a person from being locked in jail before actually being convicted of a crime. The Eighth Amendment says that bail shall not be "excessive."

After trial, if the accused is found guilty, the Eighth Amendment also forbids "excessive fines" as punishment. Furthermore, the Eighth Amendment prohibits "cruel and unusual punishment." But how should "cruel and unusual" be defined? Does the Eighth Amendment only ban those punishments that were "cruel and unusual" in 1791, such as drawing and quartering (disemboweling and cutting the body into four parts), but allow those that were not—such as cutting off ears and death by hanging? According to the Supreme Court, the Eighth Amendment "must draw its meaning from evolving standards of decency that mark the progress of a maturing society." Would a "mature" society prohibit the death penalty in all its forms, or is capital punishment necessary for justice? These are the questions of life or death—literally—that the Eighth Amendment presents.

*The whipping post and pillory were used to punish criminals publicly for their offenses.*

Library of Congress

## BEFORE THE EIGHTH AMENDMENT

The language of the Eighth Amendment came almost word for word from the Virginia Declaration of Rights of 1776, which itself was virtually identical to a provision in the English Bill of Rights of 1689. Even before these documents, however, the Massachusetts Body of Liberties, enacted in 1641, provided a right to bail and prohibited cruel and inhuman punishments.

The Massachusetts Bay Colony, founded by Puritans, sought to eliminate such English punishments as whippings of more than forty lashes, cutting off hands, and burning at the stake. The Body of Liberties allowed the death penalty for religious offenses, such as blasphemy, but not for burglary and robbery—which were capital crimes in England.

Nonetheless, the Puritans allowed many punishments that might seem "cruel and unusual" today. Physical punishments included piercing of the tongue with a hot iron, cutting off ears, branding, and whipping. The Puritans also shamed offenders by public punishment, in which lawbreakers were confined to the stocks and pillory while townspeople hurled garbage at them. Some adulterers were required to wear the letter "A" on their clothing, and others were forced to wear signs. For example, one Salem sex offender wore the following sign in 1675: "This person is Convicted for Speaking Words in a Boasting Manner of His Lascivious & Unclean Practices." The ultimate punishment, besides hanging, was banishment from the colony.

Following the example of the Massachusetts Body of Liberties and the Virginia Declaration of Rights, four states proposed some version of what eventually became the Eighth Amendment during the ratification debates over the U.S. Constitution of 1787. However, Madison's draft met with some opposition in Congress. Said one representative: "It is sometimes necessary to hang a man, villains often deserve whipping, and perhaps having their ears cut off, but are we in future to be prevented from inflicting these punishments because they are cruel?"

In its final version, the Eighth Amendment prohibited three things: excessive bail, excessive fines, and cruel and unusual punishment. But as the history of the Eighth Amendment demonstrates, Americans' definition of "cruel and unusual" has been an evolving one.

## EXCESSIVE BAIL

**EXCESSIVE BAIL** *shall not be required, . . .*

This first part of the Eighth Amendment prohibits "excessive" bail. But it does not grant a right to bail in general. It only says that where bail is available, the amount shall not be excessive. The conditions under which bail may be granted are set forth in federal and state laws.

Bail may be denied in capital cases, those involving the death penalty, and when the accused has threatened possible trial witnesses. Also, the amount of bail does not have to be something the accused can pay. Some poor people cannot afford bail at all and must stay in jail. Others use the services of a bail bondsman, who will post a person's bond for a fee. If the accused skips bail, the bail bondsman will often help the police catch that person. Sometimes the court will release defendants on their own recognizance, which means that the court trusts those persons to show up in court when required and thus will not require money bail.

Close Up Foundation/Renée Bouchard

*This bail bonding company helps defendants post bail, for a fee.*

As a rule, bail is designed to ensure that a defendant will appear for trial. Bail is based on the principle that a person is "innocent until proven guilty." Keeping accused persons in jail while awaiting trial before they have actually been convicted of a crime would violate this principle. Consequently, the Supreme Court ruled in 1951 that bail was "excessive" when set higher than necessary to guarantee the accused's appearance at trial.

But the Bail Reform Act of 1984, passed by Congress, allowed the federal courts for the first time to deny bail on the basis of danger to the community, not risk of appearing at trial. Known as preventive detention, this practice authorized judges to predict the future criminal conduct of persons accused of serious offenses and deny bail on those grounds. Opponents of preventive detention argued that the accused was being punished without trial and that protecting the community was the job of the police, not the purpose of bail.

The Supreme Court upheld preventive detention in *United States v. Salerno* (1987). The Court ruled that, since the Bail Reform Act contained many procedural safeguards, the government's interest in protecting the community outweighed the individual's liberty.

The Eighth Amendment's prohibition against excessive bail does not apply to the states because it has not been incorporated by the Supreme Court. Therefore, even after *Salerno,* state courts are still free to forbid preventive detention of state and local prisoners based on "excessive bail" provisions in the state constitutions.

# EXCESSIVE FINES

*. . . nor* **EXCESSIVE FINES** *imposed, . . .*

After the accused is convicted of a crime, the Eighth Amendment also prohibits punishment by excessive fines. Like the prohibition of excessive bail, the Excessive Fines Clause has not been incorporated to apply against the states.

There have been few Supreme Court cases on the issue of excessive fines. One case, *Browning-Ferris Industries v. Kelco Disposal, Inc.* (1989), presented the question of whether the Eighth Amendment applied to civil punishments as well as criminal punishments. In criminal law, the government is always involved as a party to the case. Civil law, however, addresses disputes between private parties, not crimes against the government.

In civil lawsuits between private parties, the plaintiff usually seeks money damages from the defendant to right an alleged wrong. Compensatory damages reimburse the plaintiff for actual harm done, such as medical expenses or lost business. Punitive damages above and beyond the actual economic loss can be awarded to punish the defendant and to warn others not to engage in the same conduct.

Private parties who bring lawsuits are sometimes called "private attorneys general" because they help enforce acceptable standards of societal behavior beyond what the law defines as a crime. For instance, if a manufacturer produces a faulty product, an injured consumer can sue for punitive damages, which would discourage the defendant from making other harmful products—even though the criminal law might not apply. Consumer advocates argue that punitive damages help protect the public from the harmful actions of major industries. Businesses counter by saying that huge punitive damage awards raise the costs of liability insurance, driving up prices for current products and delaying development of new ones.

In *Browning-Ferris Industries,* the Supreme Court ruled that the Eighth Amendment only applied to criminal cases, to "direct actions initiated by the government to inflict punishment." Punitive damages in civil cases did not involve government action, said the Court, so the Eighth Amendment did not apply. The Court noted that "[w]hile we agree . . . that punitive damages advance the interests of punishment and deterrence, which are also among the interests advanced by criminal law, we fail to see how this overlap requires us to apply the Excessive Fines Clause in a case between private parties."

However, the Supreme Court ruled in two 1993 cases that the Excessive Fines Clause does apply when a criminal law allows the government to seize the defendant's property in civil court. Particularly in drug cases, law enforcement officials have used such provisions to seize money, cars, jewelry, and real estate from defendants. The Court held that any such civil forfeitures must still be regarded as punishment for crime and therefore be subject to the Excessive Fines Clause of the Eighth Amendment.

## CRUEL AND UNUSUAL PUNISHMENT

. . . nor **CRUEL AND UNUSUAL PUNISHMENTS** *inflicted.*

This final clause of the Eighth Amendment forbids punishments that are "cruel and unusual," but it does not say what those punishments are. The Supreme Court in *Trop v. Dulles* (1958) said that the Eighth Amendment "must draw its meaning from evolving standards of decency that mark the progress of a maturing society." Therefore, as Justice Thurgood Marshall noted in a later case, "a penalty that was permissible at one time in our nation's history is not necessarily permissible today." Thus, common punishments in 1791 such as whippings and pillories are not constitutional today.

But although other forms of bodily punishment for criminals have disappeared, the death penalty remains a controversial issue. The Supreme Court has decided many cases on the constitutionality of capital punishment. It has also defined the nature of cruel and unusual punishments in noncapital cases. But the death penalty remains the most debated issue under the Eighth Amendment, probably because it concerns the ultimate issue: life or death.

### CAPITAL PUNISHMENT

The death penalty has been an established feature of the American criminal justice system since colonial times. In fact, until the mid-nineteenth century, the death penalty was the automatic sentence for a convicted murderer. State laws began to draw distinctions between degrees of murder, but the death penalty was still automatic for first-degree murderers. By the early twentieth century, however, state legislatures had given jurors more discretion in sentencing. But jurors were given no guidance by state law in choosing between life and death sentences. Jurors had total discretion in this decision that could not be reviewed upon appeal.

Murderers and rapists were executed quite frequently in the United States until the 1960s, with the rate of execution peaking at 200 per year during the Depression. But in the 1960s, the death penalty faced increased opposition. Some social scientists argued that the death penalty did not achieve its major purpose—deterrence of other murderers. Studies of execution patterns also indicated that juries did not treat like cases alike; instead, they acted randomly and unreasonably. Furthermore, where there was a pattern to death penalty sentencing, it was based on race. Blacks were executed far more often than whites for murder, and almost all those executed for rape were black men accused of raping white women.

Most criminals are sentenced under state law, not federal law. Thus, the Eighth Amendment's prohibition against cruel and unusual punishments was not relevant to the overwhelming majority of death penalty cases until the Supreme Court incorporated it to apply to the states in *Robinson v. California* (1962). Even then, some members of the Supreme Court were reluctant to address the issue of capital punishment, which they saw as inherently subjective and complex. In 1971, Justice John Marshall Harlan wrote:

> To identify before the fact those characteristics of criminal homicides and their perpetrators which call for the death penalty, and to express these characteristics in language which can be fairly understood and applied by [judges and juries], appear to be tasks which are beyond present human ability.

But only a year later, the Supreme Court undertook to do precisely that in *Furman v. Georgia* (1972). The *Furman* opinion was more than 230 pages long—the longest in Supreme Court history. All nine justices wrote separate opinions, trying to define the meaning of four words: "cruel and unusual punishment."

**FURMAN V. GEORGIA (1972).** In *Furman*, the Court ruled that the death penalty as then administered in the United States was cruel and unusual punishment because it was "wantonly" and "freakishly" imposed. Judges and juries had far too much unguided discretion under current state laws, the Court held, leading to "arbitrary and capricious," or random and unreasonable, death sentences.

The *Furman* case, for example, did not involve an especially heinous, or despicable, crime. Furman had broken into a private home in the middle of the night intending only to burglarize it, although he was carrying a gun. Furman attempted to escape when William Micke, the owner of the house, awoke. But Furman tripped and his gun discharged, hitting and killing Micke through a closed door. Furman, however, was black; Micke was white.

In *Furman,* the Supreme Court did not rule that the death penalty was unconstitutional in all circumstances. Rather, the Court held that the states, to prevent discriminatory use of the death penalty, had to give judges and juries more guidance in capital sentencing. Executions across the country were suspended as a result. In response, about three-fourths of the states and the federal government passed new death penalty laws. While reviewing these laws in 1976, the Supreme Court finally decided whether the death penalty was inherently "cruel and unusual."

**UPHOLDING THE DEATH PENALTY.** In *Gregg v. Georgia* (1976), the Supreme Court held that "the punishment of death does not invariably violate the Constitution." The Court noted that three-fourths of state legislatures reenacted the death penalty after *Furman;* therefore, the death penalty was not "unusual" punishment. Justice Potter Stewart also pointed out that, besides deterrence, another argument in support of the death penalty was retribution, or paying a criminal back for the harm done:

> In part, capital punishment is an expression of society's moral outrage at particularly offensive conduct. This function may be unappealing to many, but it is essential in an ordered society that asks its citizens to rely on legal processes rather than self-help to vindicate their wrongs.

In dissent, Justice William Brennan repeated the arguments he made against the death penalty in *Furman.* Brennan questioned "whether a society for which the dignity of the individual is the supreme value can, without a fundamental inconsistency, follow the practice of deliberately putting some of its members to death." "Even the vilest criminal," said Brennan, "remains a human being possessed of common human dignity." Brennan argued that "the law has progressed to the point where we should declare that the punishment of death, like punishments on the rack, the screw, and the wheel, is no longer morally tolerable in our civilized society."

But having upheld the death penalty as constitutional, the Court next looked at *how* the death penalty was implemented in the Georgia law at issue in *Gregg.* The Georgia law tried to eliminate unguided jury discretion by dividing a capital trial into two parts: the guilt phase and the sentencing phase. In the guilt phase, the judge or jury decided whether or not the accused was in fact guilty of the crime. In the sentencing phase, the judge or jury determined whether to condemn the convicted defendant to death based on two criteria set forth in the law: aggravating circumstances, which made the crime more serious, and mitigating circumstances, which lessened the seriousness of the crime. One aggravating circumstance, for example, was that the murder "was outrageously and wantonly vile, horrible, and inhuman." Among the mitigating circumstances were the background and character of the defendant.

The Georgia law was constitutional, said the Court in *Gregg,* because it helped limit the discretion of the judge and jury by giving them guidance. But in *Woodson v. North Carolina* (1976), the Court ruled that removing sentencing discretion altogether by making the death penalty mandatory in certain situations was "cruel and unusual" punishment. No discretion, held the Court, was just as "cruel" as unguided discretion. The Eighth Amendment's fundamental respect for humanity required that judges and juries consider the character and record of the individual offender and the circumstances of the particular crime before sentencing the defendant to death. And the Supreme Court ruled in 1994 that jurors must be told, in deciding whether a defendant should receive a life sentence or be executed, that a life sentence means no parole.

**CRIMES OTHER THAN MURDER.** As a general rule, the Supreme Court has upheld the death penalty for the crime of murder, but not for other crimes. Under the Eighth Amendment, punishment must be related to the crime, so execution is appropriate only in cases of murder—a life for a life. For instance, the Court ruled in *Coker v. Georgia* (1977) that the death penalty was "cruel and unusual" as punishment for rape. And the Court has restricted death sentences under the felony-murder rule, which allowed accomplices (those helping commit a crime) to be convicted for a murder—even if they did not actually pull the trigger—when the murder was part of a serious crime such as robbery or kidnapping.

In *Enmund v. Florida* (1982), the Supreme Court held that the death penalty under the felony-murder rule is "cruel and unusual" punishment for a person whose participation in the crime was minimal. Enmund was driving the getaway car, which was parked outside the victim's house, and had no idea the murder was happening. But in *Tison v. Arizona* (1987), the Court upheld the death penalty under the felony-murder rule when the accomplice was a "major" participant in the crime and had a "reckless indifference to human life." In breaking their father out of prison, the Tison brothers had used an armory of weapons and did not interfere when their father and another accomplice killed an entire family.

# Victims' Rights: The Stephanie Roper Committee

*"One person can make a difference and every person should try."*
*—Stephanie Roper*

Stephanie Roper Committee

*Stephanie Roper wanted to become an artist, like her mother.*

Prince George's Journal/Lon Slepicka

*Jack Ronald Jones was an unemployed maintenance worker.*

In the early hours of Saturday, April 3, 1982, Stephanie Roper was returning home from a night out with her close friend Lisa. An honor student just a month away from her college graduation, Stephanie had originally planned to spend the night at Lisa's house, but decided at the last minute to drive home.

Jack Ronald Jones, 25, and Jerry Lee Beatty, 17, had been driving around the Maryland countryside that night, while they drank beer and smoked marijuana laced with PCP. They claim they saw Stephanie's car disabled on the roadside, and offered to give her a ride back to Lisa's house—only a mile away. Once Stephanie was inside their car, however, they pulled a rifle from under the car seat and took turns raping her. Then they drove to an abandoned shack, near where Jones lived with his wife and six-year-old son, and raped Stephanie again.

Stephanie tried twice to escape, kneeing Beatty in the groin on one attempt. She pleaded for her life, but was beaten with a logging chain, fracturing her skull. As she staggered to escape, either Jones or Beatty shot her in the head with the rifle. They then set the body on fire with gasoline. At some point, her hands were cut off. Jones and Beatty then disposed of Stephanie's charred remains in a nearby swamp. Stephanie's body was discovered a week later on Easter Sunday.

At Jones's trial that fall, the jury convicted him of kidnapping, rape, and murder. The state sought the death penalty. At the sentencing hearing, the prosecutor tried to introduce testimony by Roberta Roper,

Stephanie's mother, about the devastating effects of the crime on the Roper family. The judge ruled such testimony irrelevant, although he allowed witnesses to testify on Jones's behalf. Jones also testified that he had "deep remorse" about the crime and could not understand "why something like this could happen."

As required by state law, each juror was given a form on which to check off "aggravating" and "mitigating" circumstances. The jurors found two aggravating circumstances: kidnapping and rape during the murder. They also agreed on nine mitigating factors—among them Jones's use of drugs and alcohol, his new-found religious faith, and his family's despair over his proposed execution. The jury recommended life imprisonment instead of the death penalty. But the trial judge ruled that Jones could serve his sentences for the three crimes at the same time, or concurrently. That meant Jones would be eligible for parole in less than twelve years. Beatty received the same sentence at a separate trial.

Roberta Roper was outraged. She formed the Stephanie Roper Committee, which became one of the largest victims' rights organizations nationwide. The committee took as its motto an entry from Stephanie's journal written shortly before she died: "One person can make a difference and every person should try." While the committee did not formally advocate the death penalty, it did help eliminate voluntary use of drugs and alcohol as a mitigating circumstance in Maryland. The committee also supported the use in capital cases of "victim impact evidence," in which surviving family members testified about the traumatic effects of the crime.

Some people criticized the Roper Committee for being too emotional, for having a "whiff of vigilantism" about it. Wrote one newspaper columnist: "The bills [proposed by the Roper Committee] substitute emotion for reason, and that, after all, is what [Stephanie's] killers did. The bills are no fitting memorial to her." But Roberta Roper maintained: "We are not looking for vengeance, but we must be the voice and presence of the victims who cannot be here."

The Supreme Court ruled in *Booth v. Maryland* (1987) that victim impact evidence was, in most situations, unconstitutional in death penalty cases. The Court held that such evidence generally "serves no other purpose than to inflame the jury and divert it from deciding the case on the relevant evidence concerning the crime and the defendant." Furthermore, the Court said, "the admission of these emotionally charged opinions . . . is clearly inconsistent with the reasoned decisionmaking we require in capital cases."

But only four years later, the Supreme Court overturned *Booth.* The Court held

Prince George's Journal/Lon Slepicka

in *Payne v. Tennessee* (1991) that "the state has a legitimate interest in counteracting the mitigating evidence which the defendant is entitled to put in, by reminding the sentencer that just as the murderer should be considered as an individual, so too the victim is an individual whose death represents a unique loss to society and in particular to his family."

The dissenting justices countered: "The victim is not on trial; her character, whether good or bad, cannot therefore constitute either an aggravating or mitigating circumstance." The dissent pointed out that if a defendant tried to offer evidence about the immoral

*Jerry Lee Beatty was an unemployed high-school dropout with a juvenile record.*

character of the victim, such evidence would be ruled irrelevant and inadmissible. Victim impact evidence, said the dissent, encouraged jurors to decide for the death penalty "on the basis of their emotions rather than their reason."

Roberta Roper supported the *Payne* decision because it "has restored some balance in the criminal justice system." She added, "at last 'equal justice under law' means innocent victims as well as convicted killers."

**"DEATH IS DIFFERENT."** Because death is the final and ultimate punishment, the Supreme Court has often required stronger procedural protections in death penalty cases than in noncapital crimes. The Supreme Court has heard many cases challenging the constitutionality of the death penalty under various circumstances, such as:

*When the defendant is mentally disabled.* In 1989, the Court held that "evidence of a national consensus against the imposition of the death penalty on murderers with mental deficiencies was insufficient to conclude that the Eighth Amendment bars it absolutely."

*When the defendant is a juvenile.* Also in 1989, the Court ruled that no "national consensus" existed against the death penalty for persons under 18, so the Eighth Amendment did not prohibit such executions. Furthermore, the Court added, executions of juveniles did not violate the "evolving standards of decency that mark the progress of a maturing society."

*When the defendant goes insane.* In 1986, the Court prohibited the execution of a person who goes insane while on death row. The Eighth Amendment allowed executions, said the Court, only when the "prisoner is aware of his impending execution and the reason for it."

*When killers of whites are executed more frequently.* In *McCleskey v. Kemp* (1987), the defendant introduced statistical evidence indicating that killers of whites were 4.3 times more likely to receive the death penalty in Georgia than killers of blacks. Such statistics, said the Court, did not prove actual discrimination in McCleskey's case. The Court held that because "discretion is essential to the criminal justice process, we would demand exceptionally clear proof before we would infer that the discretion has been abused."

**CRUEL METHODS OF EXECUTION.** Even when the death penalty itself is constitutional, the method used to carry it out may not be. Justice William Brennan has described the standards a form of execution must meet to be allowed by the Eighth Amendment:

> First and foremost, the Eighth Amendment prohibits "the unnecessary and wanton infliction of pain." . . . Thus in explaining the obvious unconstitutionality of such ancient practices as disemboweling while alive, drawing and quartering, public dissection, burning alive at the stake, crucifixion, and breaking at the wheel, the Court has emphasized that the Eighth Amendment forbids "inhuman and barbarous" methods of execution that go at all beyond "the mere extinguishment of life" and cause "torture or a lingering death."

Justice Brennan argued that electrocution, once the most common form of execution in America, met this test for "cruel and unusual" punishment under the Eighth Amendment. For this reason, many states now use lethal injections instead of electrocution. Other methods of capital punishment include the gas chamber, firing squad, and hanging. As of 1995, more than two-thirds of the states with the death penalty used lethal injections for executions.

# Electrocution: The Modern Version of Burning at the Stake?

*Justice William Brennan was an ardent opponent of the death penalty, in all forms. In the dissenting opinion below, from* **Glass v. Louisiana** *(1985), Justice Brennan argues that electrocution as a method of capital punishment is "cruel and unusual" in violation of the Eighth Amendment, even if the death penalty itself is not.*

Virginia Department of Corrections

*Virginia's electric chair is nicknamed "Sparky."*

[T]he Eighth Amendment requires that, as much as humanly possible, a chosen method of execution minimize the risk of unnecessary pain, violence, and mutilation. . . .

. . . There is considerable empirical evidence and eyewitness testimony, however, which if correct would appear to demonstrate that electrocution violates every one of the principles set forth above. This evidence suggests that death by electrical current is extremely violent and inflicts pain and indignities far beyond the "mere extinguishment of life." Witnesses routinely report that, when the switch is thrown, the condemned prisoner "cringes," "leaps," and "fights the straps with amazing strength." "The hands turn red, then white, and the cords of the neck stand out like steel bands." The prisoner's limbs, fingers, toes, and face are severely contorted. The force of the electrical current is so powerful that the prisoner's eyeballs sometimes pop out and "rest on [his] cheeks." The prisoner often defecates, urinates, and vomits blood and drool.

"The body turns bright red as its temperature rises," and the prisoner's "flesh wells and his skin stretches to the point of breaking." Sometimes the prisoner catches on fire, particularly "if [he] perspires excessively." Witnesses hear a loud and sustained sound "like bacon frying," and "the sickly sweet smell of burning flesh" permeates the chamber. . . . [T]he prisoner almost literally boils: "the temperature in the brain itself approaches the boiling point of water," and when the postelectrocution autopsy is performed "the liver is so hot that doctors have said that it cannot be touched by the human hand." The body frequently is badly burned and disfigured. . . .

. . . Attending physicians routinely acknowledge that electrocutions must often be repeated in order to ensure death. It is difficult to imagine how such procedures constitute anything less than "death by installments"—"a form of torture [that] would rival that of burning at the stake." . . .

. . . For the reasons set forth above, there is an evermore urgent question whether electrocution in fact is a "humane" method for extinguishing human life or is, instead, nothing less than the contemporary technological equivalent of burning people at the stake.

**WHEN IS A DEATH SENTENCE FINALLY FINAL?** Since the Supreme Court reinstated the death penalty in *Gregg v. Georgia* (1976), only 287 of the more than 3,000 prisoners on death row had been executed as of July 1995. One reason for the small percentage of executions is the number of court appeals that are made in death penalty cases. Most capital cases originate in the states and can be appealed directly through the state court system. But in addition, defendants make indirect, or collateral, appeals of their sentences through the federal court system by arguing that their constitutional rights have been violated. These federal appeals, known as petitions for the writ of habeas corpus, can last many years, long after state appeals have been exhausted.

In 1991, the Supreme Court limited the number of federal habeas corpus appeals that can be filed by death row prisoners. The Court ruled in *McCleskey v. Zant* (the same McCleskey as in the 1987 case of *McCleskey v. Kemp*) that, except in extraordinary circumstances, a death row inmate is limited to just one federal habeas corpus petition. Allowing any more than that would result in abuse of habeas corpus appeals, said the Court, and would interfere with the "orderly administration of justice." The Court also ruled in 1991 that if prisoners fail to follow the rules for state appeals, even through their lawyers' mistakes, they cannot file a federal habeas corpus appeal.

Supporters of the Court's decisions claimed that the death penalty had been losing its deterrent effect because the drawn-out appeals process created too much time between sentencing and execution. Critics of the decisions argued that the Court was denying constitutional rights to those who needed them most—death row inmates.

## NONCAPITAL PUNISHMENTS

Other punishments can be "cruel and unusual," even if the death penalty is not. For instance, the Supreme Court ruled that depriving a person of citizenship was cruel and unusual punishment in *Trop v. Dulles* (1958). The Court said that stripping an army deserter of citizenship—making the defendant a "stateless person, deprived of the right to have rights"—was too cruel a punishment for any crime. The Court has also addressed such issues as sentences that are excessive for the crime, prison conditions, and corporal punishment in schools.

**PROPORTIONALITY.** The general rule under the Eighth Amendment is that punishments must be proportional, or directly related, to the crime committed. For example, in *Robinson v. California* (1962), the Supreme Court found "excessive" a 90-day jail term for the crime of being "addicted to the use of narcotics." Robinson was not under the influence of drugs when arrested, and the only evidence against him were the scars and needlemarks on his arms. The Court believed that the defendant was being punished for the mere status of being an addict, not for actual criminal behavior.

But the Supreme Court has also been reluctant to second-guess the judgments of state legislatures on punishments for crimes. For example, in *Rummel v. Estelle* (1980), the Supreme Court upheld a Texas "three-time loser" law that gave an automatic life sentence to a person convicted of three felonies. Rummel had been found guilty of fraud three times, but the total amount of money at issue was only about $230.

In *Solem v. Helm* (1983), however, the Court retreated somewhat from *Rummel*. Emphasizing that successful challenges to proportionality of sentences will be rare, the Court declared that no penalty is automatically constitutional:

> [W]e hold as a matter of principle that a criminal sentence must be proportionate to the crime for which the defendant has been convicted. Reviewing courts, of course, should grant substantial deference to the broad authority that legislatures necessarily possess in determining the types and limits of punishments for crimes, as well as to the discretion that trial courts possess in sentencing convicted criminals. But no penalty is per se constitutional. . . .

But in *Harmelin v. Michigan* (1991), the Supreme Court upheld a mandatory life sentence without parole for a first-time cocaine conviction. Some justices wanted to overturn *Solem,* arguing that the Eighth Amendment did not require proportionality at all. Other justices maintained that "grossly disproportionate" sentences were forbidden, but because Harmelin's crime was of a "serious nature," rather than just bouncing bad checks, the fact that his sentence was the same as for a first-degree murderer was irrelevant.

**PRISON CONDITIONS.** The Supreme Court has held that inhumane prison conditions are cruel and unusual punishment under the Eighth Amendment. At the same time, the Court has said that the Constitution "does not mandate comfortable prisons," and that judges must hesitate to intervene unless prison conditions are "deplorable" or "sordid."

In *Estelle v. Gamble* (1976), the Court established minimum standards for prison health care. The government must provide medical care for those it incarcerates, said the Court, because "deliberate indifference to the serious medical needs of prisoners constitutes unnecessary and wanton infliction of pain" in violation of the Eighth Amendment. And in 1991, the Court ruled that prison inmates challenging their living conditions must prove that prison officials acted with "deliberate indifference" to their rights for the Eighth Amendment to apply, even if the conditions are otherwise inhumane.

Prison officials are also responsible for the physical safety of inmates. In *Farmer v. Brennan* (1994), the Supreme Court held that prisoners do not have to notify officials of safety risks, but they must prove that officials actually knew of or disregarded that risk.

**CORPORAL PUNISHMENT.** Are paddlings in public schools "cruel and unusual punishment" under the Eighth Amendment? Not according to the Supreme Court. James Ingraham, a junior high school student, had been hit more than twenty times with a paddle for disobeying a teacher's order. He required medical attention and missed eleven days of school.

In *Ingraham v. Wright* (1977), the Court upheld corporal punishment by school officials. The Court held that "the State itself may impose such corporal punishment as is necessary for the proper education of the child and for the maintenance of group discipline." Furthermore, the Court stated that the "school child has little need for the protection of the Eighth Amendment [because] . . . the openness of the public school and its supervision by the community afford significant safeguards against the kinds of abuses from which the Eighth Amendment protects the prisoner."

## STILL EVOLVING?

The Eighth Amendment's prohibition of "cruel and unusual punishments" depends on the "evolving standards of decency that mark the progress of a mature society." How far has American society progressed since 1791, when the Bill of Rights was ratified? Will the standard of decency in the United States someday "evolve" to prohibit the death penalty—as do most other industrialized nations? Or has the United States already "matured" as a society—recognizing that justice requires capital punishment in certain cases? Beyond the death penalty, what other punishments that are constitutional today might be unconstitutional a century from now? Will the Eighth Amendment continue to be an "evolving" one?

# The NINTH Amendment

**THE ENUMERATION** *in the Constitution* **OF CERTAIN RIGHTS** *shall not be construed to deny or disparage others* **RETAINED BY THE PEOPLE.**

The Ninth Amendment says that just because certain rights are enumerated, or listed, in the Constitution does not mean that those are the *only* rights the people have. The Ninth Amendment states that the people retain, or keep, other rights not listed in the Bill of Rights. But who determines what those rights "retained by the people" are, and who protects such rights?

Some scholars believe that the Ninth Amendment was designed only to limit the power of the federal government, and should not be used by the courts to expand the individual rights guaranteed by the Bill of Rights. Other scholars argue that, unless the courts interpret the Ninth Amendment to protect rights not listed in the Bill of Rights, the very purpose of the amendment is defeated. Consequently, the Ninth Amendment is one of the most controversial provisions in the Bill of Rights.

## HISTORY OF THE NINTH AMENDMENT

One of the arguments against adding a bill of rights to the original Constitution was that any enumeration, or listing, of rights would be incomplete. Such a list could imply that the American people had only those rights included in it. Or a bill of rights might give the federal government extra powers by implying that government *could* do all the things not expressly forbidden in the list. Thus, a bill of rights would limit Americans' freedom, not protect it.

For these very reasons, James Madison had at first opposed a bill of rights. To avoid misunderstandings, Madison included the words of the Ninth Amendment in his proposal to Congress. His original language addressed both problems: that a bill of rights would deny other rights not listed, and that it would expand the powers of the federal government. However, the final version of the Ninth Amendment did not refer to the expanded powers of the federal government, although the Tenth Amendment did.

Scholars disagree about the meaning of the changed language in the Ninth Amendment. Some argue that the Ninth and Tenth amendments mean virtually the same thing—that the federal government has limited powers, powers that were not expanded by the Bill of Rights. They maintain that the Ninth Amendment does not protect extra rights beyond those listed in the Constitution. The rights "retained by the people," they argue, are rights that must be protected by the states, not by the federal courts.

Other constitutional experts believe that Madison was trying to prevent two problems: the Ninth Amendment protects all the rights not listed in the Bill of Rights, and the Tenth Amendment restricts the powers of the federal government. These scholars argue that the Ninth Amendment means exactly what it says, and that federal courts have an obligation to protect those "unenumerated," or unlisted, rights—just as they protect other rights specifically listed. After all, these experts note, James Madison intended that the courts would "consider themselves in a peculiar manner the guardians of those rights"—including Ninth Amendment rights.

## THE FORGOTTEN AMENDMENT

The Ninth Amendment is often called the "forgotten amendment" in the Bill of Rights, because it has almost never been used as the basis for a Supreme Court decision. Some scholars believe that judges have been reluctant to rely on the Ninth Amendment because its language is vague, mentioning no specific rights. Robert Bork, a federal judge who was nominated for the Supreme Court in 1987 but rejected by the Senate, gave the following analysis of the Ninth Amendment at his confirmation hearings:

> I do not think you can use the Ninth Amendment unless you know something of what it means. For example, if you had an amendment that says "Congress shall make no" and then there is an inkblot, and you cannot read the rest of it, and that is the only copy you have, I do not think the court can make up what might be under the inkblot.

Bork and others who agree with him believe that the Ninth Amendment gives judges too much power. Its vague language, they say, invites judges to rely on their own ideas of fairness, rather than the law, to decide cases. These experts argue that such a role for judges would destroy democracy, because unelected federal court judges—based only on their personal opinions—would be overruling the laws passed by the people's elected representatives.

Other scholars take exception to Bork's comparison of the Ninth Amendment to an inkblot. They argue that the Ninth Amendment is no more vague than other phrases in the Bill of Rights that judges frequently rely on, such as "due process of law." Judges, they say, must always *interpret* the law. Judges play an important part in the constitutional system, these scholars maintain, and judges have an obligation to enforce all amendments in the Bill of Rights—including the Ninth Amendment.

Nonetheless, the Supreme Court has never defined what rights are protected by the Ninth Amendment. The Court has referred to the Ninth Amendment in a handful of cases, but the amendment has never been the basis of a decision by a majority of the justices. Although the Supreme Court has protected rights not listed in the Bill of Rights, it has not used the Ninth Amendment to do so.

## UNENUMERATED RIGHTS

Rights not specifically listed in the Bill of Rights are known as unenumerated rights. These are the type of rights to which the Ninth Amendment refers. Among the unenumerated rights the Supreme Court has recognized are the right to privacy, the right to interstate and international travel, the right to vote, and freedom of association. But the Supreme Court has used other ways to protect these rights besides the Ninth Amendment.

Sometimes, the Supreme Court decides that a right not listed in the Bill of Rights is implied by other rights that *are* listed. For instance, the

Court ruled that freedom of association is protected because it is implied by other rights in the First Amendment. The Court has also ruled that some aspects of the right to privacy are implied by rights listed in the Third, Fourth, and Fifth amendments.

The most common way the Supreme Court protects unenumerated rights has been the Due Process Clause of the Fourteenth Amendment, which says that no person shall be deprived "of life, liberty, or property without due process of law." The Court decides if a right not listed in the Bill of Rights is "fundamental" enough to be a "liberty" protected by the Due Process Clause. If so, that right is protected, even though it is not specifically mentioned in the Constitution. This method of recognizing rights is known as substantive due process, which is discussed more fully in the chapter on the Fourteenth Amendment.

Just as many constitutional law experts object to Ninth Amendment rights, they also criticize the Supreme Court for recognizing unenumerated rights using other amendments in the Constitution. These critics argue that the Court relies on its own subjective standards of justice to find "fundamental" rights, which they believe is inappropriate for an unelected judiciary. These scholars say that if the American people want to recognize such rights, they should amend the Constitution.

Other experts believe that the federal courts, including the Supreme Court, have a special role in protecting individual rights against majority rule. The very reason judges are not elected, these scholars argue, is so they will protect unpopular rights. The Constitution, created by "We the People," gives judges such power in the first place, say these scholars, and for judges to refuse to use this power would violate the Constitution.

## THE RIGHT TO PRIVACY

One of the most cherished and the most controversial rights not listed in the Constitution is the right to privacy. There are many parts of the right to privacy, as recognized by the Supreme Court—including the right to marry, to have children, to have an abortion, and the right of parents to send their children to private schools. The most famous case involving the Ninth Amendment is about the right to privacy. Most privacy cases, however, have been based on the Fourteenth Amendment.

### GRISWOLD V. CONNECTICUT (1965)

Until 1965, the Supreme Court had never seriously examined the rights protected by the Ninth Amendment. But in that year, the Court heard a case challenging an 1879 Connecticut law that prohibited the use of "any

# Case Study: Griswold v. Connecticut (1965)

*In this case about contraception for married couples, the Ninth Amendment plays a major role for the first time in a Supreme Court decision.*

**Justice Goldberg,** concurring . . .

While this Court has had little occasion to interpret the Ninth Amendment, "[i]t cannot be presumed that any clause in the Constitution is intended to be without effect." *Marbury v. Madison.* . . . The Ninth Amendment to the Constitution may be regarded by some as a recent discovery and may be forgotten by others, but since 1791 it has been a basic part of the Constitution which we are sworn to uphold. To hold that a right so deep-rooted in our society as the right of privacy in marriage may be infringed because that right is not guaranteed in so many words by the first eight amendments to the Constitution is to ignore the Ninth Amendment and to give it no effect whatsoever. . . .

. . . [T]he Ninth Amendment shows a belief of the Constitution's authors that fundamental rights exist that are not expressly enumerated in the first eight amendments and an intent that the list of rights . . . not be exhaustive . . . . The Ninth Amendment simply shows the intent of the Constitution's authors that other fundamental rights should not be denied such protection or disparaged in any other way simply because they are not specifically listed in the first eight constitutional amendments. I do not see how this broadens the authority of the Court; rather it serves to support what this Court has been doing in protecting fundamental rights. . . .

In determining which rights are fundamental, judges are not left at large to decide cases in light of their personal and private notions. Rather they must look to the "traditions and [collective] conscience of our people" to determine whether a principle is "so rooted [there] . . . as to be ranked as fundamental." . . .

In sum, I believe that the right of privacy in the marital relation is fundamental and basic—a personal right "retained by the people" within the meaning of the Ninth Amendment.

**Justice Black,** dissenting . . .

My Brother Goldberg has adopted the recent discovery that the Ninth Amendment as well as the Due Process Clause can be used by this Court as authority to strike down all state legislation which this Court thinks violates "fundamental principles of liberty and justice," or is contrary to the "traditions and [collective] conscience of our people." He also states, without proof satisfactory to me, that in making decisions on this basis judges will not consider "their personal and private notions." One may ask how they can avoid considering them. Our Court certainly has no machinery with which to take a Gallup Poll. And the scientific miracles of this age have not yet produced a gadget which the Court can use to determine what traditions are rooted in the "[collective] conscience of

our people." Moreover, one would certainly have to look far beyond the language of the Ninth Amendment to find that the framers vested in this Court any such awesome veto powers over lawmaking, either by the states or by Congress. . . . That amendment was passed, not to broaden the powers of this Court or any other department of "the General Government," but, as every student of history knows, to assure the people that the Constitution in all its provisions was intended to limit the Federal Government to the powers granted expressly or by necessary implication. If any broad, unlimited power to hold laws unconstitutional because they offend what this Court conceives to be the "[collective] conscience of our people" is vested in this Court by the Ninth Amendment, or any other provision of the Constitution, it was not given by the Framers, but rather has been bestowed on the Court by the Court. This fact is perhaps responsible for the peculiar phenomenon that for a period of a century and a half no serious suggestion was ever made that the Ninth Amendment, enacted to protect state powers against federal invasion, could be used as a weapon of federal power to prevent state legislatures from passing laws they consider appropriate to govern local affairs. Use of any such broad, unbounded judicial authority would make of this Court's members a day-to-day constitutional convention.

drug, medicinal article or instrument for the purpose of preventing conception." In that case, *Griswold v. Connecticut* (1965), a minority of three justices finally agreed on a right protected by the Ninth Amendment: the right to marital privacy, or privacy within the marriage relationship.

Most of the Court, however, did not rely on the Ninth Amendment. Justice William O. Douglas, in his opinion for the Court, held that "specific guarantees in the Bill of Rights have penumbras, formed by emanations from those guarantees that help give them life and substance." In astronomy, a penumbra is a type of shadow. Douglas used astronomy as an example to show how certain rights in the Bill of Rights have other rights implied in them, which give them "life and substance." Douglas wrote that "various guarantees" in the Bill of Rights—among them the Third, Fourth, and Fifth amendments—"create zones of privacy." The intimacy of the marriage relationship, said Douglas, involved "a right of privacy older than the Bill of Rights." The Connecticut law was struck down as unconstitutional.

But not all the justices agreed with Douglas's reasoning, even though they agreed with the Court's ruling. Some of the justices believed that marital privacy was protected by the Due Process Clause of the Fourteenth Amendment, not "penumbras formed by emanations."

Other justices argued that the Ninth Amendment was more relevant. Justice Arthur Goldberg wrote a concurring opinion on that basis, joined by Justice William Brennan and Chief Justice Earl Warren. The Ninth Amendment, Justice Goldberg wrote, was not intended to be ignored. It gave support, he argued, to the Court's protection of unenumerated rights through the Due Process Clause of the Fourteenth Amendment.

Justice Hugo Black, however, vehemently disagreed. Black argued that the Ninth Amendment was virtually identical to the Tenth Amendment, which reserved certain powers for the states. Thus, said Black, unenumerated rights should be protected by the states, not the federal courts. That was why the Ninth Amendment had been "forgotten" as a source of individual rights for the previous 150 years, according to Black. As some scholars note, however, the Supreme Court had only begun seriously to address individual rights at all, under any of the amendments, in the previous fifty years.

### AFTER GRISWOLD

*Griswold* led to other cases in which the Supreme Court upheld privacy in sexual relations, for unmarried as well as married persons. Also, the

*Justice William O. Douglas (1898-1980) served on the Supreme Court from 1939 to 1975—more than thirty-six years, the longest term in history. His judicial opinions, however, were notoriously brief. In* Griswold, *his opinion for the court was just a little over six pages long.*

Supreme Court held that the right to privacy included a woman's right to an abortion in *Roe v. Wade* (1973). Said the Court:

> This right of privacy, whether it be founded in the Fourteenth Amendment's concept of personal liberty and restrictions upon state action, as we feel it is, or, as the [lower court] determined, in the Ninth Amendment's reservation of rights to the people, is broad enough to encompass a woman's decision whether or not to terminate her pregnancy.

*Police officers arrest Michael Hardwick while protesting at the Supreme Court building. The police are wearing plastic gloves, allegedly to protect themselves from AIDS.*

The Supreme Court's decisions on abortion are discussed more fully in the chapter on the Fourteenth Amendment, since the Court relied on the Fourteenth, rather than the Ninth, Amendment to uphold abortion.

The Supreme Court's decisions, whether under the Ninth or Fourteenth amendments, continually upheld the right to sexual privacy until the case of *Bowers v. Hardwick* (1986). Michael Hardwick was arrested in his bedroom for engaging in sodomy with a consenting male adult by an Atlanta police officer with an expired warrant for a minor offense. Hardwick challenged the Georgia sodomy law on the grounds that, among other things, it violated his rights under the Ninth Amendment.

But the Supreme Court upheld the Georgia law, saying that Hardwick was asking the Court to recognize "a fundamental right to engage in homosexual sodomy." Justice Harry Blackmun dissented, pointing out that the Georgia law applied to heterosexuals as well as homosexuals. Under the Court's current rulings on sexual privacy, the law would not be constitutional if applied to heterosexuals, argued Blackmun, so it should not be constitutional when applied to homosexuals:

> . . . [T]he Court's almost obsessive focus on homosexual activity is particularly hard to justify in light of the broad language Georgia has used. Unlike the Court, the Georgia Legislature has not proceeded on the assumption that homosexuals are so different from other citizens that their lives may be controlled in a way that would not be tolerated if it limited the choices of those other citizens. . . . The sex or status of the persons who engage in the act is irrelevant. . . . Michael Hardwick's . . . claim that [the Georgia law] involves an unconstitutional intrusion into his privacy and his right of intimate association does not depend in any way on his sexual orientation.

Justice Lewis Powell, the crucial "swing" vote in the 5-4 decision, later commented that he believed his decision had been a mistake.

# The Courage of Their Convictions: Michael Hardwick

*Michael Hardwick was arrested for violating Georgia's sodomy law when a police officer entered Hardwick's bedroom with an expired arrest warrant for a minor offense. Hardwick challenged the Georgia law as a violation of the right to privacy, but the Supreme Court upheld the law in* **Bowers v. Hardwick** *(1986).*

I realized that if there was anything I could do, even if it was just laying the foundation to change this horrendous law, that I would feel pretty bad about myself if I just walked away from it. One thing that influenced me was that they'd been trying for five years to get a perfect case. Most of the arrests that are made for sodomy in Atlanta are of people who are having sex outside in public; or an adult and a minor; or two consenting adults, but their families don't know they are gay; or they went through seven years of college to teach and they'd be jeopardizing their teaching position. There's a lot of different reasons why people would not want to go on with it. I was fortunate enough to have a supportive family who knew I was gay. I'm a bartender, so I can always work in a gay bar. And I was arrested in my own house. So I was a perfect test case. . . .

I didn't realize when I went into all of this that I was going to be suing the police commissioner, nor did I realize that while in the federal courts I had to continue to live in a city where the KKK was rather strong. The case lasted about five years, and in that time I moved and got an apartment in someone else's name—my phone bills, electric bills, everything was in someone else's name. . . .

[W]hen the decision came down . . . they asked me to come out nationally. . . . [P]eople would stop me and say, I'm not a homosexual but I definitely agree with what you're doing. This is America and we have the right to privacy, and the Constitution should protect us. They were supportive once they understood the issue and how it affected them.

. . . [T]here is a very strong need for the gay community to pull together, and also for the heterosexual community to pull together, against something that's affecting both of us. I feel that no matter what happens, I gave it my best shot. I will continue to give it my best shot.

Reprinted with permission of The Free Press, a division of Macmillan, Inc., from *The Courage of Their Convictions: Sixteen Americans Who Fought Their Way to the Supreme Court* by Peter Irons. Copyright 1988 by Peter Irons.

## STILL FORGOTTEN?

The Ninth Amendment is no longer entirely forgotten. Constitutional scholars, in particular, have been intrigued by the Ninth Amendment's language and history. Some scholars even argue that the Ninth Amendment protects implied rights for individuals just as the Necessary and Proper Clause in Article I of the Constitution protects implied powers for the government.

But courts, particularly the Supreme Court, have been less willing to recognize a role for the Ninth Amendment in protecting individual rights. Lawyers continue to cite the Ninth Amendment in their arguments for their clients, but as a precedent—a basis for court decisions—the Ninth Amendment has far to go to be fully remembered.

# The **TENTH** *Amendment*

**THE POWERS NOT DELEGATED** *to the United States by the Constitution, nor prohibited by it to the States, are* **RESERVED TO THE STATES** *respectively, or to the people.*

Although the Tenth Amendment is part of the Bill of Rights, it does not refer to individual *rights* specifically, as do the first nine amendments. Rather, its focus is on limiting the general *powers* of the national government, and in that way protecting individual freedom. The greatest threat to liberty, thought many Americans of the revolutionary era, was a national government with too much power. The Tenth Amendment was designed to curb that threat.

However, a national government with too little power cannot govern effectively, as Americans discovered with the Articles of Confederation. Therefore, the U.S. Constitution of 1787 gave the federal government more power. The Tenth Amendment was an attempt to strike a balance between the power of the federal government and the power of the states. That balance has been difficult to maintain throughout America's history. Only a bloody Civil War finally resolved the ultimate question of federal versus state power. Since the Civil War, the Supreme Court has struggled to find the proper balance of the Tenth Amendment.

## HISTORY OF THE TENTH AMENDMENT

All eight states that proposed amendments to the Constitution included some version of the Tenth Amendment—the only amendment in the Bill of Rights proposed by every state. The issue of state versus federal power was thus a critical one in the ratification of the Constitution and the Bill of Rights.

James Madison included the Tenth Amendment in his original draft of the Bill of Rights to satisfy those who worried that a bill of rights could imply additional federal power. Indeed, one of the Federalist arguments against adding a bill of rights to the Constitution was that it was dangerous. In limiting the powers of the national government to deny specific rights, the Federalists argued, a bill of rights could also be interpreted to mean that the government had power in all the areas not specifically denied.

Madison's version of the Tenth Amendment made it clear that any powers not delegated to the federal government belonged to the states, or to the people. However, some members of Congress wanted the Tenth Amendment to limit the federal government to those powers specifically listed in the Constitution—just as the Articles of Confederation had done. They wanted the Tenth Amendment to say that "the powers not *expressly* delegated to the United States" were reserved to the states. Madison argued that "it was impossible to confine a Government to the exercise of express powers; there must necessarily be admitted powers by implication, unless the Constitution descended to recount every minutia."

By proposing that the Tenth Amendment limit the federal government to express powers, some Anti-Federalists in Congress were trying to weaken the strong national government created by the Constitutional Convention in 1787. One of the Anti-Federalists' chief objections to the Constitution was that it gave the national government too much power. Having lost the battle over the ratification of the Constitution, Anti-Federalists tried to resurrect the issue of federal power via the Tenth Amendment. Attempts to add "expressly" to the Tenth Amendment failed, however, both in the House and in the Senate. The history of the Tenth Amendment thus indicated that it was not intended to restrict the federal government to those powers specifically listed in the Constitution.

The question remained, however, just what powers were reserved to the states under the Tenth Amendment. Some Americans argued that the Tenth Amendment recognized states' rights—the powers of the states as sovereign governments—with authority equal to the federal govern-

ment. These Americans believed that the Supreme Court should protect states' rights no less than individual rights. Others supported nationalism, the view that the national government is supreme over the states. Nationalists said the Tenth Amendment was meant only to state the obvious, that those powers not delegated were reserved, not to be an independent source of power for the states. The Supreme Court and the American people have disagreed about the issue of state versus federal power, and the meaning of the Tenth Amendment, for more than 200 years.

## FEDERALISM

The Tenth Amendment reflects a basic principle of American government: federalism. Under federalism, power is shared by the national government and the states. The U.S. Constitution established a federal system in order to preserve the existing state governments while at the same time creating a new national government strong enough to deal with the country's problems. The nation's first form of government, under the Articles of Confederation, had been a confederation, an alliance of independent states that created a central government of very limited power. This form of government proved ineffective, leading to the Constitutional Convention of 1787.

One of the most controversial questions at the Constitutional Convention was how much power the national government should have. Many delegates at the convention feared a strong central government, but they also knew a confederation was too weak. They created a national government with strong powers, but with limits. A primary limit was that the government was one of enumerated powers, powers specifically listed in the Constitution (also known as expressed powers). However, the Constitution also included an elastic clause, which stated that Congress had the power to make all laws "necessary and proper" to carry out its enumerated powers. The Necessary and Proper Clause became the basis for the implied powers, those powers not specifically listed in the Constitution that are implied by the enumerated powers.

The powers of the national government, both enumerated and implied, are known as the delegated powers, because they were delegated, or entrusted, to the national government by the states and the people. The powers kept by the states are known as the reserved powers. The Tenth Amendment refers to both these types of powers. One of the primary reserved powers is the police power, which enables a state to pass laws and regulations involving the public's health, safety, morals, and welfare. While the Constitution recognizes the powers of both the states and the federal governments, it also contains the Supremacy Clause in Article VI, which states that the Constitution and laws of the United States are "the supreme law of the land"—higher than state laws and state constitutions.

## THE SUPREME COURT AND FEDERALISM

Although the Constitution provided general guidelines, the Supreme Court had to flesh out the particulars of the division of power between the national government and the states. Many of the early cases tested the limits of national power. The Court expanded the power of the national government until 1835, but for the next 100 years it was more favorable to state power.

### NATIONAL SUPREMACY

John Marshall, the fourth chief justice of the United States, played a paramount role in strengthening the powers of the national government through numerous Supreme Court decisions. One of these, *McCulloch v. Maryland* (1819), was the first Supreme Court case to test the nature of the implied powers. In doing so, the case also raised questions under the Tenth Amendment. *McCulloch* challenged the balance of state and federal powers in two ways: it questioned the power of the national government to establish a national bank, and the power of the states to tax an agency of the national government.

**MCCULLOCH V. MARYLAND (1819).** In 1816, Congress chartered the second Bank of the United States during a time of financial trouble for the nation. Some Americans believed that the national bank only added to these troubles by competing with state banks. Maryland passed a law

*John Marshall was the fourth, and most influential, chief justice of the United States. During his term (1801-1835), Marshall wrote many opinions that established the supremacy of the federal government over the states.*

# Case Study: McCulloch v. Maryland (1819)

*In this case, the Supreme Court holds that the powers of the United States are not limited to those expressly listed in the Constitution, but include those implied from the document itself.*

**Chief Justice Marshall** delivered the opinion of the Court. . . .

*W*e must never forget that it is a constitution *we* are expounding.

This government is acknowledged by all to be one of enumerated powers. . . . [T]hat principle is now universally admitted. But the question respecting the extent of the powers actually granted, is perpetually arising, and will probably continue to arise, as long as our system shall exist. . . .

Among the enumerated powers, we do not find that of establishing a bank or creating a corporation. But there is no phrase in the instrument [Constitution] which, like the articles of confederation, excludes incidental or implied powers; and which requires that everything granted shall be expressly and minutely described. Even the Tenth Amendment, which was framed for the purpose of quieting the excessive

jealousies which had been excited, omits the word "expressly," and declares only that the powers "not delegated to the United States, nor prohibited to the states, are reserved to the states or to the people". . . . The men who drew and adopted this amendment had experienced the embarrassments resulting from the insertion of this word in the articles of confederation, and probably omitted it, to avoid those embarrassments. A constitution, to contain an accurate detail of all the subdivisions of which its great powers will admit, and of all the means by which they may be carried into execution, would partake of the prolixity [wordiness] of a legal code, and could scarcely be embraced by the human mind. It would, probably, never be understood by the public. Its nature, therefore, requires, that only its great outlines should be marked. . . . In considering this question, then, we must never forget that it is *a constitution* we are expounding.

in 1818 requiring a tax on banks not chartered by the state. Maryland sued James W. McCulloch, an officer of the Baltimore branch of the Bank of the United States, for failure to pay the tax. Maryland won in the state courts, but the bank appealed to the U.S. Supreme Court.

The oral argument before the Supreme Court featured two prominent constitutional lawyers, Luther Martin and Daniel Webster. Martin, attorney general of Maryland, had been a delegate to the Constitutional Convention. He maintained that only the states had the power to incorporate banks because the Constitution did not give Congress that power and, under the Tenth Amendment, the powers not given to the federal government were reserved to the states. Even if Congress had the power to create a bank, Martin argued, nothing in the Constitution forbade Maryland from taxing persons or property within state borders—a power reserved to Maryland under the Tenth Amendment.

Daniel Webster represented the Bank of the United States, beginning a long career as an advocate of national power. Webster pointed out that, under the Constitution, Congress had the power "to make all laws which shall be necessary and proper" to implement its enumerated powers. A national bank, Webster argued, was a "necessary and proper" means for Congress to execute its powers to tax, to borrow money, and to regulate commerce. Furthermore, Webster said, if Maryland had the power to tax the national bank, where would such power stop? An excessive tax would drive the bank out of business—or the U.S. courts or the mails, if a state decided to tax them as well. As Webster noted, "an unlimited tax involves, necessarily, a power to destroy."

Chief Justice John Marshall, writing for the unanimous Court, agreed with Daniel Webster on both counts. Citing the Tenth Amendment's legislative history, Marshall noted that the amendment had not limited the national government to those powers specifically listed in the Constitution. The Necessary and Proper Clause gave Congress the power to create a national bank. Furthermore, the Court held, when state and national powers conflict, national power "is supreme within its sphere of action." Thus, Congress's power to create a bank was superior to Maryland's power to tax, since "the power to tax involves the power to destroy."

Marshall's opinion was criticized vehemently, especially in the South and the West. President Thomas Jefferson, himself an advocate of states' rights, called the court "a subtle corps of sappers and miners constantly working underground to undermine the foundations of the constitutional fabric." Jefferson and others believed that giving the national government implied powers created an unlimited source of federal power, which would quickly overshadow the states.

## DUAL FEDERALISM

John Marshall's successor as chief justice, Roger B. Taney, agreed with Jefferson. During Taney's twenty-eight-year term, the Supreme Court followed a policy of dual federalism, which viewed the national government and the states as equals. Both governments were sovereign, or supreme and with final authority, within their spheres of action.

Chief Justice Taney saw the Supreme Court as an arbitrator in conflicts between the "dual sovereignty" of the states and the national government. The role of the Court, Taney wrote, was "not merely to maintain

*Roger B. Taney, chief justice of the United States from 1836 to 1864, was chosen by President Andrew Jackson because he supported states' rights.*

*About 20 percent of children 10 to 15 years old had jobs in the 1890s. Many families depended on their children's income to survive. Factories and mines employed children at wages far below those of adult workers.*

the supremacy of the laws of the United States, but also to guard the states from any encroachment upon their reserved rights by the general government." Taney hoped that the Court, by "deciding in the peaceful forum of judicial proceeding the angry and irritating controversies between sovereignties," would prevent armed conflict between the states and the national government. He was wrong.

Taney's policy of dual federalism predominated for almost 100 years, even after the Civil War. While the war established the indestructible nature of the Union, it did not settle the competing claims of state versus federal power.

**HAMMER V. DAGENHART (1918).** One of the most significant cases involving the Tenth Amendment after the Civil War was *Hammer v. Dagenhart* (1918). *Hammer* involved the power of the national government under the Commerce Clause to ban goods produced by child labor from sale in interstate commerce.

The Commerce Clause in Article I of the Constitution says that only the federal government, not the states, may regulate interstate commerce. The chief issue under the Commerce Clause is how commerce is defined. A broad definition of commerce gives the national government power over almost every aspect of American life; a narrow definition limits the power of the federal government over the states. In *Hammer,* the Commerce Clause was defined narrowly.

Every state prohibited child labor when *Hammer* was decided, but minimum ages varied. Therefore, even if one state banned child labor under age 16, another state that had 14 as the minimum age could still sell its cheaper goods inside the first state. Individual states could not ban products from other states without violating the Commerce Clause. Congress attempted to provide a uniform national standard in 1916, but the act was declared unconstitutional by the Supreme Court in *Hammer*.

The Court held that Congress's power to regulate interstate commerce extended only to goods and services that were dangerous in themselves—such as liquor, lottery tickets, and prostitution—not to harmless goods that were produced by methods Congress disliked, such as child labor. Regulation of social conditions, the Court ruled, was a "local power . . . carefully reserved to the States in the Tenth Amendment." Justice Oliver Wendell Holmes, in dissent, charged that the Court was substituting its own moral judgment for that of Congress by holding the commerce power "permissible as against strong drink but not as against the product of ruined lives." Holmes's view was eventually vindicated by later Supreme Court decisions, and the commerce power became one of the most far-reaching tools of the national government.

## FEDERALISM AND POLITICS

Not all battles over federalism were fought in the Supreme Court. Many of the greatest challenges to the federal system came through politics, not court cases. These political struggles over federal power and the meaning of the Tenth Amendment helped determine the future of the Union no less than the Supreme Court. In fact, the Supreme Court was unable to prevent the gravest threat to the Constitution—the Civil War. Since the Civil War, political struggles have continued to shape the nature of American federalism.

### SECTIONALISM AND SECESSION

In 1782 the Continental Congress adopted a design for the Great Seal of the United States that included the Latin motto, *e pluribus unum:* "from many, one." From many states, one Union—but that Union proved hard to preserve. From the beginning, the states in the various geographic regions of the country—North, South, and West—struggled over their differing economic interests. Sectionalism, which put regional interests ahead of national interests, intensified the struggle between state and federal power, threatening to destroy the Union itself.

**THE VIRGINIA AND KENTUCKY RESOLUTIONS.** One of the earliest battles over the power of the states and the federal government involved two founders of the republic, Thomas Jefferson and James Madison, who came to speak for the interests of southern planters and farmers. Jefferson and Madison's political opponents, the Federalists, were mostly northerners and dominated Congress in 1798. In that year, Congress passed the Sedition Act, which punished newspaper editors who criticized the Federalists. Jefferson drafted a resolution passed by the Kentucky legislature that declared the Sedition Act unconstitutional as a violation of the First Amendment. Madison authored a similar but more far-reaching resolution for the Virginia legislature.

Jefferson and Madison argued that the Union was a compact of sovereign states, which retained the power to determine when their agent, the federal government, went beyond the scope of its delegated powers. The states thus had the power to declare acts of the federal government unconstitutional. In the words of the Virginia resolution:

> [I]n case of a deliberate, palpable, and dangerous exercise . . . of powers not granted by the [Constitution], the States who are parties thereto, have the right and are in duty bound to interpose for arresting the progress of the evil.

The Sedition Act expired in 1801 and was never tested before the Supreme Court. The Court did not establish its power to declare acts of Congress unconstitutional until 1803. Some constitutional law experts believe that Madison, who generally supported a stronger national government, would not have written the Virginia Resolution if judicial review had already been asserted. There would have been no need for a state to declare laws unconstitutional, these scholars argue, once the federal courts had claimed that power for themselves. But when the courts did exercise judicial review, an inevitable conflict emerged with those who believed the states had the same power—a conflict that eventually threatened the role of the courts themselves.

**NULLIFICATION.** Madison's language in the Virginia Resolution, and his stature as the Constitution's chief architect, lent support to many who tried to weaken the powers of the national government. Through nullification or interposition, some states claimed the authority to declare acts of the national government unconstitutional. According to the theory of nullification, the United States was a compact of states, not a government of the people, so the states had the ultimate authority in deciding when the federal government had exceeded its bounds.

*The Great Seal of the United States features the Latin motto,* e pluribus unum, *which means "from many, one."*

*John C. Calhoun (1782-1850) resigned the vice presidency in 1832 to advocate nullification in the U.S. Senate.*

*Daniel Webster (1782-1852), considered the most eloquent orator of his time, became a leading opponent of nullification in the U.S. Senate. In a famous speech in 1830, he said: "Liberty and Union, now and forever, one and inseparable!"*

Nationalists, however, argued that the Constitution created a government in which the people were the source of authority, not the states, and that the people through their elected officials and the court system would decide the scope of national power.

**THE HARTFORD CONVENTION.** An early threat of nullification came from the New England states, who protested the War of 1812 with Great Britain—an important trading partner for the region. In 1814, delegates from New England met in the Hartford Convention, where they threatened secession and passed resolutions repeating the states' rights language of the Kentucky and Virginia resolutions. The War of 1812 ended shortly after the convention, forestalling the conflict between state and national governments.

**SECESSION.** Less than two decades after the Hartford Convention, South Carolina promoted the theory of nullification and threatened to secede. South Carolina opposed the federal protective tariffs of 1828 and 1832, which hurt the economy of the South but helped Northern industries. A chief advocate of nullification was John C. Calhoun, a native of South Carolina who served as vice president of the United States from 1825 to 1832. In 1831, Calhoun supported the doctrine of nullification in his "Fort Hill Address," quoting Madison's language from the Virginia Resolution. In 1832, South Carolina adopted the Ordinance of Nullification, declaring the federal tariffs null and void and threatening secession from the Union if the federal government tried to collect the tariffs by force.

President Andrew Jackson responded by issuing the "Proclamation to the People of South Carolina." He warned the state: "Be not deceived by names; disunion by armed force is treason." Jackson asked Congress for the authority to enforce the tariff using the military if necessary; Congress granted his request in the Force Bill of 1833. To avoid armed conflict, Senator Henry Clay of Kentucky crafted a compromise tariff, which led South Carolina to suspend its Ordinance of Nullification. South Carolina's secession from the Union was averted—at least until 1860.

In 1860 South Carolina led the South in leaving the Union. Political compromises about economics and slavery had been unable to sustain the Union. Only a bitter Civil War finally resolved the nature of the Union and the states within it. After the war, the Supreme Court could hold in *Texas v. White* (1869) that the Constitution "in all its provisions, looks to an indestructible Union, composed of indestructible states."

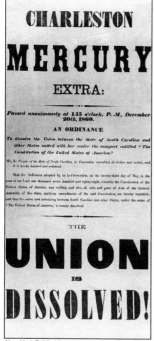

New York Public Library

*The* Charleston Mercury *announced the secession of South Carolina from the Union on December 20, 1860.*

## STATES' RIGHTS VS. CIVIL RIGHTS

Most of the contests between state and federal powers after the Civil War were fought in the courts, rather than in legislatures or on the battlefield. But the doctrine of interposition reemerged during the 1950s and 1960s in a struggle between states' rights and civil rights.

In *Brown v. Board of Education* (1954), the Supreme Court ruled that racially segregated public schools were unconstitutional under the Fourteenth Amendment, which forbade any state to deny "equal protection of the law." Southern states, in particular, decried the Court's decision as an intrusion on their rights. Education, they argued, was one of the traditional police powers reserved to the states under the Tenth Amendment, and the national government—including the Supreme Court—had no authority over education.

**NEW THREATS OF NULLIFICATION.** In January 1956, the Alabama Senate passed a resolution of nullification. In February, the Virginia legislature adopted an interposition resolution, which asserted the state's right to "interpose its sovereignty" against the Court's decision. In March, nineteen U.S. senators and eighty-one representatives issued the Southern Manifesto, which declared the sovereignty of the Southern states and decried "the Supreme Court's encroachments on rights reserved to the states and to the people." The Southern Manifesto supported "those states which have declared the intention to resist forced integration by any lawful means." Several Southern states set up "Sovereignty Commissions" to fight integration.

**SHOWDOWN IN THE SCHOOLS.** When nine black students tried to integrate Little Rock Central High School in the fall of 1957, Arkansas Governor Orval Faubus ordered the state's National Guard to prevent the students from enrolling. In a conflict between national and state powers, President Dwight Eisenhower sent in more than 1,000 troops from the 101st Airborne Division to protect the "Little Rock Nine" and allow them to enroll at Central High School.

In 1962, federal troops were also necessary to integrate the University of Mississippi. Governor Ross Barnett vehemently opposed integration of "Ole Miss," calling the time "our greatest crisis since the War Between the States." Mississippi Congressman Frank Smith criticized Barnett, saying "whether we like it or not the question of state versus federal law was settled one hundred years ago." But Barnett insisted that the federal government was "trampling on the sovereignty of this great

UPI/Bettmann

*Federal troops from the 101st Airborne Division escorted the "Little Rock Nine" to classes at Central High School.*

state" and "destroying the Constitution of this great nation." When James Meredith, the first black student to attend the University of Mississippi, finally enrolled, President John Kennedy ordered federal troops into the university to end the resulting riot.

In 1963, Governor George Wallace of Alabama also tried to prevent the integration of the University of Alabama. In a dramatic gesture, Governor Wallace stood in the doorway of the university to prevent federal officials from integrating it.

**FEDERAL SUPREMACY.** The civil rights movement helped establish the supremacy of federal law over states' rights—at least in the area of equal education. Struggles between the federal government and the states have been less vehement and less violent since the civil rights era, focusing more on courtrooms than on classrooms. Although President Ronald Reagan advocated a "New Federalism" in the 1980s, his goal was to decrease the size and cost of the federal government, not to give states the power to disobey Supreme Court rulings. Today the Supreme Court, rather than politicians, plays the most critical role in defining states' rights under the Tenth Amendment.

## MODERN FEDERALISM AND THE SUPREME COURT

By the 1940s, the role of the federal government in American society had expanded greatly to meet the challenges of the Great Depression, and the Supreme Court began to take a more expansive view of federal power as well. In the 1970s, however, the Court backtracked and decided in favor

Library of Congress

*In 1963 Governor George Wallace (left), attempting to prevent the university's integration, blocked the doorway of the University of Alabama to U.S. Deputy Attorney General Nicholas Katzenbach.*

of states' rights. In the 1980s, the Supreme Court changed directions again, and once more favored federal power. How long that trend will last is the real issue surrounding the Tenth Amendment.

### FEDERALISM AND THE NEW DEAL

The Great Depression of the 1930s presented an enormous challenge to the role of government in society, and with it came an immense change in federal-state relations. President Franklin Roosevelt believed the national government should actively help reduce the suffering caused by the Great Depression. His New Deal program consisted of many laws designed to correct problems in the economy and provide benefits to American citizens.

**COURT-PACKING.** A majority of the Supreme Court, however, disagreed with Roosevelt. They struck down as unconstitutional many of the New Deal laws passed by Congress, believing the laws exceeded the scope of federal authority. Roosevelt, outraged at what he saw as the Court's enforcement of its own personal prejudices, proposed a "court-packing" plan in 1937 for Congress to add more justices to the Supreme Court— which he of course would appoint. In that way, Roosevelt hoped to get his New Deal legislation upheld by the Court. Popular opinion caused

Library of Congress

*President Franklin Roosevelt urged Congress to increase the size of the Supreme Court— after the Court struck down many of his New Deal laws. When the Court later began upholding those laws, some pundits noted: "A switch in time saved nine!"*

Roosevelt's plan to fail, but the Court soon began upholding many New Deal laws nonetheless.

**THE COMMERCE POWER.** Much of the New Deal legislation was enacted under Congress's power to regulate interstate commerce—the same authority struck down in 1918 by *Hammer v. Dagenhart*. Critics of the New Deal charged that Congress, in passing social welfare legislation, was using the Commerce Clause as a ploy to create a national police power, giving the federal government power over the health and welfare issues traditionally reserved to the states by the Tenth Amendment.

In *United States v. Darby Lumber Company* (1941), however, the Supreme Court held that the Tenth Amendment was not an independent source of states' rights, but merely a "truism that all is retained which has not been surrendered." The Court returned to Chief Justice Marshall's interpretation of the Tenth Amendment, holding that the amendment did not deprive the national government "of authority to resort to all means for the exercise of a granted power which are appropriate and plainly adapted to the permitted end." In *Darby,* the Court overruled *Hammer v. Dagenhart* and upheld Congress's authority to fix minimum wages and maximum hours for employees of industries engaged in interstate commerce.

Since *Darby,* federal power under the Commerce Clause has greatly expanded. Congress even used the commerce power to enact the Civil Rights Act of 1964, which prohibited racial discrimination in public accommodations. The Supreme Court upheld this use of the commerce power in *Heart of Atlanta Motel v. United States* (1964).

## THE PENDULUM SWINGS

In the 1970s and 1980s, the Supreme Court took totally opposite stands on the nature of federalism under the Tenth Amendment. These pendulum swings from more federal power to more state power, then back to more federal power, created confusion both on the Court and in the legislatures. Finding the balance between federal power and state power under the Tenth Amendment has been a difficult task for the Supreme Court.

**MORE STATE POWER.** After *Darby,* the Supreme Court's interpretation of the Tenth Amendment seemed to be settled in favor of national power, until the Court ruled in *National League of Cities v. Usery* (1976). In that case, the Court noted the "limits upon the power of Congress to override state sovereignty, even when exercising its . . . powers to tax or to regulate commerce." The Court held, in a 5-4 decision, that the federal government could not interfere with "traditional" and "integral" state and local government functions, such as employee relations. In *Usery,* the Court ruled that minimum wage and overtime laws did not apply to state or local government employees.

**MORE FEDERAL POWER.** The Supreme Court overruled *Usery* less than ten years later, however, in *Garcia v. San Antonio Metropolitan Transit Authority* (1985), also in a 5-4 decision. The Court said that a city-owned mass transit system must pay its employees overtime under federal law. Although the majority opinion did not specifically mention the Tenth Amendment, it did note the "special" place of the states in the constitutional system. Nonetheless, the Court held that the *Usery* test of state sovereignty, which attempted to define "traditional" state functions, "inevitably invites an unelected federal judiciary to make decisions about which state policies it favors and which ones it dislikes." Better for the states to rely on the political process for protection of their rights, the Court said, than on the judiciary. If states believed Congress had gone too far in exercising federal power, they could elect representatives and senators more sympathetic to states' rights.

National Museum of American Art, Washington, DC/Art Resource, NY

*The message spelled out by these state license plates is contained in what famous document?*

The dissenting justices in *Garcia* declared that the majority's opinion "effectively reduces the Tenth Amendment to meaningless rhetoric when Congress acts pursuant to the Commerce Clause." "Indeed," said the dissent, "the Court's view of federalism appears to relegate the States to precisely the trivial role that opponents of the Constitution feared they would occupy."

## STILL A "TRUISM"?

The fate of the Tenth Amendment after *Garcia* is unclear. Since 1985, more justices sympathetic to states' rights have joined the Court. And Justice Rehnquist, who was in the dissent in *Garcia,* became chief justice. In *United States v. Lopez* (1995), the Supreme Court once again limited federal authority under the Commerce Clause, although it did not overrule *Garcia.* The Court struck down a 1990 federal law that created gun-free school zones, holding that Congress had not demonstrated a significant connection with interstate commerce.

One interesting note about the Tenth Amendment is its relationship to the Ninth Amendment and the role of the judiciary in enforcing both provisions. Liberal judges often see the Ninth Amendment as an important source of individual rights, but are reluctant to enforce the Tenth Amendment as a source of states' rights. Conservative judges insist on enforcing the Tenth Amendment as a guarantee of states' rights against the federal government, but dismiss the Ninth Amendment's protection of unenumerated rights. Tenth Amendment rights should be protected by the political process, not judges, say liberals; states can influence the exercise of federal power by their votes in the House of Representatives and the Senate. Ninth Amendment rights should be protected by the political process, not judges, say conservatives; the people can amend the Constitution when they want unenumerated rights protected.

The Tenth Amendment is about federalism, and federalism is about power—who gets it under the Constitution. This decision is important, because it helps determine what voices in government will have the most influence. As one political scientist has noted, "deciding *who* will act often decides *what* will be done." Those decisions, in Chief Justice Marshall's words, "will probably continue to arise, as long as our system shall exist." That is what the Tenth Amendment is all about.

# *Beyond the* **BILL** *of* **RIGHTS**

Not all rights valued by Americans are contained in the Bill of Rights. Slavery, for instance, was allowed under both the original Constitution and the Bill of Rights. Only the Civil War and three constitutional amendments would begin to remove the stain of slavery from the national charter. The Thirteenth, Fourteenth, and Fifteenth amendments—known as the Civil War Amendments— outlawed slavery, made blacks citizens, and gave black men the vote.

The Fourteenth Amendment, in particular, revolutionized constitutional law. It was used to nationalize the Bill of Rights to apply to the states. And its guarantee of "equal protection of the laws" helped eliminate discrimination not only against blacks, but against other races and women as well. This section focuses on the Fourteenth Amendment because of its critical role in U.S. constitutional law.

Since the Fourteenth Amendment was added in 1868, other amendments have extended the rights of Americans. Voting rights have been the most popular issue. Some scholars believe that Article V, which provides for the amendment process, is the secret to the Constitution's success. Amendments allow peaceful revolution when the people want change, rather than a violent overthrow of the government. The first ten amendments ensured that the Constitution would be ratified and that a new government would begin; later amendments have helped guarantee that government would not end.

# The **FOURTEENTH** *Amendment*

*Section 1.* **ALL PERSONS BORN OR NATURALIZED** *in the United States and subject to the jurisdiction thereof, are* **CITIZENS** *of the United States and of the State wherein they reside.* **NO STATE** *shall make or enforce any law which shall abridge the* **PRIVILEGES OR IMMUNITIES** *of citizens of the United States; nor shall any State deprive any person of life, liberty, or property, without* **DUE PROCESS OF LAW**; *nor deny to any person within its jurisdiction the* **EQUAL PROTECTION OF THE LAWS.**

According to Justice William Brennan, the Fourteenth Amendment gave Americans "a brand new Constitution after the Civil War." It extended citizenship to former slaves and promised them equal treatment under the law. Moreover, the Fourteenth Amendment specifically restricted the states, so it was used by the Supreme Court to apply the Bill of Rights to the states as well— thereby enormously expanding the scope of constitutional rights and the caseload of the Court.

The Fourteenth Amendment has five sections dealing with many issues that arose after the Civil War, such as paying war debts and barring Confederates from holding public office. Section 1 has had the most lasting significance in constitutional law. It provides that no person shall be denied "due process of law" (fairness in government actions) or "equal protection of the laws" (protection from unreasonable discrimination). These two rights have been the basis of most twentieth-century cases in constitutional law.

## HISTORICAL BACKGROUND

Slavery was firmly entrenched in the Constitution of 1787. Slaves had no rights under the Constitution or the Bill of Rights. Moreover, the Supreme Court ruled in *Dred Scott v. Sandford* (1857) that even free blacks could not be citizens of the United States, that they "had no rights which a white man was bound to respect."

Although the Thirteenth Amendment abolished slavery in 1865, after the Civil War many southern states passed "Black Codes"—forbidding blacks from voting, serving on juries, holding certain jobs, moving freely, owning firearms, or gathering in groups. These laws were similar to the slave codes that controlled blacks before the Civil War. To remedy such discrimination, Congress passed the Fourteenth Amendment, which gave blacks citizenship—a status previously defined only by the states. The amendment also promised blacks "equal protection of the laws." Southern states were required to ratify the Fourteenth Amendment before they could reenter the union.

The author of the Fourteenth Amendment, Representative John Bingham of Ohio, and other supporters argued during congressional debates that the amendment would also, through its Privileges or Immunities Clause, extend the protections of the Bill of Rights to the states. The Supreme Court, however, refused to go along with this interpretation. In the *Slaughterhouse Cases* (1873), the Court held that the Privileges or Immunities Clause of the Fourteenth Amendment did not apply the Bill of Rights to the states, for doing so would "change the whole theory of the state and federal governments" and "would [make] this Court a perpetual censor upon all legislation of the states."

But twenty-four years later, the Supreme Court did begin to apply the Bill of Rights to the states using the Due Process Clause of the Fourteenth Amendment. Over a period of seventy-five years, the Court eventually applied most of the Bill of Rights to the states—something it could have done all at once in the *Slaughterhouse Cases*.

*Dred Scott, a Missouri slave who had for a time been taken into free territory, sued for his freedom in* Dred Scott v. Sandford *(1857) but lost.*

## DUE PROCESS

. . . **NO STATE** *shall . . . deprive any person of life, liberty, or property, without*

**DUE PROCESS OF LAW** . . .

This part of the Fourteenth Amendment is known as the Due Process Clause. Its wording is similar to the Due Process Clause of the Fifth Amendment, but it applies to the states, whereas the Fifth Amendment restricts only the national government. Through the Due Process Clause of the Fourteenth Amendment, the Supreme Court has nationalized the Bill of Rights and applied most of its provisions to the states.

As discussed in the Fifth Amendment chapter, due process means that the government must be fair in its actions. Procedural due process means that the way the laws are carried out must be fair; substantive due process means that the laws themselves must be fair. Most cases using substantive due process have been based on the Fourteenth Amendment.

## INCORPORATION OF THE BILL OF RIGHTS

James Madison included in his proposals for the Bill of Rights an amendment that forbade the states to violate "the rights of conscience, or the freedom of the press, or the trial by jury in criminal cases." Although Madison regarded it as "the most valuable amendment in the whole list," Congress defeated the amendment. The provisions of the Bill of Rights thus limited only the federal government, not the states, as the Supreme Court held in *Barron v. Baltimore* (1833).

With the addition of the Fourteenth Amendment in 1868, however, the Court had a mechanism for applying the Bill of Rights to the states. In a series of decisions, the Supreme Court held that the Due Process Clause of the Fourteenth Amendment "incorporates," or includes within it, certain fundamental provisions of the Bill of Rights—thus applying them to the states. By 1972, the Court had incorporated most of the rights in the first eight amendments, which contain most individual rights.

**SELECTIVE INCORPORATION.** The Supreme Court applied the Bill of Rights to the states in a piecemeal fashion, rather than all at once. The Court determined whether a right was important enough to be included in "due process of law." If so, that right was applied to the states. In *Palko v. Connecticut* (1937), Justice Benjamin Cardozo set forth the test for whether a right should be incorporated. Only those rights that were "fundamental" and essential to "a scheme of ordered liberty" would be incorporated.

**TOTAL INCORPORATION.** Some justices on the Supreme Court, most notably Justice Hugo Black, argued that the Fourteenth Amendment incorporated the entire Bill of Rights, not just selected rights that the Court deemed "fundamental." That a right was even listed in the Bill of Rights made it "fundamental" to advocates of total incorporation.

# Case Study: Adamson v. California (1947)

*In this case, Justice Hugo Black argued that the original purpose of the Fourteenth Amendment was to apply the Bill of Rights to the states.*

### Justice Black, dissenting . . .

My study of the historical events that culminated in the Fourteenth Amendment . . . persuades me that one of the chief objects that the provisions of the amendment's first section . . . were intended to accomplish was to make the Bill of Rights applicable to the states. With full knowledge of the import of the *Barron* decision, the framers and backers of the Fourteenth Amendment proclaimed its purpose to be to overturn the constitutional rule that case had announced. . . .

I cannot consider the Bill of Rights to be an outworn eighteenth-century "straight jacket." . . . Its provisions may be thought outdated abstractions by some. And it is true that they were designed to meet ancient evils. But they are the same kind of human evils that have emerged from century to century wherever excessive power is sought by the few at the expense of the many. In my judgment the people of no nation can lose their liberty so long as a Bill of Rights like ours survives. . . . I fear to see the consequences of the Court's practice of substituting its own concepts of decency and fundamental justice for the language of the Bill of Rights as its point of departure in interpreting and enforcing that Bill of Rights. If the choice must be between the selective process of the *Palko* decision applying some of the Bill of Rights to the states, or . . . applying none of them, I would choose the *Palko* selective process. But rather than accept either of these choices, I would follow what I believe was the original purpose of the Fourteenth Amendment—to extend to all the people of the nation the complete protection of the Bill of Rights. To hold that this Court can determine what, if any, provisions of the Bill of Rights will be enforced, and if so to what degree, is to frustrate the great design of a written Constitution. . . .

---

Moreover, these justices feared that selective incorporation gave judges too much discretion to pick and choose among rights according to their own subjective values.

**INCORPORATION AND FEDERALISM.** Advocates of selective incorporation argued, as had the Supreme Court in the *Slaughterhouse Cases,* that applying the entire Bill of Rights to the states would destroy the nature of federalism. The states should be free, they said, to be laboratories for new standards and procedures, not bound by the specific limitations of the Bill of Rights, which some saw as "an eighteenth-century straightjacket."

# The Incorporation of the Bill of Rights

| Year | Amendment | Provision Incorporated | Supreme Court Case |
|------|-----------|------------------------|--------------------|
| 1897 | Fifth | Just Compensation Clause | Chicago, Burlington, & Quincy Railroad Co. v. Chicago |
| 1925 | First | Freedom of speech | Gitlow v. New York |
| 1931 | First | Freedom of press | Near v. Minnesota |
| 1932 | Sixth | Right to counsel in capital felonies | Powell v. Alabama |
| 1937 | First | Freedom of assembly, petition | DeJonge v. Oregon |
| 1940 | First | Free Exercise Clause | Cantwell v. Connecticut |
| 1947 | First | Establishment Clause | Everson v. Board of Education |
| 1948 | Sixth | Right to public trial | In re Oliver |
| 1949 | Fourth | Protection from unreasonable searches, seizures | Wolf v. Colorado |
| 1961 | Fourth | Exclusionary rule | Mapp v. Ohio |
| 1962 | Eighth | Prohibition of cruel and unusual punishment | Robinson v. California |
| 1963 | Sixth | Right to counsel in noncapital felonies | Gideon v. Wainwright |
| 1964 | Fifth | Protection from self-incrimination | Malloy v. Hogan |
| 1965 | Sixth | Right to confront adverse witnesses | Pointer v. Texas |
| 1966 | Sixth | Right to an impartial jury | Parker v. Gladden |
| 1967 | Sixth | Right to speedy trial | Klopfer v. North Carolina |
| 1967 | Sixth | Right to obtain favorable witnesses | Washington v. Texas |
| 1968 | Sixth | Right to trial by jury in nonpetty criminal cases | Duncan v. Louisiana |
| 1969 | Fifth | Prohibition of double jeopardy | Benton v. Maryland |
| 1972 | Sixth | Right to counsel in imprisonable misdemeanor cases | Argersinger v. Hamlin |

However, proponents of total incorporation maintained that the specific language of the Bill of Rights was less of an intrusion upon the states than the subjective definition of due process used by the Supreme Court, which gave the states no standards to follow.

TWO SYSTEMS OF JUSTICE. Incorporation had the greatest impact on the criminal justice system, in part because much of the Bill of Rights protected defendants. As long as the Bill of Rights did not apply to the states, America had two systems of justice. Federal prosecutors were required to have search warrants, trial by jury, counsel for the defendant, and other rights protecting the accused, but state prosecutors were not. This double standard encouraged disobedience of the Constitution, as the Supreme Court noted in *Mapp v. Ohio* (1961) regarding the exclusionary rule:

> Presently, a federal prosecutor may make no use of evidence illegally seized, but a State's attorney across the street may, although he supposedly is operating under the enforceable prohibitions of the same [Fourth] Amendment. Thus the State, by admitting evidence unlawfully seized, serves to encourage disobedience to the Federal Constitution which it is bound to uphold. . . .

Eventually, the Supreme Court abolished the dual system of justice by incorporating almost all the provisions of the Bill of Rights dealing with the criminal process.

**RIGHTS NOT INCORPORATED.** Of the first eight amendments in the Bill of Rights, those provisions that have not been incorporated are: the Second Amendment's right to keep and bear arms; the Third Amendment's ban on quartering troops; the Fifth Amendment's right to a grand jury indictment; the Seventh Amendment's guarantee of trial by jury in civil cases; and the Eighth Amendment's prohibition of excessive bail and fines. The Supreme Court has not regarded these rights as "fundamental" enough to be a necessary part of due process.

Normally, when a right is incorporated, the same standard applies to the states as to the federal government. But although the Sixth Amendment right to a jury trial in criminal cases has been incorporated, states are not required to have twelve-person juries and unanimous verdicts in noncapital cases, although the federal government is. So at least a small vestige of the double standard in criminal justice still remains. But so much of the Bill of Rights was applied to the states under selective incorporation that, as Justice Black noted with pleasure, it came close to being total incorporation after all.

### SUBSTANTIVE DUE PROCESS

Besides incorporation, the Due Process Clause of the Fourteenth Amendment has also been used to uphold rights not specifically listed in the Constitution, as mentioned in the Ninth Amendment chapter. Using substantive due process, the Court determines which "liberty" or "property" interests are fundamental and cannot be denied by state law, even if the law is enacted according to fair procedures. From the 1880s to the 1930s, the Court mainly protected property interests; since the 1930s, the Court has focused on liberty interests.

**PROPERTY INTERESTS.** The rapid industrial growth of the late 1880s created many social problems—such as unsafe working conditions, long hours, low pay, and child labor. State legislatures passed laws attempting to correct these problems, under the rationale of promoting the general welfare. But critics of the laws, mainly businessmen, argued that the government should follow a *laissez-faire* policy of leaving the economy alone. Economic regulations, businessmen said, protected the "special interests" of the workers at the expense of property rights.

The Supreme Court upheld a *laissez-faire* economic policy in a series of cases. In the most notorious of these, *Lochner v. New York* (1905), the Court struck down a New York law that limited the work week of bakers to sixty hours. The law, said the Court, restricted bakers' "liberty of contract" to work for however long they pleased—even though bakeries, not bakers, were challenging the law.

In a famous dissent, Justice Oliver Wendell Holmes argued that "the Fourteenth Amendment does not enact Mr. Herbert Spencer's *Social Statics,*" referring to a popular author who advocated Social Darwinism—the theory that "survival of the fittest" applies in business as well as in nature. "A constitution," Holmes maintained, "is not intended to embody a particular economic theory, whether of paternalism . . . or of *laissez faire.*"

The *Lochner* decision became a symbol of the Supreme Court using substantive due process to impose its own subjective values. Critics argued that the Court was acting as a "super legislature," second-guessing the value choices of the people's elected representatives. The Court received so much criticism for its reversal of economic regulations, particularly during the New Deal, that it began to reverse itself. In *United States v. Carolene Products Company* (1938), the Court announced that economic regulations would be presumed constitutional and that a state had only to prove a "rational basis" for enacting the law—a very weak test. But in the famous Footnote 4 of that decision, the Court said that states must prove a "compelling interest"—a very difficult test—for laws affecting fundamental personal liberties.

**LIBERTY INTERESTS.** While the Supreme Court abandoned the field of economic regulation, it started to play a much greater role in protecting personal liberties. This role began in the 1920s, when the Court in *Meyer v. Nebraska* (1923) used substantive due process to strike down a

Nebraska law that forbade the teaching of languages other than English. And in *Pierce v. Society of Sisters* (1925), the Supreme Court struck down an Oregon law requiring parents to send their children to public schools, rather than private schools. In the 1950s, the Supreme Court also protected the right of international travel using substantive due process. More recently, the Court has upheld the right to privacy—including a woman's decision to have an abortion—and the right to die.

*The Right to Privacy.* As discussed in the Ninth Amendment chapter, the Supreme Court has used substantive due process under the Fourteenth Amendment to protect rights not specifically listed in the Constitution. The most famous of these rights is the right to privacy. In *Roe v. Wade* (1973), the Supreme Court ruled that the right to privacy was "founded on the Fourteenth Amendment's concept of personal liberty" and was "broad enough to encompass a woman's decision whether or not to terminate her pregnancy."

In *Roe,* the Court set forth guidelines for how states could regulate abortions by dividing a pregnancy into three-month periods, or trimesters. During the first trimester, the state cannot prohibit or regulate abortions. During the second trimester, the state's interest in the mother's health increases, so that it can regulate how abortions are performed but not outlaw them. During the third trimester, the state has an interest in the "potentiality of human life" as the fetus becomes more viable, or able to live outside the mother's body. States may prohibit third-trimester abortions, unless the life or health of the mother is endangered.

Since *Roe,* the Supreme Court has held that states and the federal government do not have to pay for abortions under Medicaid programs for poor people. The Court has also upheld laws that require minors to notify their parents before obtaining an abortion, as long as they can go before a judge instead of telling their parents if necessary. Generally, the Court has struck down laws that attempt to regulate abortions before the third trimester for reasons other than a woman's health. But in *Webster v. Reproductive Health Services* (1989), the Court's majority argued that a state's interest in protecting human life began before viability. Some justices suggested that *Roe* be overturned and that abortions be regulated by the states instead.

Many states took *Webster* as an invitation to pass more restrictive abortion laws. In *Planned Parenthood of Southeastern Pennsylvania v. Casey* (1992), the Supreme Court upheld *Roe v. Wade*—to the surprise of many experts—but it abandoned *Roe's* trimester framework. Rather, the Court held that states were free to regulate abortions as long as they did not place an "undue burden" on a woman's right to choose an abortion. The

Jane Roe Women's Center

*Norma McCorvey was the actual "Jane Roe" in* Roe v. Wade *(1973). Plaintiffs in controversial cases sometimes use the aliases "Doe" or "Roe" to protect their anonymity.*

Court defined "undue burden" as placing a "substantial obstacle in the path of a woman seeking an abortion of a nonviable fetus."

*The Right to Die.* Besides abortion, the Supreme Court has also used substantive due process to uphold the right to die. In *Cruzan v. Director, Missouri Department of Health* (1990), the Court held that the right to refuse medical treatment was a "liberty interest" protected by the Fourteenth Amendment. But the other issue in *Cruzan* was whether this right applied to a person who was incompetent, or unable to make choices for herself, like Nancy Beth Cruzan.

In 1983, Cruzan was critically injured in an automobile accident. Although paramedics were able to revive her, Nancy's brain was without oxygen for about twelve minutes. She seemed unresponsive to her surroundings and was unable to swallow food or water. Doctors surgically inserted a tube into her stomach through which she received food and water to keep her alive. By 1987, her parents were convinced that Nancy was in a "persistent vegetative state" and would never get better. They wanted to have the feeding tube removed and allow Nancy to die, arguing that Nancy would not have wanted to live another thirty years (which her doctors believed was possible) as a "vegetable." But Nancy's nurses, the hospital, and the state of Missouri opposed the action—even though her care cost the state more than $100,000 per year.

The trial court ruled for Nancy's parents, who argued that they were the best persons to exercise Nancy's right to die on her behalf, since Nancy could not do it herself. But the Missouri Supreme Court ruled that the state needed "clear and convincing evidence" of Nancy's wishes,

Tribune Media Services: Reprinted with permission.

and overturned the lower court. The U.S. Supreme Court held that, although the Fourteenth Amendment protected a right to refuse medical treatment, states could require strong evidence that an incompetent person actually wanted to die in such circumstances, rather than turning that decision over to relatives.

Nancy's parents sued again in Missouri court, producing evidence from several of her friends that in specific conversations Nancy had said she would not want to "live like a vegetable." The court ordered the feeding tube removed, and, almost eight years after her accident, Nancy died. The *Cruzan* case prompted many Americans to draft living wills stating that they do not want to be kept alive by medical technology if they are terminally ill or in a persistent vegetative state.

## EQUAL PROTECTION

. . . **NO STATE** shall . . . *deny to any person within its jurisdiction the* **EQUAL PROTECTION OF THE LAWS.**

This part of the Fourteenth Amendment is known as the Equal Protection Clause, which forbids unreasonable discrimination. All laws discriminate in some fashion; a law forbidding burglary discriminates against burglars, for instance. But under the Equal Protection Clause, a law must have a good reason for treating people differently, especially if it discriminates on the basis of race or gender. Since the Equal Protection Clause only applies to the states, the Supreme Court has ruled that the

Due Process Clause of the Fifth Amendment also prohibits unreasonable discrimination by the national government.

When a law draws distinctions between groups, the courts will normally defer to the government if it can show a "rational basis" for the legislation—a very weak test. However, if the law affects "suspect" classes (such as race) or "fundamental" rights (such as education or voting), it must undergo "strict scrutiny"—the most difficult test. The government must then prove a "compelling interest" in the law.

Early on, the Supreme Court established in the *Civil Rights Cases* (1883) that the Equal Protection Clause, like the Bill of Rights, limits only state action, not discrimination by private parties. Although the Court held in the *Slaughterhouse Cases* (1873) that the Equal Protection Clause applied only to blacks, in later decisions equal protection was extended to other groups as well.

## RACIAL DISCRIMINATION

Despite the Fourteenth Amendment, the Supreme Court for many years upheld racial segregation, arguing that separate facilities for whites and blacks could still be equal before the law. But during the 1950s, the Court reversed its position, striking down segregation in education and other areas of public life. Resistance to the Court's actions was great, however, and only a grassroots movement of thousands of Americans finally ensured that blacks would enjoy "equal protection of the laws" in reality, not just in court decisions.

**SEPARATE BUT EQUAL.** In the late nineteenth century, many southern states passed "Jim Crow" laws, named for a minstrel show character. These laws strictly segregated blacks from whites in schools, restaurants, streetcars, hospitals, and cemeteries. In *Plessy v. Ferguson* (1896), the Supreme Court upheld a Louisiana law that required segregated railroad cars. The Court ruled that as long as the facilities for blacks and whites were equal, segregation did not violate "equal protection of the laws," a doctrine known as "separate but equal."

Homer Plessy, the plaintiff, had argued that segregation laws imposed a "badge of inferiority" on blacks. But the Supreme Court responded: "If this be so, it is not by reason of anything found in the act, but solely because the colored race chooses to put that construction upon it." In a famous dissent, Justice John Marshall Harlan declared: "Our Constitution is colorblind, and neither knows nor tolerates classes among citizens."

The *Plessy* doctrine of "separate but equal" denied the reality that segregated facilities for blacks were hardly ever equal to those for whites. In education, particularly, black schools were vastly inferior to white schools. The National Association for the Advancement of Colored People (NAACP) began challenging "separate but equal" by demanding equal facilities for blacks in graduate schools. The NAACP won several cases that required blacks to be admitted to all-white graduate schools because the black schools were inferior and could not be made equal. The next step was challenging segregated elementary and secondary schools.

**SEPARATE IS INHERENTLY UNEQUAL.** In several cases across the country, the NAACP sought to overturn segregated public schools. In *Brown v. Board of Education of Topeka, Kansas* (1954), which combined all the NAACP cases, the Supreme Court overturned the *Plessy* doctrine of "separate but equal." Chief Justice Earl Warren, writing for the unanimous Court, declared: "We conclude that in the field of public education the doctrine of 'separate but equal' has no place. Separate educational facilities are inherently unequal."

In its decision, the Court cited a study by psychologist Kenneth Clark that asked black children to choose whether a black doll or a white doll was "better." The black children chose the white doll. The Court said such studies contradicted the *Plessy* holding that segregation laws did not treat blacks as inferior:

> To separate [school children] from others of similar age and qualifications solely because of their race generates a feeling of inferiority as to their status in the community that may affect their hearts and minds in a way unlikely ever to be undone. . . . Whatever may have been the extent of psychological knowledge at the time of *Plessy v. Ferguson,* this finding is amply supported by modern authority.

**"ALL DELIBERATE SPEED."** Integrating the nation's public schools was an enormous task. The Supreme Court held hearings on how to implement *Brown* and in 1955 ruled that desegregation was to begin "with all deliberate speed." However, many school districts were more deliberate than speedy.

In Little Rock, Arkansas, schools were still not integrated three years after the *Brown* decision. A federal judge ordered that nine black students be admitted to Central High School in the fall of 1957, but Governor Orval Faubus surrounded the school with the Arkansas National Guard to prevent integration, citing threats of violence. Faubus removed the

Supreme Court Historical Society

*As head of the NAACP Legal Defense Fund, Thurgood Marshall won twenty-nine of the thirty-two cases he argued before the Supreme Court, including* Brown. *In 1967, Marshall became the first black justice of the Supreme Court.*

UPI/Bettmann

*Elizabeth Eckford is threatened by a mob as she attempts to integrate Little Rock Central High School in 1957.*

troops under a federal court order, but a mob of angry white residents threatened the "Little Rock Nine" when they enrolled. President Dwight Eisenhower sent in the 101st Airborne Division of the U.S. Army to ensure the safety of the students. But the Little Rock public schools closed for the 1958/59 school year, until the federal courts reopened them in August 1959.

Across the country, other school districts resisted integration. Finally, in 1969, the Supreme Court ruled that "all deliberate speed" had come to an end. Schools were to be integrated immediately. In 1971, the Court upheld busing as a method of achieving integration. The Court also struck down segregation in other areas besides education—including recreational facilities, transportation, and prisons and jails—and it overturned laws barring interracial marriages. However, in the 1990s, the Supreme Court issued several decisions allowing school districts to end court-ordered desegration plans, even if their schools still had racial disparities.

# The Courage of Their Convictions: Fannie Lou Hamer

The youngest of twenty children of Mississippi sharecroppers, Fannie Lou Hamer (1917-1977) became a national leader of the civil rights movement. Her motto was, "I'm sick and tired of being sick and tired."

In her autobiography, *To Praise Our Bridges,* Fannie Lou Hamer described when, at the age of 44, she first tried to register to vote:

> I . . . stayed on the plantation until 1962, when I went down to the courthouse in Indianola to register to vote. That happened because I went to a mass meeting one night.
>
> Until then I'd never heard of no mass meeting and I didn't know that a Negro could register and vote. . . . When [the civil rights workers] asked for those to raise their hands who'd go down to the courthouse the next day, I raised mine. Had it up high as I could get it. I guess if I'd had any sense I'd a-been a little scared, but what was the point of being scared. The only thing they could do to me was kill me and it seemed like they'd been trying to do that a little bit at a time ever since I could remember.

When she tried to register to vote, Fannie Lou Hamer was forced to take a literacy test, in which she had to explain one of the 286 sections of the Mississippi state constitution. Whites were often coached on their answers. Hamer failed the test, which asked about *de facto* laws. "I knowed as much about a *de facto* law as a horse knows about Christmas Day," said Hamer later.

*Fannie Lou Hamer testifies at the 1964 Democratic National Convention.*

On the way home, police stopped the old school bus in which Hamer and others who had tried to register were riding. The police fined the driver $100 because the bus was "too yellow" and could be mistaken for a real school bus. The bus had often carried plantation workers without any trouble—until those same people wanted to vote.

When she returned home, Fannie Lou Hamer was forced to leave the plantation, and her husband was eventually fired. Hamer began to work as a civil rights organizer. As she said: "There was nothing they could do to me. They couldn't fire me, because I didn't have a job. They couldn't put me out of my house, because I didn't have one. There was nothing they could take from me any longer."

In 1963, Fannie Lou Hamer successfully registered to vote on her third try. She helped organize the Mississippi Freedom Democratic party (MFDP), which held alternative elections to the all-white Mississippi Democratic party. At the 1964 Democratic National Convention in Atlantic City, New Jersey, the MFDP sought to be seated as the official Democratic delegation from Mississippi.

Fannie Lou Hamer testified on national television. "If the Freedom Democratic party is not seated now, I question America," she said. "Is this America, the land of the free and the home of the brave, where we have to sleep with our telephones off the hook because our lives be threatened daily, because we want to live as decent human beings in America?" Hamer also described beatings she had received for attending voter registration meetings. President Lyndon Johnson scheduled a news conference to interrupt

*I'm sick and tired of being sick and tired.*

Hamer's televised testimony because he thought it might endanger his reelection.

Known for her powerful voice, Fannie Lou Hamer led the MFDP delegation in freedom songs on the convention floor. One reporter asked Hamer if she wanted equality with the white man. "No," she replied, "I don't want to go down that low. I want the true democracy that'll raise me and that white man up—raise America up."

The MFDP delegates were not seated in 1964. But Fannie Lou Hamer ran for Congress in an MFDP counterelection to the regular Democratic primary. Although Hamer was not seated in Congress, the U.S. House of Representatives did investigate elections in Mississippi—and the federal courts eventually ruled them illegal. At the 1968 Democratic National Convention, Fannie Lou Hamer and her delegation from Mississippi were seated, to a standing ovation. From the cotton fields of Mississippi to the arenas of national politics, Fannie Lou Hamer was sick and tired no more.

**THE CIVIL RIGHTS MOVEMENT.** Equal rights for blacks were not gained by court decisions alone. Thousands of people across the nation risked their lives—and many died—to make sure those court decisions were enforced. The *Brown* case mobilized nationwide opposition to segregation. Initially, the focus of this opposition was the South, where most blacks lived, but the civil rights movement eventually spread to the North as well.

Rosa Parks sparked the civil rights movement in 1955 when she refused to give up her bus seat to a white man in Montgomery, Alabama. Her action began a yearlong bus boycott by blacks, led by Dr. Martin Luther King, Jr., a young minister. After his success in Montgomery, King became a national leader of the civil rights movement, using nonviolent tactics such as boycotts and demonstrations to confront racial injustice.

The highlight of the civil rights movement was the March on Washington in August 1963. More than 200,000 people met at the Lincoln Memorial in Washington, D.C., to demonstrate for stronger civil rights laws. In his famous speech, "I Have a Dream," King noted that although President Lincoln had issued the Emancipation Proclamation freeing slaves 100 years earlier, blacks still did not have equal rights under the law. "I have a dream," King said, "that my four little children will one day live in a nation where they will

UPI/Bettmann

*Dr. Martin Luther King, Jr., led the March on Washington in 1963 to support civil rights.*

not be judged by the color of their skin, but the content of their character."

The March on Washington spearheaded the passage of the Civil Rights Act of 1964, which outlawed discrimination based on race in public accommodations. The act also banned discrimination based on race, religion, or sex in employment and in programs that received federal funds. Section 5 of the Fourteenth Amendment gives Congress the power to pass civil rights laws enforcing the amendment. Congress can also use its commerce power under Article I to prohibit discrimination in interstate commerce, as held in *Heart of Atlanta Motel v. United States* (1964). Congress has passed other civil rights laws since 1964 based on these powers.

**AFFIRMATIVE ACTION.** Civil rights laws do nothing to remedy the effects of past discrimination. For example, a black person may be severely disadvantaged in the job market because of unequal education even though formal discrimination has been outlawed. Therefore, the federal government has enacted a policy of affirmative action, which requires those who receive federal funds to take positive steps to provide training and job opportunities for those who have traditionally been discriminated against in the past—such as blacks, other racial minorities, and women.

Some people charge that affirmative action leads to reverse discrimination, because women or racial minorities are hired over white males who may be better qualified. But the Supreme Court upheld affirmative action to some extent in *Regents of the University of California v. Bakke* (1978). The university's medical school at Davis reserved a fixed number of slots for nonwhite students each year. Alan Bakke, a white male, had twice been denied admission to medical school, even though less qualified nonwhites had been admitted. Bakke charged that the university's quota system violated the Equal Protection Clause.

The Supreme Court ruled that a strict quota system, in which race was the sole factor for admission, violated the Fourteenth Amendment. But the Court also held that the university could consider race as one of many factors in an admissions decision. As Justice Harry Blackmun noted: "In order to get beyond racism, we must first take account of race. There is no other way. And in order to treat some persons equally, we must treat them differently. We cannot—we dare not—let the Equal Protection Clause perpetrate racial supremacy."

Since *Bakke,* the Court has issued many decisions that curtail affirmative action programs. Most of these decisions have been based on federal statutes that prohibit job discrimination, rather than the Fourteenth Amendment. Generally, the Court has held that affirmative action in employment must result from specific acts of discrimination against specific individuals, rather than a general claim that blacks and women have been discriminated against in the past.

**SUSPECT CLASSIFICATIONS.** The Supreme Court has held that distinctions based on race are inherently "suspect." Consequently, whenever a law or a government action classifies people on the basis of race, the Court requires "strict scrutiny"—the most rigorous test. The government must show a "compelling interest" in the classification, which is very difficult to prove.

In *Richmond v. Croson* (1989), the Court ruled that strict scrutiny applies to programs that discriminate against *any* race, not just those races that have traditionally been discriminated against in the past. Thus, an affirmative action program must prove a "compelling interest" for discriminating against white men. And in *Miller v. Johnson* (1995), the Supreme Court held that race may not be the dominant factor in drawing congressional districts, even to comply with the Voting Rights Act.

However, in at least one notorious instance, the Court allowed racial classifications. During World War II, Japanese-Americans were forced to obey certain curfews and to abandon their homes on the West Coast, even though none of them were specifically charged with disloyalty or spying. In *Korematsu v. United States* (1944), the Supreme Court upheld the relocation order. Said the Court, "pressing public necessity may

Library of Congress

*Japanese-Americans were forcibly removed from their homes on the West Coast and sent to relocation camps during World War II.*

sometimes justify racial restrictions." More than forty years later, Congress voted to compensate the Japanese-Americans for their lost homes and businesses.

## OTHER FORMS OF DISCRIMINATION

Besides race, the Equal Protection Clause is also at issue in other types of discrimination. These include discrimination based on gender, alienage, and poverty. In addition, the Equal Protection Clause is involved when rural people are more represented than urban people in state legislatures.

**SEX DISCRIMINATION.** The Fourteenth Amendment mentions "persons," not men or women. Sex discrimination was first challenged in *Bradwell v. Illinois* (1873). The Supreme Court upheld a state law that prohibited women from practicing law. Said one justice:

> Man is, or should be, woman's protector and defender. The natural and proper timidity and delicacy of the female sex evidently unfits it for many of the occupations of civil life. . . . The harmony . . . of interests . . . which belong . . . to the family institution is repugnant to the ideas of a woman adopting a distinct and independent career from that of her husband. . . .

U.S. Army

*Although women may enlist in the armed forces, Congress may prohibit women from being drafted or serving in combat without violating the Due Process Clause of the Fifth Amendment.*

But during the 1970s, the Supreme Court issued a number of decisions that struck down sex-based distinctions. As the Court noted in *Frontiero v. Richardson* (1973):

> There can be no doubt that our nation has had a long and unfortunate history of sex discrimination. Traditionally, such discrimination was rationalized by an attitude of "romantic paternalism" which, in practical effect, put women, not on a pedestal, but in a cage.

In *Frontiero,* the Court for the first time struck down a federal law that discriminated on the basis of gender, using the Due Process Clause of the Fifth Amendment. The law had given certain medical and housing allowances to a male soldier for his wife and dependents, but not to a female soldier and her husband.

Some of the laws overturned by the Court discriminated against women, while others gave women preferential treatment. The Court has struck down

- a state law that preferred men over women as administrators of estates;
- a state law forbidding the sale of beer to men under 21, but to women under 18;

- a provision in the federal Social Security law that gave benefits to families with unemployed fathers, but not with unemployed mothers;
- a state law allowing unwed mothers, but not unwed fathers, to block adoption of their children;
- a state rule giving women smaller retirement pensions than men who paid the same premiums, on the grounds that women lived longer; and
- a regulation forbidding men to be admitted to a nursing program at a state-run university for women.

Not all sex-based classifications are unconstitutional, however. The Supreme Court has upheld

- a state law forbidding women to be guards in all-male prisons;
- statutory rape laws, which punish a man if he has sex with a girl under 18, even if she is a willing partner; and
- federal laws that require men, but not women, to register for the draft and exclude women from future drafts.

Discrimination based on gender is not inherently "suspect," as is race. Therefore, the Supreme Court uses a less strict test for gender classifications than "compelling interest," but more strict than "rational basis." Supporters of the Equal Rights Amendment, which was proposed by Congress in 1972 and defeated in 1982, argued that it would have made sex discrimination just as unconstitutional as race discrimination. Currently, however, sex discrimination is more permissible than race discrimination under the Fourteenth Amendment.

**ALIENS.** The Equal Protection Clause protects "persons," not citizens. Therefore, the Supreme Court has held that states may not discriminate against legal immigrants in most cases—although Congress can, since it has absolute power over the people it admits to the country. States may not forbid aliens to practice law or deny them welfare benefits. But states may prohibit aliens from voting, serving on juries, running for public office, or teaching elementary and secondary school—since these are all linked to the practice or promotion of citizenship.

The Equal Protection Clause even applies in some instances to aliens who are in the country illegally. In *Plyler v. Doe* (1982), the Supreme Court struck down a Texas law prohibiting illegal aliens from attending public school. The law, said the Court, "imposes a lifetime of hardship on a discrete class of children not accountable for their disabling status."

Smithsonian Institution

*The proposed Equal Rights Amendment stated: "Equality of rights under the law shall not be denied or abridged by the United States nor by any state on account of sex."*

"Great Scott! We've lost our vote!"

Sanders in the *Kansas City Star*

**POVERTY.** The Supreme Court has held that "poverty standing alone is not a suspect classification." However, the Court has also prohibited the states from requiring fees that would deny poor people certain basic rights, such as automatically imprisoning a poor person who cannot pay a fine or requiring a poll tax to vote.

In *San Antonio School District v. Rodriguez* (1973), residents of poor school districts challenged a Texas law that based school funding on taxes within each district, rather than distributing funds equally statewide. Said the Court:

> At least where wealth is involved, the Equal Protection Clause does not require absolute equality or precisely equal advantages. Nor indeed, in view of the infinite variables affecting the educational process, can any system assure equal quality of education except in the most relative sense.

But the Texas Supreme Court later ruled that education funds must be distributed equally across the state and ordered the legislature to come up with a new funding formula. In 1991, Texas enacted a "Robin Hood" law implementing the court's ruling. Thus, a state supreme court can recognize a right under a state constitution even when it is not recognized under the U.S. Constitution by the U.S. Supreme Court.

**RURAL VS. URBAN.** State legislatures traditionally had the power to determine the apportionment, or allocation and distribution, of legislative seats. Many state constitutions required that the legislature reapportion itself based on changes in population. However, as population shifted from rural to urban areas, legislators were reluctant to redraw district lines and put themselves out of office. Consequently, rural areas were over-represented in state legislatures and urban areas were underrepresented—so that a rural person's vote could be worth as much as forty-three times that of an urban person.

The courts would normally not get involved in reapportionment disputes, holding that such cases were "political questions" to be resolved by the legislatures. But in *Baker v. Carr* (1962), the Supreme Court ruled that federal courts could hear challenges to reapportionment plans under the Equal Protection Clause. And in *Reynolds v. Sims* (1964), the Court applied the "one person, one vote" rule to both houses of a state legislature. Population, said the Court, was the only basis for apportionment of legislative seats:

> Legislators represent people, not trees or acres. Legislators are elected by voters, not farms or cities or economic interests. . . . The Equal Protection Clause requires that the seats in both houses of a bicameral state legislature must be apportioned on a population basis.

## A NEW CONSTITUTION

In the words of Justice Thurgood Marshall: "While the Union survived the Civil War, the Constitution did not. In its place arose a new, more promising basis for justice and equality, the Fourteenth Amendment." Under the Fourteenth Amendment, the Bill of Rights was applied to the states, vastly expanding the reach of constitutional law. And under the Fourteenth Amendment, blacks and other Americans began to enjoy "equal protection of the laws." The Fourteenth Amendment was not just another amendment to the Constitution; it made possible a new Constitution.

*THE BILL of RIGHTS*

Amendment I *Congress shall make no law respecting an establishment of religion, or prohibiting the free exercise thereof; or abridging the freedom of speech, or of the press; or the right of the people peaceably to assemble, and to petition the Government for a redress of grievances.* Amendment II *A well regulated Militia, being necessary to the security of a free State, the right of the people to keep and bear Arms, shall not be infringed.* Amendment III *No Soldier shall, in time of peace be quartered in any house, without the consent of the Owner, nor in time of war, but in a manner to be prescribed by law.* Amendment IV *The right of the people to be secure in their persons, houses, papers, and effects, against unreasonable searches and seizures, shall not be violated, and no Warrants shall issue, but upon probable cause, supported by Oath or affirmation, and particularly describing the place to be searched, and the persons or things to be seized.* Amendment V *No person shall*

# To die for.

*be held to answer for a capital, or otherwise infamous crime, unless on a presentment or indictment of a Grand Jury, except in cases arising in the land or naval forces, or in the Militia, when in actual service in time of War or public danger; nor shall any person be subject for the same offense to be twice put in jeopardy of life or limb; nor shall be compelled in any criminal case to be a witness against himself, nor be deprived of life, liberty, or property, without due process of law; nor shall private property be taken for public use, without just compensation.* Amendment VI *In all criminal prosecutions, the accused shall enjoy the right to a speedy and public trial, by an impartial jury of the State and district wherein the crime shall have been committed, which district shall have been previously ascertained by law, and to be informed of the nature and cause of the accusation; to be confronted with the witnesses against him; to have compulsory process for obtaining witnesses in his favor, and to have the Assistance of Counsel for his defense.* Amendment VII *In Suits at common law, where the value in controversy shall exceed twenty dollars, the right of trial by jury shall be preserved, and no fact tried to jury, shall be otherwise reexamined in any Court of the United States, than according to the rules of the common law.* Amendment VIII *Excessive bail shall not be required, nor excessive fines imposed, nor cruel and unusual punishments inflicted.* Amendment IX *The enumeration in the Constitution, of certain rights, shall not be construed to deny or disparage others retained by the people.* Amendment X *The powers not delegated to the United States by the Constitution, nor prohibited by it to the States, are reserved to the States respectively, or to the people.*

*PREPARED by THE AMERICAN BAR ASSOCIATION*
*IN CELEBRATION of LAW DAY USA*

# RIGHTS *in the Future*

Since the Bill of Rights was ratified in 1791, seventeen other amendments have been added to the U.S. Constitution. Six more amendments were proposed but never ratified. More than 10,000 suggested amendments have been introduced in Congress. What amendments might future generations of Americans add?

As the Bill of Rights begins its third century, the winds of freedom are blowing around the world. In China, in the republics of the former Soviet Union, in Eastern Europe, people are demanding their rights. Experts in U.S. constitutional law have been helping newly democratic nations write their own constitutions. The U.S. Bill of Rights serves as a reference point, if not always as a model. In 1990, when Americans asked Soviet officials who were revising their constitution how they would deal with human rights, one replied: "For us it will be in the body of the constitution. It will not be an amendment."

But no constitution, no bill of rights alone can guarantee human freedom. Only the people themselves can do that. People like Fannie Lou Hamer, Clarence Earl Gideon, Dollree Mapp, Mary Beth Tinker, Michael Hardwick, Bridget Mergens, and Ishmael Jaffree. People who are willing to risk their security—and sometimes their lives—to make the Bill of Rights not just empty promises on paper, but a living reality. As long as some Americans are stubborn and daring enough to follow "the courage of their convictions," the rest of the nation will continue to enjoy its freedom.

# Glossary

**accommodationists**—those who believe that government must accommodate, or make allowances for, the role of religion in society

**accusatory system**—system of justice in which the government must find evidence to prove its case

**actual malice**—when a false statement is made knowingly or in reckless disregard of the truth; standard required to prove libel in cases involving public figures

**adversary system**—system of justice that relies on a battle between two opposing parties to determine the truth

**affirmative action**—positive action to remedy past discrimination, generally by giving preferences to racial minorities and women over white men

**aggravating circumstances**—factors that make a crime more serious

**apportionment**—the allocation and distribution of seats in a legislature

**arraignment**—court proceeding at which the defendant enters a plea

**bail**—money bond or property posted by the accused to allow pretrial release from jail and ensure that he will appear at trial

**bill of attainder**—legislative act that convicts a person of a crime without a trial

**black codes**—laws that regulated the lives of newly freed slaves

**capital**—cases or crimes that involve the death penalty

**censorship**—government's denial of free expression

**challenge for cause**—an attorney's ability to exclude a potential juror for bias

**charge**—the judge's advice to the jury about the law of a case

**chilling effect**—discouraging citizens from exercising their rights

**civil law**—branch of law that deals with disputes between private parties, such as contracts and injuries to persons and property

**common law**—law based on customs and court decisions, but not written in a legal code

**compelling interest**—what the government must prove under the strict scrutiny test to have a law upheld; very difficult to prove

**compensatory damages**—money reimbursing the plaintiff for actual harm done, such as medical expenses or lost business

**complexity exception**—argument that juries should not be used in complex civil cases

**concurring opinion**—written explanation of the views of one or more judges that supports the decision of a majority of the court but offers different reasons for reaching that decision

**constitution**—the most important and most fundamental law of a society

**constitutional democracy**—a government in which the people rule, but are limited by a constitution

**constitutional law**—law based on a constitution; under the U.S. Constitution, "the supreme law of the land"

**content-neutral**—requirement that the government cannot forbid speech based on its content or the nature of the message

**criminal law**—branch of law under which the government punishes a person for a crime

**cross-examine**—to ask questions challenging the testimony of witnesses

**curtilage**—the area immediately surrounding a home

**defamation**—damaging another person's reputation through falsehoods

**defendant**—a person accused of a crime in criminal law or against whom a claim is made in civil law

**delegated powers**—the powers, both expressed and implied, that were delegated to the national government by the states and the people

**democracy**—a form of government in which the majority rules

**dissenting opinion**—written explanation of the views of one or more judges that disagrees with the decision reached by a majority of the court

**double jeopardy**—trying a defendant twice for the same offense

**dual federalism**—doctrine that views the national government and the states as equals

**due process**—requirement that the government be fair in its actions

**Elastic Clause**—phrase in the U.S. Constitution giving Congress the power to make all laws "necessary and proper" to carry out its expressed powers; also known as the Necessary and Proper Clause

**eminent domain**—the government's power to take private property for public use

**enumerated rights**—rights specifically listed in the Constitution

*ex parte*—involving only one party to a case, such as a grand jury proceeding

*ex post facto* **law**—law that makes an action criminal after the fact

**exclusionary rule**—legal rule that forbids illegally seized evidence from being admitted at trial

**executive privilege**—doctrine that in some circumstances the president may refuse to testify before Congress or appear in court

**expressed powers**—powers specifically listed in the Constitution; also known as enumerated powers

**federalism**—sharing of power by the national government and the states

**felonies**—serious crimes punishable by prison sentences of more than one year

**felony-murder rule**—legal rule that allows accomplices to be convicted for a murder, even if they did not actually pull the trigger, when the murder was part of a serious crime such as robbery or kidnapping

**general warrants**—orders authorizing government agents to search wherever and whomever they wish

**grand jury**—(French for "large jury") a group of citizens, usually twenty-three, that investigates the evidence of a crime and decides whether or not the accused should be prosecuted

**habeas corpus**—(Latin for "having the body") a requirement that an officer who has custody of a prisoner show cause why the prisoner should not be released; designed to prevent illegal arrests and unlawful imprisonments

**hearsay**—testimony in which one person testifies about something someone else said, rather than something that person actually experienced

**heckler's veto**—the ability of a hostile onlooker to disrupt an otherwise peaceful assembly or speech

**implied powers**—those powers not specifically listed in the Constitution that are implied by the expressed powers; based on the Elastic Clause

**incorporation**—applying provisions of the Bill of Rights to the states through the Due Process Clause of the Fourteenth Amendment

**indictment**—formal criminal charge issued when a grand jury believes the prosecutor has presented enough evidence to justify a trial

**information**—a sworn statement by a prosecutor that there is sufficient evidence for a trial

**injunctions**—court orders prohibiting a specified action

**inquisitional system**—system of justice in which the accused is questioned under oath to determine if he is guilty

**interposition**—doctrine under which states interpose their sovereignty to declare an act of the federal government null and void; also known as nullification

**Jim Crow laws**—laws that segregated blacks from whites

**judicial activism**—legal philosophy in which the courts willingly overturn precedents and statutes

**judicial restraint**—legal philosophy in which the courts refrain from overturning precedents and statutes

**judicial review**—power of the courts to declare a law unconstitutional

**just compensation**—fair payment when the government takes private property for public use

**legal rights**—rights that come from laws, statutes, and court decisions

**libel**—defamation through the written word

**majority opinion**—written explanation of a decision made by a majority of the judges of a court

**militia**—citizens who defend their communities in emergencies

**misdemeanors**—minor crimes punishable by small fines or short jail terms

**mitigating circumstances**—factors that lessen the seriousness of a crime

**national police power**—using the federal power over interstate commerce to regulate health and welfare issues traditionally reserved to the states by the Tenth Amendment

**nationalism**—the view that the national government is supreme over the states

**natural rights**—rights that people have simply by being human

**nontestimonial evidence**—physical evidence such as fingerprints, handwriting samples, fingernail clippings, and blood specimens

**nullification**—doctrine under which states have the authority to declare an act of the federal government null and void; also known as interposition

**obscenity**—anything that depicts sex or nudity in a way that violates society's standards of decency

**original jurisdiction**—authority of a court to hear and decide a case for the first time

**overbreadth**—when a law is written too broadly; for example, restricting protected speech as well as unprotected speech

***parens patriae***—philosophy that in juvenile proceedings the court is acting as a "benevolent parent," not a prosecutor, and is trying to rehabilitate instead of punish

**parochaid**—aid to parochial, or religious, schools

**particularity requirement**—requirement that a warrant specifically describe the place to be searched and the persons or evidence to be seized

**peremptory challenge**—an attorney's ability to exclude a potential juror without giving any reason

**petit jury**—(French for "small jury") a trial jury that usually consists of six to twelve persons and decides whether the accused is guilty of the crime

**plaintiff**—the person who claims to be injured in a civil case

**police power**—one of the primary reserved powers; allows a state to regulate the public's health, safety, morals, and welfare

**precedent**—a previous court decision that is usually binding on related cases that follow

**prerogative courts**—special courts created by English rulers during the sixteenth and seventeenth centuries that did not use juries

**presentment**—formal criminal charge issued by a grand jury without going through a prosecutor

**preventive detention**—denying bail for persons accused of serious offenses based on predictions of their future criminal conduct

**prior restraint**—censorship of a work before it is published

**probable cause**—reasonable grounds for an arrest or a search

**procedural due process**—requirement that the way laws are carried out must be fair

**proportionality**—rule under the Eighth Amendment that punishment must be directly related to the crime committed

**public forum**—a place such as a street or park that is traditionally used for freedom of speech and other First Amendment rights

**punitive damages**—damages above and beyond the actual economic loss to the plaintiff used to punish the defendant

**pure speech**—spoken words alone, such as debates and public meetings

**quarter**—to provide food and housing for soldiers

**rational basis**—the least difficult test for a law to pass; if the government can make any argument at all in favor of the law, it will be upheld

**reserved powers**—the powers kept by the states under federalism

**retribution**—paying a criminal back for the harm done

**reverse discrimination**—argument that affirmative action programs discriminate against white men who are better qualified than racial minorities or women

**sectionalism**—putting regional interests ahead of national interests

**sedition**—urging of resistance to lawful authority or rebellion against the government

**selective incorporation**—incorporating the Bill of Rights piecemeal, rather than all at once

**self-incrimination**—forcing a defendant to testify against herself

**separationists**—those who believe in strict separation between church and state

**sequester**—to isolate jurors from the community and the news media

**shield laws**—laws that protect reporters against revealing confidential information

**slander**—defamation through the spoken word

**sovereign**—having supreme authority

**speech-plus**—speech combined with action, such as demonstrations

**standing army**—permanent army composed of professional soldiers

**Star Chamber**—the best-known English prerogative court, which held its proceedings in secret and used an inquisitional system

**state action**—doctrine that the government or its agents must act in order for the Constitution and the Bill of Rights to apply

**states' rights**—the powers of the states as sovereign governments

**statutory law**—the written codes or statutes created by legislatures

**strict scrutiny**—the most difficult test for a law to pass; used by courts in cases involving fundamental rights and suspect classes

**subpoena**—(Latin for "under penalty") a court order requiring a witness to testify and/or turn over relevant documents to the court

**substantive due process**—requirement that the laws themselves must be fair, not just their procedures

**Supremacy Clause**—phrase in Article VI that makes the Constitution and laws of the United States "the supreme law of the land"

**suspect class**—a classification, such as race, that receives the highest form of protection under the Equal Protection Clause

**symbolic speech**—conduct that conveys a message in itself, without spoken words; also known as expressive conduct

**total incorporation**—incorporating the Bill of Rights all at once, rather than piecemeal

**unenumerated rights**—rights not specifically listed in the Constitution

**vagueness**—when a law is not clear and specific enough for reasonable people to know what action is forbidden

**venires**—groups of potential jurors

**venue**—the location of a trial

**voir dire**—process in which the prosecuting and defense attorneys question jurors about their personal biases and their knowledge of a case

**warrant**—court order authorizing some action, such as an arrest or a search

**writ of assistance**—a type of general warrant allowing British customs officials to search colonial homes and businesses for smuggled goods

**writ of mandamus**—(Latin for "we command") court order forcing government officials to carry out their duties

# For Further Reading

The following books and articles will provide information for further research on some of the issues covered in *The Bill of Rights: A User's Guide*.

Alderman, Ellen, and Caroline Kennedy. *In Our Defense: The Bill of Rights in Action*. New York: William Morrow and Co., Inc., 1991.

Barker, Lucius J., and Twiley W. Barker, Jr. *Civil Liberties and the Constitution*, 6th ed. Englewood Cliffs, N.J.: Prentice Hall, 1990.

Barnett, Randy E., ed. *The Rights Retained by the People: The History and Meaning of the Ninth Amendment*. Fairfax, Va.: George Mason University Press, 1989.

Brant, Irving. *The Bill of Rights: Its Origin and Meaning*. Indianapolis: Bobbs-Merrill Company, Inc., 1965.

Chandler, Ralph C., Richard A. Enslen, and Peter G. Renstrom. *The Constitutional Law Dictionary*. Vol. I. Santa Barbara, Calif.: ABC-Clio, Inc., 1985.

Douglas, William O. *A Living Bill of Rights*. New York: Anti-Defamation League, 1961.

Halbrook, Stephen P. *That Every Man Be Armed: The Evolution of a Constitutional Right*. Albuquerque: University of New Mexico Press, 1984.

Hall, Kermit L., ed. *By and For the People: Constitutional Rights in American History*. Arlington Heights, Ill.: Harlan Davidson, Inc., 1991.

Hentoff, Nat. *Free Speech for Me—But Not for Thee: How the American Left and Right Relentlessly Censor Each Other*. New York: Harper Collins, 1992.

Irons, Peter. *The Courage of Their Convictions: Sixteen Americans Who Fought Their Way to the Supreme Court*. New York: The Free Press, 1988.

Kammen, Michael. *A Machine That Would Go of Itself: The Constitution in American Culture*. New York: Alfred A. Knopf, 1986.

Kammen, Michael, ed. *The Origins of the American Constitution: A Documentary History*. New York: Penguin Books, 1986.

Levinson, Sanford. "The Embarrassing Second Amendment." *The Yale Law Journal*. Vol. 99, No. 3 (December 1989), pp. 637-659.

Levy, Leonard W., Kenneth L. Karst, and Dennis J. Mahoney, eds. *Encyclopedia of the American Constitution.* New York: Macmillan, 1986.

Lewis, Anthony. *Gideon's Trumpet.* New York: Vintage Books, 1964.

_____. *Make No Law: The Sullivan Case and the First Amendment.* New York: Random House, 1991.

Lieberman, Jethro K. *The Enduring Constitution: A Bicentennial Perspective.* Saint Paul, Minn.: West Publishing Company, 1987.

Lockard, Duane, and Walter F. Murphy. *Basic Cases in Constitutional Law,* 2nd ed. Washington, D.C.: Congressional Quarterly Inc., 1987.

Mason, Alpheus Thomas, and Donald Grier Stephenson, Jr. *American Constitutional Law: Introductory Essays and Selected Cases,* 9th ed. Englewood Cliffs, N.J.: Prentice Hall, 1990.

Mee, Charles L., Jr. *The Genius of the People.* New York: Harper & Row, 1987.

Rubel, David. *Fannie Lou Hamer: From Sharecropping to Politics.* Englewood Cliffs, N.J.: Silver Burdett Press, Inc., 1990.

Rutland, Robert Allen. *The Birth of the Bill of Rights, 1776-1791,* rev. ed. Boston: Northeastern University Press, 1983.

Schwartz, Bernard. *The Bill of Rights: A Documentary History.* New York: Chelsea House, 1971.

Urofsky, Melvin I. *A March of Liberty: A Constitutional History of the United States.* New York: Alfred A. Knopf, 1988.

Veit, Helen E., Kenneth R. Bowling, and Charlene Bangs Bickford, eds. *Creating the Bill of Rights: The Documentary Record from the First Federal Congress.* Baltimore: The Johns Hopkins University Press, 1991.

Wagman, Robert J. *The First Amendment Book.* New York: Pharos Books, 1991.

Williams, Juan. *Eyes on the Prize: America's Civil Rights Years, 1954-1965.* New York: Viking, 1987.

# Case Index

# Subject Index

## ALSO FROM CLOSE UP PUBLISHING . . .

Now that you have finished *The Bill of Rights: A User's Guide*, why not try our other titles on American government and history? Thousands of readers across the nation rely on Close Up's timely, unbiased treatment of domestic and global policy issues in our respected collection of books, teacher's resources, videotapes, and simulation activities.

## Bill of Rights Video Series

 Each of these four engaging videos explores personal, legal, and constitutional questions relating to a particular Bill of Rights issue. Each 30-minute documentary features personal stories on opposing sides of the issue along with the insights of constitutional experts.

> *For Which It Stands: Flag Burning and the First Amendment*, 1992.
> *To Keep and Bear Arms: Gun Control and the Second Amendment*, 1994.
> *One Nation Under God? School Prayer and the First Amendment*, 1995.
> *Sentenced to Die: Capital Punishment and the Eighth Amendment*, 1995.

**$39.95 each. A FREE teacher's guide accompanies each video.**

## *Ordinary Americans: U.S. History Through the Eyes of Everyday People*

 Read about the birth of a nation, the start of a democracy, and the development of a people in *Ordinary Americans*. This unique anthology of nearly 200 primary source documents includes letters, diary entries, and other writings by the people who witnessed and participated in events throughout U.S. history. Readings are organized by time period from the pre-Columbian era to the 1990s. More than half of the activities, lessons, and handouts in the 190-page teacher's guide feature multicultural themes.

**1994. $16.95. Teacher's guide, $15.95.**

## *Current Issues: Critical Issues Confronting the Nation and the World*

 **Standard Edition and new Lower-Reading-Level Edition**

Updated annually, *Current Issues* presents a concise synopsis of ten domestic and ten foreign policy issues with thorough background information not found in newspapers and magazines. Featuring the same content as the standard edition, the new lower-reading-level edition includes highlighted vocabulary words and definitions as well as shorter sentence structures. The *Current Issues Teacher's Guide* provides enough lesson plans, activities, reproducible handouts, and unit tests for up to 21 weeks of teaching.

**Updated annually. $12.95. Teacher's guide, suitable for both texts, $14.95.**

For more information on other titles from Close Up Publishing or to request a FREE catalog of our materials, please call 800-765-3131, or write Close Up Publishing, Department H36, 44 Canal Center Plaza, Alexandria, VA 22314-1592.

A purchase order or payment must accompany each order. Shipping and handling charges are not included. Prices are subject to change.